DRINKING, HOM   ION

in Colonial Mexican Villages

William B. Taylor # DRINKING, HOMICIDE & REBELLION *in Colonial Mexican Villages*

STANFORD UNIVERSITY PRESS STANFORD, CALIFORNIA

Stanford University Press
Stanford, California
© 1979 by the Board of Trustees of the
Leland Stanford Junior University
Printed in the United States of America
Cloth ISBN 0-8047-0997-1
Paper ISBN 0-8047-1112-7
Original printing 1979
Last figure below indicates year of this printing:
04 03 02 01 00 99 98 97 96 95

Original edition published with the assistance
of the National Endowment for the Humanities

Stanford University Press publications are distributed
exclusively by Stanford University Press within the
United States, Canada, Mexico, and Central America;
they are distributed exclusively by Cambridge
University Press throughout the rest of the world.

To Barbara

ACKNOWLEDGMENTS

Friends and colleagues contributed at every stage to the preparation of this book. Nancy D. Mann, Waldemar R. Smith, and Fritz L. Hoffmann read the first draft and offered much valuable criticism. Important suggestions on the research design and shorter versions of Chapters 2, 3, and 4 came from Arnold Bauer, Mary G. Berg, Charles Hale, Lewis Hanke, James Lockhart, Ralph Mann, and Ronald Spores. José Hernández Palomo and E. William Jowdy sent me information on documents from Spanish archives. Salvador Victoria Hernández helped in many ways during my trips to the National Archive in Mexico City. James B. Given and Stanford University Press kindly let me read Professor Given's *Society and Homicide in Thirteenth-Century England* before publication. Political boundaries on the maps are derived from Peter Gerhard's *A Guide to the Historical Geography of New Spain.*

I am especially grateful to Woodrow Borah and Charles Gibson for their advice and support over the years and to J. G. Bell for his steady confidence.

Generous grants from the American Philosophical Society, the National Endowment for the Humanities, and the University of Colorado made the research possible. A timely APS grant-in-aid in 1973 allowed me to begin the archival research in Mexico City and Oaxaca. An NEH fellowship in 1974–1975 and a Faculty Fellowship in 1976 supported further research in the United States and Mexico and gave me time to organize and write.

W.B.T.

CONTENTS

MAPS

TABLES

DRINKING, HOMICIDE & REBELLION
in Colonial Mexican Villages

Introduction

This book is about patterns of social behavior in Indian peasant communities of central and southern Mexico after the severe hazards of the sixteenth century had passed, leaving the pressures of a mature colonial system on the lives of an expanding population. Without attempting to force connections among peasant norms, behavior, and circumstances, I am interested in what colonial peasants believed and said about themselves, what they actually did and said in specific situations, and what their relations were to the powerful outsiders whose presence defined their position as peasants.

The beliefs and acts presented here suggest the fundamental importance of the village in Mexican peasant life. Political conquest and the economic and social sanctions of colonial rule disturbed native society at all levels, but European intrusion was most destructive of the indigenous elite, which rested on a massive rural base. Beyond the sharp decline of the elite, many kinds of local adjustment in rural Mexico had to be made to colonial rule. *Encomienda*, epidemic disease, *repartimiento*, *reparto de efectos*, and *congregación* forced changes in peasant life and traditional culture, but somehow peasant communities survived, and not merely at the pleasure or weakness of Spanish masters. The land-based communities were more resilient than the forests of central Mexico, which were destroyed for timber, and than the millions of individuals who succumbed to the fearsome epidemics of the colonial centuries. They were not crushed and swept aside; nor did they endure only in remote areas of refuge. I have found much evidence of decline and destruction, but I have also found energy and ingenuity in the ways Indian peasants coped with and survived within the Spanish system. In the heartland of colonial Mexico the most enduring native American adaptation to colonial demands centered on the land-holding village. It usually was the basic unit of common interest for peasants in central and southern Mexico, giving this community a special importance and a moral basis. The strong association of individuals as members of a single community is documented in various ways—in their conscious identity and especially in their social behavior.

In emphasizing the peasant village, I am not unwittingly subscribing to the traditional "local community" focus of cultural anthropologists, which has been called into question by a number of scholars who stress the individual, the domestic unit, or the extended family as the political, economic, and social basis of peasant society, and by others who stress the essential relationships between peasants and the outside world.[1] I recognize also that Spanish colonial administration, by dealing with the rural village as a corporate, legal unit of the empire, generated more documentation on the local community than it did on groups within the village, such as neighborhoods and families.

I have already used two terms—peasant and Indian—that require some explanation. "Peasant" is an ambiguous term, used in many different ways by anthropologists and historians. For the purposes of this study, "peasants" indicates settled villagers engaged mostly in farming on their own or rented lands, whose productive agricultural activities, utilization of surpluses (including their labor), and culturally distinct characteristics are influenced to a significant extent by powerful outsiders. The peasant villages of central and southern Mexico in the colonial period were partially autonomous communities with some (often little) control over their productive activities and the administration of community affairs. Distinctive local variations in such colonial peasant characteristics will become apparent in later chapters.

"Indian" is an even more elusive term, which I use sparingly. I occasionally speak of Indian peasants as distinct from *mestizos*, mulattoes, and Spaniards in order to suggest a continuity of peasant life and local history from pre-Hispanic to colonial times. Obviously, the European invention that lumped native Americans into a subordinate social and legal category, to the advantage of the Spanish rulers, did not create an Indian bloc. The subjects knew themselves as Indians only to the extent that they had learned their place from Spanish masters. Descendants of pre-Hispanic Americans in the colonial period were inclined to think of themselves as, for example, "the people of Metepec" or "the people of Teotitlán." They knew they were Indians when they dealt with the formal institutions of Spanish rule. A castelike legal status must have affected Indian attitudes and social behavior, but, in using the term, I stop short of inferring a colonial Indian psychology or set of grotesque character traits including collective depression, anxiety, irresponsibility, and self-destruction formed by the supposedly irresistible force of Spanish rulers. In other words, colonial Indian peasants were descended from pre-Hispanic villagers; they still spoke modified versions of native languages and displayed other distinctive cultural traits that suggest a localized social identification. Structurally, they occupied a separate, subordinate position in a stratified society that fortified the ethnic categories of Indians and non-Indians.

How can historians document the values and living patterns of Indian villagers and the structure of colonialism from the peasants' vantage point? The behavior of villagers resists historical inquiry in many ways. The use of written records to study essentially nonliterate people means that most of the documentation is *about* peasants rather than *by* peasants. As a result, most peasant and Indian history deals with relations between Spanish rulers and Indian subjects or filters the subjects' behavior through the words of Spanish witnesses or of the Indian elite. This is the outsider's view of rural society, telling us more about Spaniards and rulers than about peasants.

To approach the social history of peasants as a long-term development in the patterns of events, ideas, perceptions, and actions in human relationships requires a different type of documentation—a fairly continuous and homogeneous body of case evidence reporting numerous events and illuminating details that can be directly compared. In searching for new information of this type, I have found that the records of criminal trials furnish especially abundant and fairly continuous evidence of peasant behavior as well as the voices of peasants themselves speaking of the world in which they lived. I worked in two large collections of criminal records for this study. They are the *Ramo Criminal* of the Archivo General de la Nación (Mexico), a collection of 748 volumes of criminal trials (in 741 numbered volumes) for central Mexico, including the modern state of Mexico and portions of the states of Hidalgo, Guerrero, and Morelos; and the municipal archive of Teposcolula, with its long series of criminal trials for the *alcaldía mayor* of Teposcolula, which encompassed much of the Mixteca Alta of Oaxaca during the colonial period. These collections give emphasis to two regions: rural districts of central Mexico that were connected with the urban capital of Mexico City; and rural Oaxaca communities, which were situated farther from the major centers of Spanish settlement (see Maps 1–2). My archival research also included state and municipal archives in the Valley of Oaxaca, Inquisition trials, civil litigation, and administrative records for Indian affairs, colonial justice, and royal revenues. These sources and their uses for social history are explained at greater length in Chapters 2–4 and the notes.

In seeking to move beyond the very general view of the colonial setting presented in Chapter 1 to a deeper understanding of peasant life and the tension of village societies within the larger world of eighteenth-century New Spain, I have examined three types of actual events in the social life of peasant communities, which are documented through the words of the peasants as well as those of colonial officials. Drinking, homicide, and community uprisings lead us to poles of opposition and harmony in community relations. Between these poles are other less dramatic events and habits that are more genuinely typical of everyday life, although they are more difficult to document in a satisfactory way with numerous examples. In using the more dramatic events, I have tried to look beyond the individual communities to patterns in the actions of many individuals, relations among events and people, and the relations of Indian communities to the larger colonial world. Colonial trial records, casting their wide net of interrogation into the circumstances and results of homicides and uprisings as well as documenting the acts themselves, permit us to steer a middle course between individual biographies and depersonalized social analysis, enabling us to study the history of peasants in terms of the behavior of groups united by certain common interests. In addition to being manifestations of stress and protest, the patterns of behavior in these dramatic events and the nature of the trial records can suggest norms, desires, and aspects of everyday life that are ordinarily undocumented because they are taken for granted.

Initially, I intended to use archival records to study drinking patterns in peasant societies after the Spanish conquest. During the course of this investigation, it became clear that evidence of drinking could best be understood in relation to other kinds of social behavior. Collective drinking led to questions of local rituals and community values. Alcoholism and individual drinking habits as social problems led to larger patterns of crime, breaches of norms, and antisocial behavior in rural communities. In uniting the archival material with the general subject of peasant history, I have written core chapters on the original topic of drinking patterns, as well as on the subjects of community uprisings and homicide. Together, these subjects have a certain symmetry: collective behavior in uprisings; individual, personally destructive behavior in homicides; and collective and individual acts of drinking. Although interrelationships are explored in the concluding chapter, I want to emphasize that I chose these three types of dramatic behavior because they bear directly on the social life of peasant communities and because the documentation available is extraordinarily rich, not because there might be strong causal connections among them. I have concentrated on the eighteenth century because it provides the richest runs of trial records. I have, however,

1. Apam y Tepeapulco
2. Chalco
3. Coyoacán
4. Cuernavaca
5. Cuautitlán
6. Lerma
7. Malinalco
8. Metepec
9. Mexicalcingo
10. Meztitlán
11. Otumba
12. Pachuca
13. San Cristóbal Ecatepec
14. Tacuba
15. Temascaltepec y Sultepec
16. Tenango del Valle
17. Texcoco
18. Toluca
19. Tulancingo
20. Xochimilco
21. Zacualpa
22. Zumpango de la Laguna

23. Antequera
24. Cuatro Villas
25. Guaxolotitlán
26. Mitla y Tlacolula
27. Nochistlán
28. Teposcolula
29. Zimatlán y Chichicapa

MAP 1. Alcaldías mayores represented in the documentation on drinking, homicide, and uprisings

MAP 2. Towns mentioned in the text

Towns mentioned in the text

CENTRAL MEXICO

1. Acolman
2. Amecameca
3. Apam
4. Atlacomulco
5. Atlatlauca
6. Chalco
7. Chimalhuacán
8. Coyoacán
9. Cuauhtitlán
10. Cuautla
11. Cuernavaca
12. Ecatepec
13. Huixquilucan
14. Iscateupa
15. Ixmiquilpan
16. Ixtlahuaca
17. Lerma
18. Malinalco
19. Metepec
20. Mexicalcingo
21. Mexico City
22. Meztitlán
23. Ocuituco
24. Otumba
25. Pachuca
26. Real del Monte
27. Sultepec
28. Tacuba
29. Temascaltepec
30. Tenancingo
31. Tenango del Valle
32. Teotihuacán
33. Tepeapulco
34. Tepoztlán
35. Tetela
36. Texcoco
37. Tlacotepec
38. Tlalmanalco
39. Toluca
40. Tulancingo
41. Tututepec
42. Xochimilco
43. Zacualpa
44. Zinguilucan
45. Zumpahuacán

OAXACA

46. Achiutla
47. Almoloyas
48. Antequera
49. Apuala
50. Chalcatongo
51. Chilapa
52. Coixtlahuaca
53. Huajuapan
54. Macuilxóchitl
55. Mitla
56. Nochixtlán
57. Tamazulapa
58. Tejupan
59. Teotitlán del Camino
60. Teotitlán del Valle
61. Teozacualco
62. Teposcolula
63. Tilantongo
64. Tilcajete
65. Tlacochahuaya
66. Tlacolula
67. Tlalixtac
68. Tlaxiaco
69. Yanhuitlán
70. Yolotepec
71. Zimatlán
72. Zoyaltepec

taken some liberties with the time limits. Indian drinking requires a retrospect into the early colonial period, and rural rebellion imposes its own requirement of a forward glance into the nineteenth century.

The rural history of Mexico in the late colonial period can be told only as it survives, not as it actually was. Written records permit access to many elements of complexity and of the uniqueness and individuality of events, but often at the cost of precision, control, and generalization. As E. H. Carr says, however, "The historian is not really interested in the unique, but what is general in the unique."[2] Thus, I have emphasized what is general or revealing about uprisings, homicides, and drinking and have resisted the temptation to write about many particular cases. Detailed notes and references at the end of the book will guide readers interested in learning more about cases and events that support the patterns discussed in the text

At all stages of the research and writing, I wanted to move beyond both black legends of Spanish cruelty and wholesale destruction of Indian life and white legends of Spanish benevolence. Such legends rest heavily on what Spaniards said about themselves or on assumptions that change means either breakdown or "progress" measured by European standards. In both cases the subordinate peasants are viewed as passive objects of the colonial process, people whose way of life could only disintegrate or imitate superior European culture.

In attempting to organize the data and interpret the patterns of drinking, homicide, and collective violence, I have been guided by a number of concepts and hypotheses developed by anthropologists, sociologists, and fellow historians, as well as some that occurred to me as I traveled in Mexico and puzzled over my stacks of note cards. Several of these concepts affect my approach in a general way and need to be mentioned at the outset.

My approach to criminal records is not limited to the pathological side of peasant history. I am equally interested in how violent incidents can reveal patterns of social behavior and their relations to cultural premises and external conditions—patterns and relations that can be translated from behavior recorded in criminal trials.* Trial records

---

*Mousnier, p. 15, points out the special interest of these patterns: "There are facts, even important ones, of which contemporaries are unaware, others that they prefer not to admit or confess to, and others again that are so basic that they seem commonplace to such a degree that contemporaries do not take the trouble to describe them, and they come to our notice only through a few words dropped in passing in some document. The historian's task is to bring out these forms of social behavior by analyzing a substantial number of accounts, offered in the form of memoirs, letters, and chronicles, and a substantial number of legal transactions, revealed by notaries' records and the proceedings of courts."

also provide direct oral expressions of a situation by the participants that can suggest norms, the "rules, more or less overt, which express the 'ought' aspects of interpersonal relationships."[3] Using criminal records to identify the situations in which people commit breaches of norms allows the historian to observe the interplay of the conditions of peasant life, cultural premises (contemporary interpretations of conditions), and behavior. In unstable circumstances many social elements that are taken for granted in everyday life, such as ideologies and social values, rise to the surface of consciousness and are documented in written records.

In speaking of unstable circumstances and departures from ideal behavior, I do not mean that conflict was in fact an aberration disturbing a naturally stable society, only that norms and behavior cannot be assumed to coincide. I am inclined to view conflict—which is not usually *violent* conflict—and temporary accommodation as perennial among and within the groups that formed colonial society. When I speak of the durability of villages, I am not suggesting the absence of conflict but, rather, conditions that allowed villages to survive or to transcend the "monotonous" conflicts endemic in colonial society.

This is not a full history of the regions of central Mexico and Oaxaca marked out on Map 1. It is, rather, an examination of three types of social behavior well documented for rural villages in these areas, based on criminal trials and related records. Using other kinds of records, a number of scholars have studied and are studying selected aspects of places within the same two regions. In many ways, their studies provide an important context for the patterns of social behavior discussed here. I should note in particular Charles Gibson's work on the Valley of Mexico, John Tutino on Chalco, Wayne Osborn on Meztitlán, Mario Colín on the hinterland of Toluca, James Lockhart on several parts of central Mexico, and Ronald Spores, Woodrow Borah, Sherburne F. Cook, and Barbro Dahlgren de Jordan on the Mixteca Alta. Peter Gerhard's massive *A Guide to the Historical Geography of New Spain* provided essential information on political boundaries and sources for local history.

Chapter 1 The Colonial Setting

The areas of central Mexico and Oaxaca well represented in the colonial records by homicides, uprisings, and drinking follow fairly definite political boundaries. For central Mexico, all of the communities were located within the Intendancy of Mexico (created in 1786); for Oaxaca, they fell within the alcaldías mayores of Teposcolula, Cuatro Villas, Antequera, Guaxolotitlán, Teotitlán del Valle, Nochistlán, and Zimatlán (see Maps 1–2). These political boundaries do not chop the history of rural Mexico into arbitrary units. They encompass major subregions of two of the six ethnohistorical regions of Middle America shaped by the complex interplay of natural environment and cultural developments: central Mexico and Oaxaca.* The Intendancy of Mexico covers much of the core region of central Mexico surrounding Mexico City, an area of continuous human settlement for at least three thousand years and the heartland of colonial society in New Spain. The alcaldía mayor of Teposcolula corresponds roughly to the Mixteca Alta in the western portion of the modern state of Oaxaca, a major subregion of the Oaxaca ethnohistorical region, and the alcaldías mayores of Teotitlán del Valle, Antequera, Cuatro Villas, and Zimatlán cover the Valley of Oaxaca, another major geographical and cultural subregion. Together, these two subregions accounted for more than half of the Oaxaca population and were mainstays of the region's colonial economy.

Both Oaxaca and the Intendancy of Mexico are located in the mountainous central highlands of Mexico, 5,000 to 8,000 feet above sea level. The rugged spines are interspersed with basins of small to moderate size, from 30 to 300 square kilometers. Especially in Oaxaca, snug valleys and *barrancas* are the characteristic land forms; in central Mexico the valleys are larger—the Valley of the Mezquital, the Valley of Toluca, and the great Valley of Mexico—and in the Bajío on the northern rim of the central Mexico region, the mountains open up to a

---

*Middle America's ethnohistorical regions are identified and discussed by Cline in vol. 12 of the *Handbook of Middle American Indians*, pp. 166–82. The other four regions are northern Mexico, western Mexico, southeastern Mexico and Guatemala, and Central America.

broad plateau, the *mesa central*. The weather generally is semiarid and temperate to cool. In both regions life-giving rains are concentrated in the late spring and summer months. In pre-Hispanic times seasonal rains and some irrigation from year-round water sources supported a productive maize culture, supplemented by a variety of wild plants and secondary native crops, including maguey, beans, squash, chiles, tomatoes, zapotes, nuts, sweet potatoes, avocados, and herbs. The Mixteca Alta was the driest of our subregions, the least easily brought under irrigated farming, and the most susceptible to erosion.

SOCIAL ORGANIZATION BEFORE THE CONQUEST

Central Mexico and Oaxaca were among the most thickly peopled Indian areas of Latin America in the colonial period, their dense indigenous populations concentrated in village communities often no more than three or four kilometers apart. The central Mexico area, defined by Woodrow Borah and Sherburne F. Cook as stretching from the Chichimec frontier (roughly following the northern boundary of the *gobierno* of Nueva España on Map 1) south—through the Bajio and the populous states of Hidalgo, Mexico, Morelos, Tlaxcala, Puebla, Guerrero, Veracruz, and Oaxaca—to the Isthmus of Tehuantepec, was occupied by a very large population in the early sixteenth century, supporting perhaps as many as twenty-five million people when the Spaniards arrived in 1519. This population was devastatingly reduced by epidemic disease and relentless labor demands during the following century to little more than one million in 1605. It began to grow again in the late-seventeenth and eighteenth centuries. To the end of the colonial period the population of both central Mexico and Oaxaca remained predominantly Indian peasant.

Each region had a measure of internal linguistic unity. The Mixteca Alta was and still is inhabited principally by Mixtec-speaking people and their Hispanicized relatives, with enclaves of Trique, Chatino, Chocho, Popoloca, Ixcateco, and Amuzgo peoples. The Valley of Oaxaca villagers spoke local dialects of Zapotec, with an important addition of Mixtec-speakers in the south. In central Mexico, Nahuatl was widely spoken and was becoming the lingua franca of politics even among other linguistic groups such as the Otomís, Mazahuas, and Tarascans.

Both central Mexico and Oaxaca were situated within the area of "High Indian Culture," which supported elaborate societies of artisans, traders, and hereditary elites of priests and warriors who shared political power.[1] Intensive food production by farming villages under the sway of political centers sustained these complex societies. In both regions incipient state organizations developed to extract surplus wealth and labor from the countryside, enabling the elites to carry on their building programs, military ventures, and regulation of public life.[2] The "city state," with an administrative center and outlying dependent villages occupying a well-defined territory, was the basic unit of native state organization in central and southern Mexico at the time of the conquest.* In central Mexico, the administrative centers often were fairly large, compact settlements, the political and economic hearts of their sustaining areas. Compact settlements supported by a hinterland of small hamlets of farmers were also found in the Valley of Oaxaca, but in the Mixteca Alta, food-producing villages and hamlets were organized around sparsely occupied political centers.[3]

Combinations of petty states into larger political organizations based on military conquest and alliance occurred in the fifteenth century in both regions but were stronger in central Mexico. In the Mixteca Alta, Tilantongo had a preeminent place in regional associations, based on its earlier power under the warrior-leader Eight Deer in the eleventh century;[4] in the Valley of Oaxaca, Monte Albán may have been a major seat before its decline in the eleventh century, and Zaachila is thought to have been something of a Zapotec capital in the fifteenth and sixteenth centuries. In Oaxaca, these larger groupings had limited continuity; the lasting organization in this region of little valleys divided by rugged mountains was the smaller city state. In central Mexico, with larger valleys and better lines of communication, political organizations and cities were more highly developed and based on tighter central control. Important ethnic units, such as the Tepaneca in the Valley of Mexico, groups of Otomí people centered at Meztitlán, and the Tlaxcalans, formed substantial social and political provinces. The great urban nucleus was Tenochtitlán in the Valley of Mexico, the largest city on the American continent before the arrival of Europeans and a major political center.

In the late fifteenth century the Tenocha-Mexica ("Aztecs") of Tenochtitlán-Tlatelolco had allied with two other major city states in the Valley, Texcoco and Tlacopan, to extend state centralization and tribute demands. But even this famed "Aztec Empire" fell far short of a unified political command in central Mexico. According to the recent

---

*Bray, p. 162; C. N. B. Davies, p. 219. "City state" is a convenient, approximate term. As Lockhart has noted, these units may have been less cities and states and more "the association of a group of people with a given extended territory," "Capital and Province," p. 101.

findings of Warwick Bray, Nigel Davies, and Frances Berdan, the integrated state of the Triple Alliance existed primarily in the Valley of Mexico, and even there it had to contend with fifty or sixty semiautonomous city states.[5] It appears that the Triple Alliance rulers were not able to impose much political or cultural uniformity on their tributaries. The "empire" outside the Valley was a far-flung but loosely organized tribute system sustained by Triple Alliance occupation of strategic locations with a garrison and sometimes the symbolic presence of a governor. Tribute was the integrating institution. The political system lacked most of the instruments of centralized state control —such as police, formalized laws enforced by a system of courts, religious conversion, resettlement, and protection of state sovereignty by local subjects.[6]

Within the extensive territory of the Triple Alliance tribute network, independent regional confederations, or *señorios*, existed in Michoacán, Tlaxcala, Yopitzinco, Meztitlán, Cholula, Huejotzingo, Acapulco, and Acatepec; other provinces on the periphery of the tribute area were often in rebellion.[7] The Triple Alliance "empire," then, was loosely organized and tended to atomization rather than centralization and uniformity. Still, the leagues of city states and a few great towns engaged in extensive trade and forced redistribution of goods were striking features of the native society of central Mexico when Cortez encountered them.

EARLY COLONIAL DEVELOPMENTS

Disasters of several kinds struck Indian Mexico with the arrival of Spaniards and their rapid dispersion in search of wealth. The military conquest, the best-known disaster, affected Oaxaca less than it did central Mexico, the main area of state organization and concerted armed resistance. But in both regions the military conquest was the blow that native society as a whole was best prepared to withstand. The pre-Hispanic past was filled with wars that, like the conquest, were waged by warrior elites for control of a peasant population not directly involved. During the conquest the rural farmers were spectators at one more in a long series of political battles fought by outsiders.

The physical destruction caused by military conquest and its immediate political consequences fell heaviest on the Indian elites above the city-state level. Tenochtitlán was virtually leveled by 1523, and the "empire" collapsed with the removal of the warrior groups, state officials, and high priests. Provincial chieftains outside Triple Alliance control in central Mexico and Oaxaca also quickly lost their authority to the Spanish invaders, and Indian cities lost their preeminence as centers of native life. Ethnic unities that had supported state organization, such as that of the Valley Zapotecs at Zaachila, also began to decline. Native priests at all levels were systematically attacked in the consolidation of Spanish power. Lands worked for their benefit by subject villagers were confiscated and redistributed, and priests were killed, brought to trial, or harried into secrecy.

Although only the upper levels of the native elite were systematically removed, this fragmentation of native political organization set in motion a half-century of turmoil for the entire native nobility. Old sumptuary regulations of food, drink, and dress broke down, and local nobles found it difficult to enforce old customs of marriage and labor service.[8] After the conquest, some *macehuales* (commoners) eagerly denounced the arbitrary acts and pagan habits of nobles in order to diminish their authority; and some subject towns and hamlets of landless farmers attached to noble estates (*mayeque*) seized the opportunity to declare their independence.[9] On the other hand, the majority of natives—rural villagers and peasant families—did not suffer a fall from social eminence with the Spaniards' arrival. Where they had once worked to provide the surplus that maintained native priests and nobles, they now labored to sustain more demanding and less divine rulers.

Although peasant villages and local traditions were not broken apart by the political effects of the conquest, other sixteenth-century disasters did jeopardize rural life. Epidemics of European introduction, apparently measles, smallpox, and typhus, scourged the Indian population. Millions of natives died in the pandemics of the 1530's, 1540's, and 1570's.[10] The Indian depopulation was dramatic everywhere, but especially in the coastal regions where whole communities ceased to exist. In the highland regions of central Mexico and Oaxaca, many communities, although drastically reduced, survived these devastations.

The balance of rural life in the sixteenth century was also seriously upset by the Spaniards' coercive labor practices, their monopolization of trade in certain important goods, their congregación, or resettlement, programs, and their introduction of European livestock. The encomienda system, under which zones of Indian communities were assigned to serve individual Spanish colonists, permitted virtually uncontrolled use of Indian labor in central Mexico and Oaxaca through at least the 1540's. The increased royal regulation of all spheres of Indian life after 1535 under Viceroy Antonio de Mendoza began the gradual decline of encomienda power but did not much alter the heavy labor demands. Transformation of the encomienda based on personal service into the encomienda based on tribute after 1549 signified a radical change in the private authority of privileged colonists, but other state-administered legal devices such as the repartimiento, or labor draft, and penal servitude were found to reintroduce obligatory service. Labor demands were also made on native society by the Church for its building projects and the maintenance of parish priests, and by the Crown through taxation and labor drafts for public works of all kinds. The eventual replacement of *encomenderos* with royal *alcaldes mayores* brought with it the reparto de efectos, the officeholder's lucrative monopoly on the sales of certain items, such as horses and chocolate, at inflated prices. Alcaldes mayores in the late colonial period reportedly pressed their monopoly goods on peasant subjects in order to coerce low-cost production of valuable export products, such as cochineal. Numerous complaints against such abuses led the Crown to cancel the reparto de efectos privilege in 1790.

Relocation of Indian peasants by Catholic missionaries during the 1540's and by the viceregal government in the 1590's forcibly uprooted the surviving members of some communities. For central Mexico and Oaxaca, these congregación programs affected the Otomí people of modern Hidalgo most extensively and encouraged the growth of head towns, or local administrative capitals, in the Mixteca Alta.[11] Many attempts at resettlement ultimately failed; peasants who were settled in the congregaciones gradually returned to their original homes and fields. The dramatic increase of European livestock altered the ecological balance of pre-Hispanic times, although perhaps not as drastically as it first appears. Much open grassland was available for grazing, which did not interfere with peasant agriculture (although grazing must have reduced the wild foods gathered by Indians). Stray cows, sheep, and goats nevertheless inevitably spilled onto Indian fields, destroying crops.

The periodic epidemics, limited resettlements, labor requirements, and ranching activities were not frontal attacks on peasant life, but they did bring confusion. During the first fifty years of European rule rapid changes introduced a new fluidity to the way of life of rural Indians. A general Hispanicizing of formal aspects of life took place, in public religious activities, eating habits, dress, and property rights, and most completely among the surviving nobility at the local level and in the old city-state centers that became colonial head towns.[12] Political reorganization within the Spanish Empire also involved a considerable Hispanicization at local levels. Local governments of large Indian communities were modeled after the old annually elected municipal councils of Spain (*cabildos*), and their relation to the state followed bureaucratic channels established by the Crown. Contemporary Spanish ideas of urban planning and architecture—including the true arch and the grid plan, consisting of a central plaza with streets leading out at right angles from it—were widely imposed.

From the vantage point of pre-Hispanic society, excess and individual license must have seemed the rule in this early period of adjustment, whether in Indian religious rites, such as a kind of confession, which had been performed only once in a lifetime before the conquest, eating habits, the frequency of public celebrations, or vagrancy by young men. A climate of restlessness and "psychological unemployment" in which old habits lost their meaning accompanied the new conditions of uncertainty.[13] Work lost much of its transcendent value as a sacred act and must have appeared to Indians another kind of excess. Migration—from village to city and from one rural area to another—seems to have been common enough in pre-Hispanic times, but it reached new dimensions in the sixteenth century.[14] With the collapse of closed groups of native traders, more Indians set off on their own as peddlers and muleteers; and some small communities were abandoned through congregación, flight from disease, or resolve to escape the growing burdens of mandatory labor and taxation.

Not all early changes drained the existing communities. In the struggle between encomienda and royal authority, royal officials helped to establish the corporate rights of villages. The Crown's aims in the early sixteenth century, its views of Indian subjects, and the limits of Spaniards' abilities to achieve their political and economic goals in this vast territory contributed to the selective survival of rural communities. America was in fact as well as in name a "New World," inhabited by millions of natives who could not be fitted neatly into a European world of laws and social relations. The sedentary indigenous people were not considered analogous—as non-Christians and potential Spanish subjects—to the Muslims who had been absorbed in the Christian reconquest of the Iberian peninsula between the eighth and fifteenth centuries. Unlike the Muslims, native Americans had not rejected Christianity; nor, for the most part, were they committed to resisting Spanish intrusion. The numerous sixteenth-century laws regarding Indians contrast sharply with the terse edicts concerning treatment of Africans, a group with whom Spaniards had dealt in the Old World and who needed to be defined legally only in terms of special New World conditions, primarily for purposes of punishment and control.

Early Indian laws reveal two underlying attitudes that promoted the survival of rural communities and the preservation in them of a strong corporate identity: a paternalistic preoccupation with the well-being of Indians as new and different royal subjects; and the economic and political motives inherent in colonial rule. Royal paternalism carried with it a view of sedentary converted Indians as perpetual minors, "niños con barbas" (children with beards), as an eighteenth-century priest put it, who needed special protection and consideration in order to learn the ways of Christian civilization and the obligations of royal vassals. Royal laws frequently enjoined "looking out always for the welfare of the Indians" and "giving greater protection to the Indians."[15] The special status of Christian natives extended to the judicial system, for, unlike other royal subjects in America, Indians were not under the rigorous authority of the Inquisition in the late colonial period. In most civil and criminal proceedings involving Indians, the special Juzgado de Indios had appellate jurisdiction. To protect Indian communities in their daily lives, the Crown issued a series of laws designed to keep non-Indians out of the *pueblos de indios*.[16] The impossibility of enforcing these laws was made evident by the racial mixture that had taken place in rural Mexico by the end of the colonial period (although central Mexico and Oaxaca were still predominantly "Indian").* Protective segregation and a degree of political autonomy for communities did not mean that the Spanish rulers intended Indian life to carry on unchanged. Segregation was intended to save Indians from the worst features of non-Indian ways and to allow for the best features of Christian Spain to be formally introduced under royal guidance. The Indians were, for example, to be taught Castilian so that they could better understand Christian doctrine.[17]

Paternalism and interest in converting the indigenous population were not incompatible with economic exploitation and imperial defense. The colonial economy depended heavily on Indian labor and productivity for its wealth. In particular, the sixteenth-century colonial system received substantial revenues from Indian tribute and relied on Indian agriculture to supply the predominantly nonagricultural Spanish population, which clustered in newly formed towns. This dependence on Indian agriculture explains early laws declaring that Indians should engage in farming and must have sufficient time to cultivate their fields.[18] The colonial experience of the city of Antequera in the Valley of Oaxaca illustrates the Spaniards' expectation that Indians

---

* Mörner, *La corona española*. Miscegenation, however, was not the same as intermarriage, which establishes conditions favorable to more rapid transfer of culture.

would satisfy their needs for food and basic supplies. As early as 1532 the cabildo of Antequera petitioned the king to order that Indians in the district sell food to Spaniards in the city. Bishop López de Zárate complained on behalf of the city in 1538 that Valley natives were not cultivating all the lands available to them, and that as a result there was a shortage of wheat and maize. In 1551 the cabildo again urged the Crown to order Indians to produce wheat, silk, and other crops for the Spaniards, arguing that otherwise the natives would produce only enough to pay the royal tribute and would become lazy and quarrelsome.

The Crown expected Indians to pay tribute and to provide certain labor services, and central Mexico and Oaxaca were particularly rich sources for both. Spanish administrators, traders, and ranchers as well as city-dwellers depended on the Indian peasants' ability to produce a surplus above subsistence needs to meet these obligations. In collecting its taxes, the colonial administration maintained local Indian districts at the *altepetl*, or city-state, level. The boundaries of encomiendas and alcaldías mayores usually built on these old jurisdictions, although the Spaniards went much further than had native political organization in centralizing state authority through the *audiencias* and viceroyalties. The colonial tax system grafted onto native boundaries contributed to the survival of local nobles, granting them entailed estates and other colonial privileges in exchange for their responsibilities as collectors of the royal tribute and organizers of the labor drafts.

The special status of Indians affected their property rights. Early laws proclaimed that villages were to be confirmed in their landholdings and, further, were to be assured of the lands they needed for planting and livestock. These decrees and principles remained largely academic except in cases adjudicated by the courts. Alcaldes mayores and lieutenants appointed to carry the alcalde mayor's authority to specific sections of the district reportedly meddled in municipal elections, exacted illegal services, extorted local funds, and abused the reparto de efectos.[19] The sale of lieutenancies from the sixteenth century on must have added to the potential for abuse of office by local royal representatives. Although royal officials had ample opportunity to take advantage of their authority, it is still fair to say that the legal rights of villagers—their corporate identity, property rights, and recourse to the judicial system—discouraged unrelieved abuse and gave villagers a political instrument with which to defend themselves.

Catholic priests were central to the penetration of Spanish authority into the Mexican countryside and to encouraging village life. Iberian Catholicism in the sixteenth century was a component of the government—not a separate compartment but an all-pervasive influence on the formation and implementation of state policy. The temporal monarch was also the head of the Church, clerics were leading advisers to the king in the writing of American law, and the early missionary priests were entrusted with secular responsibilities in addition to their religious duties. In sixteenth-century central Mexico and Oaxaca, conversion and parish duties were carried out by the mendicant orders, imbued with a special zeal for their calling by the reforms of the Franciscan order and the influence of Erasmus in Spain in the late fifteenth century.[20] Franciscans and Augustinians were active in the central Mexico region from the 1520's, and the Dominicans evangelized Oaxaca from the 1530's. Although they were eventually replaced by secular priests in many rural parishes, the Regular clergy left an indelible mark—in political ties to the Spanish Empire, in folk culture, in the dissemination of the new public cult, in the large amount of peasant social capital that was invested in impressive church-monasteries, in the establishment of new forms of religious government, such as *cofradías* (sodalities that played an important part in formal religious observances in most rural communities) and lay offices, and in the support of community identity. Long after the missionary zeal of the sixteenth century had passed, rural priests still embodied Spanish authority in remote parishes and had substantial influence in local affairs. They served informally as judges, sometimes oversaw tax collection, reported to provincial officials on local conditions, and hallowed the cycles of seasons and individual lives according to the new religion.

The peasant labor force remained a vital source of enrichment for the Spanish state and for private capital throughout the colonial period, increasingly so as the rural population began to grow again from the late seventeenth century. But as the native population approached its lowest point from 1576 to 1640 and the easily exploited veins of silver played out, colonists had to search for supplementary sources of wealth. Landownership and nonpeasant labor became increasingly important, especially in the hinterland of colonial towns and cities where the demand for food could no longer be supplied through tribute or labor drafts from the villages. Grain production joined with the long-standing interest in ranching to create *haciendas*, rural estates in which capital was invested in permanent buildings, irrigation works, and a large, mostly seasonal labor force. Trade across the Atlantic in both directions diminished as the Spanish economy continued a downward movement that had manifested itself in the periodic bankruptcies of the royal treasury under Philip II and his successors. The result seems to have been a regionalizing of economic activities in New Spain—growth of local manufactures, such as textiles, domestic wares (*artes útiles*), and sumptuary goods including religious art, to replace European imports in regional markets; growing contraband trade by the Dutch, English, and French; and the opening of a modest intercolonial trade.[21]

THE PEASANT VILLAGE IN THE EIGHTEENTH CENTURY

This prolonged period of imperial retrenchment and the growth of local interests eventually gave way to more dramatic changes in rural life in the eighteenth century. The population of selected districts in central Mexico grew by 85 per cent between 1644 and 1742. Between 1750 and 1800 the rural Indian population of Mexico as a whole grew by 44 per cent, with even larger increases in the most populous rural districts of central Mexico and Oaxaca.[22] New economic activities directed toward the European market blossomed, often closely regulated by a more vigorous and absolutist monarchy under the Spanish Bourbons; mining and transatlantic commerce revived; there was new vitality in the viceregal capital at Mexico City; administrative reforms, such as the creation of intendancies and a standing army, expulsion of the Jesuits, and consolidation of some Church wealth under royal stewardship, were undertaken to increase royal revenues, tighten the bonds of loyalty to the Crown, improve colonial defenses, and reduce the power of long-entrenched institutions, especially the Church. All of these developments contributed to the centralization of authority and to a sense of movement, if not always to great change.

For peasant communities of central Mexico and Oaxaca, these eighteenth-century developments meant intensified demands from the larger social system; but again, these were not frontal attacks on peasant life. They were piecemeal and administrative, rather than pervasive and structural as were the Bourbon attacks on the Church. Population growth and new markets led to greater peasant activity beyond community boundaries, more pressure on the land, increased circulation of goods, and a more commercial outlook. Administrative reforms increased tax obligations and attempted to transfer community wealth from cofradías to the *cajas de comunidad* (village treasury), but most of the political changes of the eighteenth century had little direct impact on peasant life.* In subregions where mining and export

---

*Rural communities may have been more strongly affected by the administrative reforms through their parish priests. This supposes a uniformly great influence of parish priests on the political stands of their congregations, a debatable supposition, as we shall see in Chapter 4.

agriculture developed, demand for year-round labor regularly exceeded supply, and peasant groups were vulnerable to becoming satellites of the entrepreneurial enterprises through loss of lands, indebtedness, or voluntary movement into full-time wage employment. In some activities and subregions, especially textile and cochineal production in the Mixteca Alta and the Sierra Zapoteca of Oaxaca, peasants were integrated into expanding markets without losing their control over the means of production or experiencing much change in village life. Here, peasants produced cochineal on their own lands and wove cotton textiles at home, receiving low prices from the urban merchants who bought from them and sometimes coerced production by advancing money or goods against the next season's crop or the next month's production of cloth.

Compared to the violence and disorder of the conquest before it and the violence that was to follow in the nineteenth century, the stability of the period from 1650 to 1800, in which villages were relatively free to elaborate on their early adjustments to colonial rule, was a respite. The simplification of pre-Hispanic native society during the sixteenth century—with the elimination of the state leaders, priests, merchants, and serflike mayeque, and the weakening of hereditary privilege at the local level—was giving way to new complexities, especially in the head towns. Historians sometimes think of the large rural population as homogeneous or only slightly varied, but hereditary nobles and political *caciques* were still distinguished in Oaxaca and most of central Mexico by their wealth and personal influence. Almost every rural head town had its small bourgeoisie, composed of notaries, skilled artisans, state officials, tavernkeepers, and traders. Communal property and communal obligations tended to equalize village life, unless officials used community property to enrich themselves, but differences did exist in wealth and independence within the farming-artisan peasantry of many communities: differences among farmers based on the amount and quality of land owned, and among these and tenant farmers, part-time wage-earners, and landless wage-earners.

The populous reorganized villages of the late-seventeenth and eighteenth centuries were neither much like their pre-Hispanic ancestors nor molded by their Spanish masters into new communities of a European stamp. Where they persisted—and they persisted all over the two regions represented in the documentation on drinking, homicide, and rebellion—these communities bore the marks of major changes in religion, political relationships, and economic activities. They maintained, however, a continuing base of maize agriculture, rural community identity, and certain conceptual habits that connected them to a more distant past and suggest a complex process of development rather than unrelieved decay or destruction under the pressure of colonial demands.[23] Remnants of presumably pre-Hispanic life can be found in eighteenth-century central Mexico and Oaxaca—in maize farming, housing, crafts, food, tools, local market systems, fertility rites, rites of passage, and other prosaic features of village economy and family life; in pictorial land deeds; in the informal groups of elders who were respected as advisers and decision-makers, whether or not they held public office; in the local political jurisdictions that served Spanish purposes of orderly administration and tax collection; occasionally in religious celebrations that served the whole community; and especially in native languages, which, although they did not remain unchanged, were by no means replaced systematically by Castilian during the colonial period.[24] Such survivals were overshadowed by the widespread adoption of Spanish forms—in dress, many elements of folk culture, tools (especially the plow and steel knives), domesticated animals, the public religious cult, the Gregorian calendar, and political institutions, among many others. In fact, most of the obvious cultural traits of late colonial peasants were more European than pre-Hispanic.[25]

But measuring survivals of native culture against the adoption of Spanish culture is a misleading way to evaluate changes in peasant communities, for change involved more than the simple alternatives of survival of old traits and replacement by imported ones, with peasants in a largely passive role. Some facets of Spanish culture, such as *compadrazgo* (ritual co-parenthood), the potter's wheel and kiln, the oxen and plow, served to strengthen local communities and increase their productive capacity. These were eagerly adopted. Others, such as cofradías and the ladder system of religious and political offices, channeled local wealth into the coffers of church and state but at the same time institutionalized and strengthened village identity.[26] The ties to the colonial economy of producers, traders, part-time laborers outside the village, and muleteers must also have been voluntary in many cases and promoted an attachment to the growing cash economy. Habits that were neither pre-Hispanic nor Spanish in form grew out of a fruitful combination of old and new beliefs (such as the cult of the Virgin of Guadalupe, which combined a Catholic image with Indian mother-worship, or the worship of San Isidro Labrador, which combined another Catholic image with peasant preoccupations with farming and fertility). Or they developed out of a transfer of socially useful behavior from one institution to another (such as the transfer of the social prestige of ritual sponsorship from pagan to Catholic cere-monies).[27]

Passive resistance to imposed systems was another possible response to the colonial process. It is documented in the repeated complaints by eighteenth-century priests of peasants' "tibieza"—their secrecy and cold treatment of priests and their habits of hiding infants and the deceased in order to avoid paying the clerical fees for baptism and the last rites—despite their obvious reverence for Christ, the Virgin Mary, the patron saints, holy relics, and the sacred grounds of the Church. Passive resistance is also evident in refusals to allow outsiders, particularly the alcalde mayor and his lieutenant, into the community except when taxes were due, and in refusals to grow wheat or to rent land to Spaniards and other outsiders.[28]

The corporate strength of peasant societies in eighteenth-century central Mexico and Oaxaca centered in the village community and, to a lesser extent, in the *municipio* network that built upon native group-ings of head towns and hamlets. Local identity was supported by an internal structure largely formed out of the sixteenth-century disasters and the continuing pressure of colonial demands for products and ser-vices. Patterns of residence within colonial peasant communities, pos-sibly pre-Hispanic in origin, seem to have been mainly patrilocal or neolocal in neighborhoods of male relatives, and the marriage pat-terns, abetted by Church doctrine, tended toward unions outside the *barrio* or neighborhood lineage group.[29] Patrilocal residence was part of a pattern of descent through the male line, another dimension of social identity and continuity within communities. Community structure—such as inheritance patterns—must also have been altered, in ways we can only guess, by the century of death that followed the Spaniards' arrival. The Crown encouraged the economic and social organization of colonial life around towns and villages. Peasants were required to form local governments to respond to royal orders, to col-lect taxes, to provide labor service, and to maintain a church, a com-munity treasury, and sometimes a hospital. All of these institutions encouraged local people to think of themselves as a distinctive, sep-arate community. Oaxaca is most notorious for the atomization of social life in this period, with each little hamlet struggling to achieve the status of an independent head town, but central Mexico experienced similar urges to local independence. The district of Sultepec in the southwest portion of the Intendancy of Mexico, for example, had fifty-four *cabeceras*, or head towns, in 1801.[30]

Two general characteristics of peasant village survival in the heartland of elaborate Indian societies of central Mexico emerge from all the social behavior I have examined: the most enduring patterns of renewal of peasant society arose within the discrete landholding village, which gained importance in the colonial period at the expense of ethnic and regional ties; and most of the protective adjustments of surviving villages took place in Old Regime terms—protesting abuses rather than the legitimacy of a remote colonial sovereign, and accommodating, often uneasily, within the colonial system in ways that were perceived as mutually advantageous by the colonial lords and the peasant villagers.

The essential building block for this kind of village society was landownership. Land grants were assigned to villages from the first years of colonial rule. Communal ownership of land was part of the Castilian tradition of corporate towns and it allowed the pueblos to fulfill their economic obligations to the State. But ownership of lands by villages in New Spain was not a Spanish invention. A close association between rural communities and specific areas of land long antedated the arrival of Europeans, and validation of ownership for nobles and communities seems to have been the purpose of some of the surviving pre-Hispanic codices that inspired similar title documents painted by Indian officials in the colonial period. Belonging to a landholding village did not guarantee a comfortable life for peasant families. Private property was increasingly important in the colonial period, and small groups of native ranchers, nobles, and traders emerged in many local communities; nevertheless, substantial tracts of land, especially pasture land, continued to be held by community organizations, such as cofradías and the caja de comunidad, to support their activities or by the community as a whole in the form of *ejidos*. By the eighteenth century there may have been relatively little village land left to support individual families. Most village farmers, even in well-landed communities, had little material wealth to show for their efforts—several pieces of farm land, a houseplot bordered by maguey or cactus, a home of adobe or reeds, a storage bin for corn and fodder, a small sweatbath, a change of clothes, a knife, kitchen utensils, a few farm implements, chickens, and perhaps a yoke of oxen or a mule and a few sheep and goats.

In neither of our regions was uniform prosperity or pervasive decay of village societies the rule. Some village communities even in the Valley of Mexico, such as Huitzilopochco and Tepetlaostoc, achieved new and remarkably even prosperity for their citizens in the eighteenth century, but even more communities disappeared or under-

went divisive internal changes at this time.[31] Within the general simi-
larities already discussed, differences existed between the peasant
societies of central Mexico and those of Oaxaca at the end of the colonial period. The principal difference between the two regions was the
dominant position of Mexico City in central Mexico. The Valley of
Mexico was the center of statecraft and wealth in the fifteenth century,
and its supremacy was accentuated in the colonial period by the
greater range of activity in the urban capital of Mexico City, the concentration of rich and powerful residents, and the city's authority over
a much larger area than that ruled from Tenochtitlán. Life in central
Mexico was shaped in many ways by the city's insistent demands for
crops and taxes and its position as the center of patronage and state
authority. Rural communities in central Mexico changed in response to
these demands, some specializing in production of pottery, vegetables, pulque, soap, brooms, and herbs for the urban market. Indians
from virtually all villages occasionally came to the city to sell their
wares, settle political business, and spend their meager earnings. Citizens of rural central Mexico communities were more likely to be
drawn into the city as full-time residents and laborers than were peasants from other regions. Migration to Mexico City was one way for
Indian peasants of central Mexico to avoid paying tribute; complaints
accumulated after the mid-seventeenth century of both vagrant Indians and residents of the settled Indian *parcialidad* of Santa María
la Redonda attempting to pass as tribute-exempt mestizos in the city.[32]

Villages in central Mexico, especially those in the Valley of Mexico,
generally had a more proletarian aspect than those in most other peasant areas of New Spain. Whole communities in some cases, large
numbers of adults in others, abandoned farming to become muleteers,
bakers, potters, brickmakers, or common laborers on private estates
or in public-works projects, such as street-paving and construction.
Some villagers of the Mixteca Alta and the Valley of Oaxaca also traveled to Mexico City for political business and trade and were in closer
contact with the urban markets of Puebla and Antequera, but the urban influence was less intense in Oaxaca and centered in head towns
and large communities along the colonial trade routes.[33]

Private estates producing for regional markets loomed somewhat
larger in the lives of peasant villagers of central Mexico. Not only were
more large haciendas competing with villages for good land and requiring substantial pools of day laborers during the planting and harvest
seasons, but many more small ranchos were also interspersed among
the rural villages of central Mexico.[34] By the eighteenth century some

TABLE 1.   *Indian Population of Intendancies in Central Mexico, 1810*

Intendancy	Population	Indian Population	Percentage of Indians
Mexico	1,600,000	1,000,000	62.5%
Puebla	800,000	600,000	75
Oaxaca	600,000	530,000	88.3
Michoacán	400,000	170,000	42.5
Veracruz	190,000	140,000	74
Tlaxcala	90,000	65,000	72.2

haciendas that combined sheep-ranching with farming were beginning to set up small *obrajes* (textile mills) on the estates, increasing the demand in the countryside for reliable full-time laborers and placing new pressure on neighboring villages.[35] For their size, villages in Oaxaca seem to have retained relatively more productive land and more control over flour mills, a common capital investment in the farming regions.[36]

Indians were the largest social group in both regions. In 1810, 62.5 per cent of the population of the Intendancy of Mexico was still classified as rural Indian; 88.3 per cent of Oaxaca's population was also identified as Indian (see Table 1). For the viceroyalty as a whole, less than half of the population in 1793 (39.9 per cent) was said to be Indian. Between them, the intendancies of Mexico and Oaxaca accounted for more than one-third (34 per cent) of the Indians of New Spain in 1793, and the Indians of these two provinces were concentrated in the subregions used in this study.[37] These proportions point as well to an important contrast between central Mexico and Oaxaca at the end of the colonial period: the countryside of central Mexico harbored more non-Indians. The smaller proportion of indigenous peasants was combined with a higher population density in central Mexico: fifteen inhabitants per square kilometer in central Mexico compared to eight inhabitants per square kilometer in Oaxaca. The numerous *rancheros* and overseers living on private estates were Creoles and mestizos, as were some of the resident laborers on the large estates. Contacts between Indian villagers and non-Indians in central Mexico were frequent but not especially sociable. Peasant farmers complained that alcaldes mayores were trying to force them to live in settlements dominated by Spaniards, and priests complained that the Indians were not allowing devout, law-abiding *gente de razón* (non-Indians, especially Spaniards, mestizos, and mulattoes) to live in the parish seats.[38] When rural villages staged political riots, gente de razón seemed always closer at hand to aid the militia in central Mexico than in the Mixteca Alta. Non-Indians dominated numerically in many of the rural administrative and commercial towns of central Mexico, such as Toluca, Actopan, Cuernavaca, and Coyoacán, as well as in the mining communities of Pachuca, Real del Monte, Taxco, Sultepec, and Temascaltepec. The administrative and commercial cabeceras of Oaxaca generally were more Hispanicized and had more non-Indian residents than their *sujetos* (politically subordinate communities), but even the cabeceras—Teposcolula, Nochistlán, Tlacolula, Zimatlán, and Ocotlán—were still largely composed of Indian peasant farmers.

The fierce corporate identity of many landholding villages was inevitably inconsistent with the peasant condition within the imperial system, sometimes sharply so. Peasants' strongest allegiances were to community and family, but these local groups were never entirely closed or isolated from the larger social order. Villages were linked to larger societies by regional peasant markets, fading ethnic identities, political jurisdictions of head towns and sujetos, and marriage patterns in which wives were sometimes sought outside the community or at least outside the barrio, or neighborhood, lineage group. These wider associations were based on practical considerations and rarely signified regional solidarity. To varying degrees the villagers of central Mexico and Oaxaca were subordinate to the state and dependent on colonial officials, landowners, merchants, and other outsiders for the terms on which their products and labor were exchanged.* Their inferior status made them objects of paternalistic control, subject to demeaning treatment, such as public whippings, and to the formal slighting of their credibility in court testimony.

---

*Institutionalized forced labor was less apparent in the eighteenth century. Labor drafts continued but were much diminished and technically exceptions to the law. Peonage, penal servitude, and illegal coercion were also made use of, but, generally, labor was secured in less obviously coercive ways.

Chapter 2 Drinking

E
arly colonial administrators and priests often remarked on the pervasive, uncontrolled drinking of Indians in central and southern Mexico. Taken at face value and compared to evidence of restricted drinking before the conquest, these early reports of a surge of Indian drunkenness commonly have been taken by historians to indicate a demoralized, self-destructive Indian response to the harsh realities of epidemic disease and Spanish colonization.[1] This view of drinking as cause or consequence of Indian demoralization needs careful examination because the subject of Indians and drugs in past time contains fundamental questions that are not well documented in these standard sources: Who drank before the conquest? What? When? How much? In what ways did these patterns change after the conquest? What were the beneficial and harmful effects of more drinking?

PRE-HISPANIC DRINKING

Knowing how Indians drank before the arrival of Europeans is essential for evaluating changes in the colonial period. The major published sources on pre-Hispanic drinking in central Mexico and Oaxaca are the few surviving Indian codices, Sahagún's monumental *Florentine Codex*, the *Codex Mendoza*, the writings of sixteenth-century Spanish colonists, such as Motolinía, Mendieta, and Zorita, scattered references in other clerical accounts, and the *Relaciones Geográficas*, which were composed in the 1570's.[2] The pre-Hispanic and early colonial codices provide clues to the divine significance of native fermented drinks (distillation was unknown in the New World before European colonization) and their ritual uses but relatively little information on actual drinking patterns. The *Florentine Codex* contains more explicit information on elite drinking, sacred uses and additives, and pre-Hispanic legal restrictions on drinking, but since most of Sahagún's informants were high nobles from Tlatelolco, it presents Indian life from a socially and geographically restricted viewpoint. It tells us a great deal about the norms and beliefs of the Aztec nobility, but its application to Indian life generally is problematical. Motolinía and Zorita must be taken seriously, but they offer short general impressions about drinking based on unspecified sources. In their allusions to drunken Indians, the early chroniclers may be telling us more about their concerns as urban magistrates, missionaries, and Spaniards than about the real uses of alcohol in native societies. At best, relying on Sahagún, Motolinía, Mendieta, Durán, Zorita, and related sources for documentation of Indian values and behavior tends to present pre-Hispanic history with an Aztec bias, which may not correspond to patterns of behavior in peasant communities within or outside the Aztec tribute territory. The Aztec overlay in most of the early Spanish accounts tends to standardize pre-Hispanic morals and the uses of alcohol according to formal rules of a state that had limited control over the social life of central Mexico.

The *Relaciones Geográficas* also depend heavily on noble Indian informants. They are further limited because they were compiled more than fifty years after the conquest and because the reports are not in all ways comparable. Two generations after the conquest, recollections of real-life complexities in pre-Hispanic times were fading, whereas the rules remained vivid, at least in the minds of the descendants of the rulers. Many reports mention severe punishment for unlawful drinking in pre-Hispanic times, but few describe actual drinking practices.* On the other hand, they bear the stamp of a specific time and place; they provide information on many localities in central Mexico and Oaxaca; and they paraphrase directly the testimony of Indian witnesses. Early Inquisition trials of Indian nobles for idolatry are another firsthand source of information on pre-Hispanic drinking. Trials from Ocuytuco

---

*The *Relaciones Geográficas* were compiled in the late 1570's, a period of major adjustments in rural communities. Resettlement of peasants had been attempted with some success in the preceding decades; Gerhard, "Congregaciones de indios," pp. 347–95, has brought to light new documentation that suggests that these congregaciones had a greater impact on rural communities than previously imagined. The most devastating epidemic of the colonial period was sweeping the countryside at this time, and the legitimacy and prerogatives of the local hereditary nobility were eroding. Native noble informants for these reports often lamented the "liberty" and laziness of commoners at the cost of order, especially the decline of sumptuary laws, which favored the nobility. Such views of embattled Indian nobles are found in the following reports for central Mexico and Oaxaca: *Papeles de Nueva España* IV, pp. 74, 80, 106, 141–42, 146, 186, 221, 244; VI, pp. 15, 29, 55, 57, 73, 76, 124, 141, 185, 278, 294, 301. Benjamin Keen (p. 129) describes the nostalgia of one noble descendant for the good life of leisure and consumption before the conquest. Quite early in the colonial period the nobility continued its sumptuous banquets in secret in order not to arouse the macehuales, AGN *Inquisición* 30 exp. 9 (Ocuytuco, Morelos, 1539).

(Morelos, 1539), Coatlán (Oaxaca, 1544), and Yanhuitlán (Oaxaca, 1544) include testimony of Indian witnesses on the ritual use of pulque at funerals, weddings, and fertility celebrations.[3]

Taken together, these sources suggest a general pattern of restricted use but also a rich variety of rules and drinking occasions in different communities. Indian notions of moderation seem to have focused on the occasions when alcohol could be used and by whom rather than on how much was drunk. On ritual occasions when drinking was permitted, adult male participants could apparently drink themselves into a stupor without shame.[4] There were few if any totally abstinent communities in central Mexico and Oaxaca before the conquest. Only the *Relación Geográfica* for Tecciztlán says directly that the people did not drink pulque. Other reports in this series state that certain groups such as priests or macehuales did not drink or that people did not "become drunk," not that drinking was unknown in the community.* Another possible example of abstinence or at least severely restricted drinking is recorded in Chimalpahín's chronicle of Amecameca history. In 1476, after the execution of Prince Cahualtzin for chronic drunkenness, "no one became drunk, in spite of the fact that the ancients were very attached to drunkenness during their idolatrous ceremonies."[5]

The principal alcoholic drink throughout central Mexico was derived from the maguey, a large agave or century plant with thick, fleshy leaves. Maguey is a hardy perennial, extremely resistant to drought and frost. It played a leading role in native life and religion because of its many uses and is described at length in many of the *Relaciones Geográficas*. With corn, it was a staff of peasant life in pre-Hispanic and early colonial times. The fermented juice from its heart—pulque—was the common people's intoxicant, but this vitamin-rich juice was also an important dietary supplement and was substituted for water during the dry months of every year and the periodic droughts.† It was considered an essential medication, especially good for diarrhea and stomach ailments and as the medium for medicinal roots and herbs.[6] The maguey's spiny leaf was used for food, fuel, and roofing material. It was shredded for thread and fiber, which was woven into rope, tumplines, sandals, and blankets. Its sharp tips served as needles.

---

*PNE VI, pp. 15, 29, 57. Acosta (pp. 297–98) was under the impression that the general drunkenness he observed in the late sixteenth century contrasted with total ignorance of alcohol before the arrival of Europeans.

†Pulque contains vitamin B, protein, and considerable vitamin C. Next to corn tortillas, it is still the leading food source for Otomí Indians of the Mezquital Valley in Hidalgo, R. K. Anderson et al., pp. 883–903.

One maguey required eight to ten years to mature (somewhat longer at higher altitudes) and then produced sixty to ninety gallons of juice for pulque over a period of a few months.[7] In extracting the juice, the central leaves were cut back and the heart pierced with a sharp knife. Then a bowl was scraped around the hole to catch the accumulating juice. Twice daily, the *tlachiquero*, or collector, gathered the juice by sucking through a long gourd with a hole at each end. The juice was taken to vats made of animal hides or wood, where it was added to a starter and allowed to ferment. After a few days of fermentation the result was pulque, a frothy brew with an alcohol content of about 4 per cent. The juice of the maguey was also cooked to the consistency of syrup. This extract was traded in central Mexico before and after the conquest. Various roots and herbs were added to pulque for their preservative and intoxicating properties.

One clearly pre-Hispanic additive to pulque was *cuapatle* (the bark of the *Acacia angustissima*), which was widely used throughout the pulque zone of central and southern Mexico although its use was forbidden by the Crown in 1529. It is mentioned as a standard additive in various *Relaciones Geográficas* for central Mexico and Oaxaca.[8] Motolinía speaks of cuapatle or *ocpatli* as the "medicine" or "cure" that caused the fermentation of pulque.[9] Other sixteenth-century sources more accurately speak of the bark "giving strength" to the pulque rather than causing fermentation.[10] Henry Bruman, who studied pre-Hispanic drink areas in Mexico, has identified cuapatle as a source of digitoxin, a heart stimulant, which would indeed make the drug effect of the beverage stronger.[11]

Pulque in both Oaxaca and central Mexico was the chief ritual intoxicant. It was believed to have been invented by the gods, and its use was primarily in the service of the gods. A close association among maguey-pulque, fertility, and agriculture in pre-Hispanic central Mexican religions is suggested by the importance of Mayahuel, the goddess of pulque, who appears in the *Codex Vaticanus A* in an earth-mother form with four hundred breasts and whose headdress in the Mixtecan *Borgia Codex* seems to link her with Tlaloc, god of rain and the focal point of peasant religion.[12] The association of pulque with divine femininity is repeated in the colonial period with the Virgin of Guadalupe, who was acclaimed as the mother of maguey, and the Virgin of los Remedios, whose carved image was found on a maguey plant by a Christian cacique.[13]

Reports of large fields of maguey and of extensive taxation, which usually indicate trade in pulque, suggest drinking on a fairly important scale at the time of the conquest.[14] Cultivation of maguey and production of pulque were concentrated in the districts of Cuauhtitlán, Apam, and Tula, northeast of Mexico City in the modern states of Mexico and Hidalgo, which were also centers of an industry that expanded geographically during the colonial period.[15] Pulque origin myths suggest that the fermentation of maguey juice was practiced centuries before the arrival of Europeans among the Otomí Indians of Hidalgo.[16] The *Codex Mendoza* records nine towns in the states of Mexico and Hidalgo producing maguey syrup for tribute to the Señorío of Tenochtitlán at the time of the conquest.[17] Another community, Aoxocopan, and two neighboring settlements provided about 62,500 liters of pulque in tribute each year.[18] The *Relaciones Geográficas* also provide evidence of pre-Hispanic production. The Atitalaquia report, covering part of the district of Tula in southern Hidalgo, speaks of the pre-Hispanic settlement pattern being dispersed in order for community members to tend their maguey fields.[19] The *Relación Geográfica* for Tepeapulco on the plains of Apam in southeastern Hidalgo comments on the "very great quantity of these shrubs [magueyes] in this province," which echoes the observation of Bernal Díaz del Castillo that there were large stands of maguey in central Mexico at the time of the conquest.[20] The church at Tepeapulco, constructed in the 1530's or 1540's, makes heavy use of the maguey as a decorative motif in sculptured columns and paintings, visual evidence of its importance to local people in the early sixteenth century and of the early missionaries' syncretic approach to religious conversion.[21] Cuauhtitlán's position in pre-Hispanic pulque production in the Valley of Mexico is suggested by its manufacture of "Toltec pulque cups" and large jars for transporting liquids.[22]

Restriction of drinking to the native nobility or at least regulation of public drinking by the nobility seems to have been the law, although not necessarily the practice, in tributary provinces of the Triple Alliance and in Oaxaca.[23] Periodic ritual drinking limited to the nobility and coupled with severe punishment—death, whipping, or public humiliation—for commoners who drank (exempting the old and sick) and for nobles who were chronic drunkards, is demonstrated by various *Relaciones Geográficas*, the *Codex Mendoza*, the Ocuytuco trial, and an early civil suit against the cacique of Tlacolula (Oaxaca).[24] Drastic punishment of commoners who drank and special drinking rights for military men, however, are especially evident in the heart of the Aztec domain in and near the Valley of Mexico.[25] The only clear example of capital punishment for drinking in areas outside this region was its application to priests in Malinaltepec (southeastern Guerrero), who were forbidden to drink during their seven years of service.[26] The idea that only the old and sick were permitted to drink regularly seems to originate with the *Codex Mendoza*, an early colonial pictorial manuscript that recorded "laws of the lords of Mexico," again emanating from the Aztec capital. Later sources on this point, such as Zorita, Mendieta, Keen, Wolf, and Guerra, do not provide evidence of this rule applying outside the Aztec domain and seem to be based on the *Codex Mendoza*.[27]

Mass drinking in pre-Hispanic villages may not have been exceptional. There is evidence of general drinking and mild punishment for drinking violations in at least five Oaxaca communities and perhaps also in the state of Mexico on the periphery of Aztec domination.[28] Examples from the *Relaciones Geográficas* and early Inquisition trials suggest that the more common pattern of mass drinking by men and women in Mesoamerica was confined to community ritual occasions associated with principal gods, the agricultural calendar, and benchmarks in the life cycle of native nobles: once a year in the case of Meztitlán (Hidalgo), twice a year in Ucila (Oaxaca), four times a year in Chinantla (Oaxaca), and as often as every twenty days in Teotitlán del Camino (Oaxaca) and Acolman (Mexico).[29] Although they are not clear about the frequency of collective drinking, eight *Relaciones Geográficas* for the bishopric of Oaxaca describe religious celebrations in honor of pagan idols with popular drinking and dancing.[30] Fray Jacinto de la Serna, who served as a parish priest in the Valley of Toluca (Mexico), described sixteen moveable feasts, several of which included popular drinking.[31] Popular drinking is recorded in harvest and rain ceremonies, births, weddings, funerals, and the warrior's rite of passage, as well as during feasts dedicated to particular gods.[32] The drinking celebrations were prolonged affairs, lasting for several days or more. On these ritual occasions pulque was sometimes thrown into a fire as an offering to the gods, as well as consumed by the faithful.

It is not particularly surprising to find that there were various drinking patterns before the conquest. The documented patterns, however, divide into two main types: drinking only by the nobility, with harsh sanctions imposed on violators; and popular drinking on ritual occasions with milder punishment for violations. These two types follow a rough regional division. Ideal patterns of sumptuary drinking by the nobility and severe rules against drunkenness usually occur in communities controlled by warrior overlords, especially those in or near the Valley of Mexico that were under the direct administrative control of the Triple Alliance. Religious rituals with drinking in this area seem to have been restricted to a select group of nobles, or at least ritual use by others was dictated by the nobility.[33] Of the communities documented in the *Relaciones Geográficas*, mass drinking was more common outside the zones controlled by an entrenched warrior elite and perhaps is an old pattern in central Mexico that the Aztecs were attempting to suppress because of its association with rituals affirming the sanctity of the local community. Oaxaca provides strikingly more evidence of community drinking at the time of the conquest than does central Mexico. Within central Mexico, community drinking was apparently more common in regions that were independent or that may have paid tribute to the Triple Alliance but were not ruled from Tenochtitlán, such as Meztitlán (Hidalgo) or Totolapa and Acolman (Mexico).[34]

In both of these configurations religious ritual and periodic heavy drinking are the outstanding features. Ritual—the formal, symbolic expression of values, attitudes, and expectations—permeated the use of alcohol just as it, along with a view of the insignificance of humanity in the face of Nature personified, permeated pre-Hispanic life in general. Even the Aztecs, who attempted to place tight sumptuary controls on drinking, were not ancient prohibitionists and did not view the physical effects of alcohol in a uniformly negative way. Sahagún reports that the Aztecs called pulque *centzonttotochtli*, or "four hundred rabbits," because of its almost infinite variety of effects on the behavior of those who drank it.[35] Pulque, then, was an important drink in our regions before the conquest: not really a forbidden drink, but a powerful, almost sacred substance, with unpredictable effects, and generally controlled by rules of periodic, ritual use.

EARLY COLONIAL USES OF ALCOHOL

Indian drinking in the aftermath of the Spanish conquest received at least passing mention by most early colonial chroniclers. Despite this body of commentary, the transition to colonial drinking patterns is difficult to present in convincing detail of time and place. In independent sources various types of change are discernible, but the scale of new social behavior—when and where it is representative—is difficult to determine before the eighteenth century. Additionally, the documentation is much more abundant for central Mexico, especially the hinterland of the viceregal capital in Mexico City, than for other regions. This concentration of evidence presents problems of comparison among regions and tends to give a metropolitan bias to Spanish comments on Indian drinking in general.[36] Nevertheless, enough information is available on drinking practices in the early colonial period to answer three general questions: Was there more drinking in central Mexico and Oaxaca after the conquest? Did ritual social and religious drinking continue? Did increased drinking contribute to destructive social behavior?

Since the extent of pulque consumption before the conquest is an open question, it is difficult to estimate the magnitude of increase in the sixteenth century. Nevertheless, pulque and Spanish wine and brandy were clearly consumed on an impressive scale, and liquor was certainly becoming an important commercial product for Spanish traders and Indian peasants alike.

One type of evidence of more drinking in the sixteenth century is the reports of macehuales drinking in central Mexico communities where only nobles had been allowed to drink before the conquest.[37] This development is consistent with a general breakdown of sumptuary laws limiting foods such as meat and cacao and certain types of clothing to the nobility. Attempts by alcaldes mayores and noble informants in the *Relaciones Geográficas* to explain the Indian depopulation quite often center on new customs of eating, drinking, and dress.[38] Obviously, since they gloss over disease and working conditions, these sources are not balanced accounts of the causes of depopulation, but they do respond to the dramatic decline with their perceptions of other kinds of change after the conquest. A few reports of women and children drinking and of chronic community drunkenness also suggest that the pool of alcohol consumers within the population was increasing.[39] Production of pulque for household use, a common practice in the eighteenth century, probably developed early in the colonial period when the nobles' ability to enforce sumptuary rules was failing.

Other tangible signs of increased drinking and changing attitudes toward liquor are the growing production of pulque for sale and the establishment of taverns and inns in the countryside. Whereas Cuauhtitlán seems to have been the main provider of pulque in the northern section of the Valley of Mexico in pre-Hispanic times, other northern communities closer to Mexico City were reported to be actively involved in the maguey industry in the sixteenth century: Tequixquiac, Tecama, Acolman, Chiconauhtla, Ecatepec, Xaltocan, Teotihuacán, Tepexpam, and Tequicistlán.[40] The *Relaciones Geográficas* for the archbishopric of Mexico report eighteen towns specializing in maguey and the sale of pulque and maguey syrup.[41] All of these towns are located in the modern states of Mexico and Hidalgo, the heartland of pre-Hispanic cultivation of maguey, and all are within seventy-five miles of Mexico City. Commercial production of pulque by villages in Oaxaca is less evident, although Macuilxóchitl in the Valley of Oaxaca was a producer according to its 1576 report, and Malinaltepec, formerly in the bishopric of Oaxaca, now in the state of Guerrero, reportedly bought pulque from other towns.[42] Many other Oaxaca and central Mexico towns mentioned in the *Relaciones Geográficas* cultivated maguey for local uses.[43]

Commercialization of peasant production in the sixteenth and seventeenth centuries is documented in numerous petitions by individual producers for licenses to sell pulque in Mexico City or other market centers in and near the Valley of Mexico.[44] These petitions begin in the late 1580's when the viceroys and audiencias were being called upon by the Crown to control both commerce in liquor and social unrest in the towns and cities of New Spain. The petitions were granted with pro forma regularity until the Mexico City riot of 1692. The liquor trade was actively encouraged by the colonial government and city fathers in the seventeenth century because taxes on alcoholic beverages, especially pulque, had become a major source of revenue for public works.[45] One 1629 petition stated that many villages near Mexico City depended on the sale of pulque for their livelihoods.[46] To sell in Mexico City, petitioners had to live within five leagues (approximately thirteen miles) of the city, a regulation designed to protect against spoilage of the fermented juice before it reached the market, for without preservatives or refrigeration pulque goes bad in less than a week. Producers for outlying markets such as Xochimilco and Pachuca likewise had to be within a five-league radius of the market. This encouraged further specialization of the traditionally maguey-oriented economies of such communities as Cuauhtitlán and Apam. Commercialization of pulque and mezcal is not well documented in Oaxaca before the eighteenth century and then it was on a much more modest scale than in the vicinity of Mexico City.[47] Prior to the 1692 prohibition of pulque production, there seems to have been some trade in pulque in the weekly regional markets and along the major roadways of rural Oaxaca, and some production for sale in Antequera by villages nearby.[48] There are Indian petitions for licenses to sell pulque in the Mixteca Alta, but the general picture is one of less commercialization of liquor in Oaxaca before the eighteenth century.

Inns and taverns were established in villages situated on the main colonial thoroughfares in the sixteenth century.[49] They dispensed wine and pulque to thirsty travelers and exposed the local people to new drinking habits, transient visitors, and retail trade. These roadside inns and taverns usually were operated by village officials under royal license and were intended as revenue-producing enterprises for the community coffers as well as the royal treasury. One danger was that these *mesones* would be rented or sold to unscrupulous outsiders and no longer be regulated by community officials.[50] When this happened, the innkeepers did not simply look to travelers for their business, but catered also to the villagers and encouraged heavier daily drinking.

Proximity to Mexico City was vital to the commercialization and heavy consumption of pulque. The city was not only a huge market for the pulque produced by nearby villagers, it was also a favorite place for peasants to drink. Indians living in the four residential areas of Mexico City were known to be especially heavy drinkers.[51] A Franciscan friar living in the sanctuary of Churubusco (formerly a Culhua community and rural area in the southern portion of the Valley of Mexico, now engulfed by the city) in the late seventeenth century reported that "in the villages near the sanctuary, hundreds of men are continually drunk."[52] Pulque traders of both sexes spent longer periods of time in the city than other rural central Mexicans. Traders from pulque towns such as Cuauhtitlán and Teotihuacán were inclined to establish part-time or permanent residence in Mexico City rather than carry on their business from the fields.[53] For them, as well as for those who came to the city to sell flowers, fodder, firewood, and vegetables or to pursue disputes before the colonial courts, the city was a time-out setting, an island of temporary personal liberty where the village rules on drinking and social respect did not apply.[54] By the late eighteenth century as many as 2,000 nonresident Indians entered the city every day to carry on their business and experience the pleasures of the metropolis.[55] The Plazuela del Volador was a favorite meeting place for Indian peasants, many of whom drank themselves into oblivion and spent the night passed out in the streets.[56] Personal violence is strikingly linked to Indian drinking in early Mexico City. Following the 1692 revolt, the parish priest of two Indian sectors of the city reported that during his long tenure he was accustomed to find forty or more drunken, seriously wounded Indians in the emergency room of the Indian hospital almost every night.[57]

As early as the 1580's the colonial government began to experiment with ways of controlling the consumption of liquor in the city. In 1579, 1585, and 1586 the sale of wine, pulque, and maguey syrup was ordered confined to a few specific sites.[58] In 1608 the viceroy, responding to the special excesses of Mexico City, ordered that only one respectable old woman be licensed to sell pulque for every one hundred Indians (except in towns specializing in maguey).[59] Later laws in 1635 and 1639, responding to clandestine trade and the unresolved problem of regulating vendors, provided that *pulque blanco* (unadulterated pulque) could enter the city only during the daytime and that only two Indian women were to be licensed for each of the four Indian residential areas in Mexico City and one woman for each town within five leagues of the city. The 1639 order conjures up a picture of 250 *pulquerías* operating without license in Mexico City, each of them surrounded by "an army of Indians from dawn to dusk."[60] These efforts at order and control in the pulque trade must have been especially ineffectual after 1629, when peasants were encouraged and protected in their pulque commerce by municipal and viceregal governments engrossed in the tax revenue produced by the sale of pulque. The strategic importance of Mexico City in the patterns of alcohol production and use by peasants became even more evident in the eighteenth century as did the use of distilled drinks and other postconquest concoctions.

Commercialization of pulque contributed to social stratification within communities, as individual peasant entrepreneurs acquired personal fortunes from large-scale exploitation of the maguey fields. One striking example from eighteenth-century Oaxaca is Juan Luis Sánchez, an Indian of San Martín Tilcajete, who produced pulque for sale in Antequera. At the time of his death in the 1760's, Sánchez owned sixty pieces of arable land with 10,000 maguey plants, four houses in Tilcajete, a house and a pulquería in Antequera, a hacienda with 700 head of cattle and sheep and numerous personal effects.[61]

The sale of imported Spanish wines and brandies in peasant villages is another, probably more disruptive change in drinking habits in the sixteenth century. As a new beverage purchased by or sometimes forced upon villagers rather than produced by them, the new Spanish wine was less likely than pulque to carry a close association with community ritual.[62] Itinerant Spanish traders found the sale of wine lucrative, sometimes even a means of manipulating drunken Indians into selling their property at bargain prices.[63] Documentation of the sale of Spanish wine to villages in Oaxaca and central Mexico is concentrated in the late sixteenth and early seventeenth centuries, when the Crown attempted to control the trade; first in 1572 by licensing vendors, and then by laws forbidding the sale of Spanish wine to Indians in 1594, 1637, and 1640.[64] Despite prohibition, this lucrative enterprise, which began early in the colonial period, attracting bishops as well as enterprising laymen to the quick profits, continued well into the seventeenth century.[65] In central Mexico, the wine problem was apparently most serious in the Indian city of Cholula. In 1572 Spaniards were forbidden to sell there without license; yet in 1614 thirty-six private taverns continued to operate clandestinely.[66] Wine sellers were active in the highlands, central valleys, and coastal regions of Oaxaca in the late sixteenth century, but they seem to have found the best rural market near the coast, where several *Relaciones Geográficas* reported Indians of Ocelotepec, Cuauhuitlán, and Miahuatlán to be addicted to the new drink.[67] The men of Ocelotepec were said to spend all their gold on wine. The reporter for Tlalixtac in the Valley of Oaxaca claimed that when it came to Spanish wine, one Indian could drink for twenty Spaniards.[68]

The other side of the wine market issue is that some Indian towns sought to protect themselves against the economic and social costs of the new drinks by denouncing aggressive traders to the viceroy and demanding enforcement of the prohibitions. This was especially true in the Mixteca Alta after 1605, in Ixmiquilpan (Hidalgo) in 1617, in Pungaravato (Guerrero) in 1590, and in the city of Tlaxcala from 1602 to 1616.* The wine trade was also limited by the fact that imported wine was too expensive for long-term wide distribution among peasants.[69]

One important feature of early colonial drinking is the continuation of ritual celebrations as a form of worship in which devotion was measured by the degree of intoxication. Some of the early Spanish accounts imply ritual feasting, rather than heavy daily drinking, in their condemnation of "drunken orgies."[70] Peasants' attempts to keep outsiders from selling pulque and wine in their communities may also represent an effort to maintain local rules of ritual consumption.[71] In

---

*Simple stills for the distillation of liquor had been introduced into Mexico before the end of the sixteenth century. Production and distribution of distilled beverages in the early colonial period are an important but poorly documented facet of the social history of alcohol. Sixteenth-century sources generally do not make a clear distinction between fermented and distilled drinks. Imported "vino" may have referred to brandy as well as wine so that what I have said about Spanish wine may apply to brandy as well, Bruman, "Aboriginal Drink Areas," p. 230. Bruman states that distillation in sixteenth-century Mexico was carried on by Spaniards but is not documented in Indian communities (p. 228). A reference in 1600 to miners of Taxco selling "vino de azúcar" may be an early reference to cane alcohol, Zavala, pp. 400–401. Development of the early sugar industry, which probably promoted distillation in the late sixteenth century, is discussed in Sándoval, *La industria del azúcar*. Negative evidence of distilled sugar cane and maguey juice in early seventeenth-century Mexico is provided in the 1631 and 1635 viceregal ordinances prohibiting their production and consumption, AGN *Ordenanzas* 2 fols. 55v-58v, BNM 1358 exp. 23, fols. 363–66.

some cases early colonial rituals followed pre-Hispanic religious practices with native nobles indulging in drinking feasts, using "heaven's water" (pulque) in honor of the powerful god Tezcatlipoca or the stars, or in order to preserve political ties with the lords of other communities. In these feasts pulque was offered to the gods and sprinkled onto a fire.[72] Drinking feasts lasting for several days continued to accompany marriages and annual celebrations throughout the colonial period.[73] Whether a sign of syncretism or a covert flouting of the new religion, these traditional drinking rites were sometimes practiced according to the Christian calendar. The Ocuytuco nobles, for example, drank to the stars on Sunday nights, and the nobles of Miahuatlán held their annual feast on St. Andrew's day.[74]

The most apparent changes in ritual drinking in the early colonial period, however, were increasing participation by macehuales and an emphasis on rituals with secular rather than religious meaning. Some early drinking was a conscious attempt to ward off Spanish intrusion; nobles of central Mexico in the 1530's and 1540's were accused of encouraging commoners' drinking bouts in order to make them unresponsive to the missionary efforts of Catholic priests. Animal sacrifices accompanied by community drinking were thought to protect the community from new diseases brought by the Spaniards.[75] The secularizing of pulque's symbolic power in the early colonial period is suggested by its strong association with planting and harvest ceremonies, marriage, birth, death, and healing. It was used as a kind of non-Catholic "holy water" (in the words of a seventeenth-century priest) for dedicating new houses, and at the time of the first tapping of a mature maguey.[76] Pulque was also emerging as an article of exchange, consumed in ways that confirmed obligations, social responsibilities, and membership in the community.[77] In one documented example dated 1762, Pascuala Vanegas, a widow from the village of Santa María Asunción Ocotlán in the Valley of Oaxaca, spoke of toasting the Indian alcalde with a cup of pulque when he called on her.[78]

Much of the early colonial evidence about Indians' behavior under the influence of alcohol comes from the reports of political officials and priests. These tend to be sweeping statements of excessive drinking and general indictments of pulque and *tepache* (pulque mixed with sugar and other substances) as the cause of virtually all sins and social problems, including idolatry, rebellion, poverty, illness, violent crime, infidelity, and incest. Some of the observations, such as those of Motolinía, are sober, measured indictments. Some deal in vague metaphors of epidemics and cancers; others conjure up the jaws of Hell. At least one friar, Baltasar de Medina, thought vividly of the use of alcohol in terms of "a deluge of this drink [pulque], and the Indians, not only shipwrecked in their pulque jars on the moist shores of Mexico City, but also on their tiny islands and in their flimsy dwellings exposed to this sea's savage blows."[79] In 1732 the bishop of Michoacán, who had lived for many years in Mexico City, concluded that drink among Indians was the wellspring of all vice.[80]

There is a core of truth to these observations, as the wine trade, the growing consumption of pulque, and the social problems of Mexico City indicate, but they contain a fundamental exaggeration of the Spanish clergy and colonial officeholders, characteristic of Hispanic attitudes toward alcohol and Indians. One key to this exaggeration is a basic difference in the ways Spaniards and Indians defined moderation. Grape wine to Spaniards was a symbol of civilization and Catholic heritage and a culturally essential part of the diet. One Mexican friar called it "a most noble, useful, and necessary drink in these Kingdoms; a drink venerated and honored by Christ; and as the most noble of drinks, He chose to transform it into His most precious blood."[81] Spaniards generally valued a Mediterranean ideal of drinking mostly at mealtimes and being able to "hold" their liquor without losing control of their dignified demeanor and "natural reason."[82] Drunkenness to the point of passing out was considered barbarous, disgusting, ridiculous, and a blot on a man's honor. This notion of moderation was expressed in a number of colonial Spanish sources, sometimes in rather exalted terms; a Mercedarian monk in Mexico City near the end of the seventeenth century stated that "God created wine for the enjoyment of mankind, not for drunkenness."[83] Baltasar Gracián, the Spanish *arbitrista* whose work was widely known in seventeenth-century Mexico, expressed Spain's superiority to her European neighbors in terms of her more civilized attitude toward alcohol: "In Spain, drunkenness has never reached the status of 'Merced' ['You,' the polite form of address], but in France it has already become 'Sir,' in Flanders 'Excellence,' in Germany 'Most Serene Sir,' in Sweden 'Your Highness,' and in England 'Your Majesty.'"[84] "Drunkard" was one of the most offensive insults a Spaniard in Mexico could utter.[85]

Indians defined moderate drinking according to traditional conceptions of appropriate occasions and gastronomic privileges rather than according to the amount consumed or whether the drinkers showed their intoxication. Solitary, daily drinking was generally condemned by peasants, as by the Indians of San Miguel (Temascaltepec), who looked down on neighboring hacienda workers as "professional drinkers."[86]

But periodic heavy drinking in ritual situations, often to complete saturation, was accepted as the standard of moderation—not considered behavior that brought ridicule or shame on the drinker.[87]

It is not surprising, then, to find Spaniards condemning the "excessive drunkenness" of Indians, with examples of Indians who became unconscious, vomited, and lost motor control and with comparisons between the occasional individual excesses of Spaniards and the inebriation of whole peasant communities in Mexico, rather than with observations of heavy daily drinking by Indian peasants.[88] The crucial point for the social historian—which is not considered by most of these Spanish commentators—is how often these communal drinking binges happened and under what circumstances. Spanish concern for Indian drunkenness as distinct from Indian drinking is evident from the beginning of colonial rule, first with a 1529 law to control the use of additives in pulque, followed by a viceregal code in 1546 that set down rules of corporal punishment for Indians who became drunk on any liquor.[89] The perfect Indian drinker from a Spanish viewpoint was Don Fernando Tapia, a rich cacique of Querétaro, who "ate and drank in the Spanish manner with his high table, chairs, and tablecloths. . . . Considering that all Indians are so given to drink, he had one especially excellent trait. No one could truthfully say that he saw him drunk even though he always had one or two casks of wine ready in his cellar."[90] Colonial Spaniards, however, had little confidence that the average Indian could conform to such a standard. Indians by nature and by law were perpetual minors, "niños con barbas" (physically adults but children in mind and spirit). They were not so much malicious as moral weaklings who were easily led astray. In less generous moments, local Spanish officials in the sixteenth century considered native Americans to be "brutes," "uniformly barbarous," "stupid and brutal," "extremely short on intelligence," "without judgment," and "barbarous people of vile inclinations."[91] Applying these sentiments to the use of alcohol, Spanish colonial authorities considered Indians incapable of moderation: "If the Indians drank pulque the way Spaniards drink wine (which is not the case, nor has it been, nor is there any hope of their ever doing so) it could be permitted . . . but these are Indians and it is proven that their custom is to get drunk, and it is for that reason that they drink."* This accurate but highly selective

* AGI *Mexico* 333, informe de Fr. Antonio de Escaray, July 2, 1692. This attitude also is well documented in "Apunte del genio, condición y trabaxos de los yndios, 1799," UT Mexican MS G-273, fol. 1r-v: "It customarily gets them drunk and launches them into a stupor because it is a very unrefined drink, the color of *horchata*. It dulls

observation that Indians drank to get drunk reinforced Spanish preconceptions of Indian habits and was made by many other appalled
Spaniards as well: "The Indian uses it [pulque] to get drunk and unless
he is intoxicated he doesn't believe that he has been drinking."[92]
Drunkenness, then, was a natural inclination of Indians in the minds
of the colonial officials: a barbarous vice of a barbarous people.[93]

Beliefs about the physical effects of alcohol also affected the Spaniards' portrayal of Indian drinking. Alcohol was generally thought to
deprive people of their natural judgment and to give free reign to
baser, animal instincts.[94] In Freudian terms Spanish beliefs about
alcohol and the courts' judgments on crime soaked in liquor followed
a view that alcohol dissolved the superego and broke down the restraints that gave order to society. As one late colonial official put it:
Under the influence of alcohol "the child does not accept his father,
the vassal his lord, nor the Christian his God."[95] To colonial priests
and officials, a drunken state suggested more about Indians than merely disgraceful or uncivilized behavior. The Church considered Indian
drunkenness tantamount to idolatry. This recurring worry, in light of
the view that Indians were normally weak and potential backsliders,
tended to exaggerate the priesthood's impressions of the extent and
damage of alcohol. Officials responsible for social control and the maintenance of colonial authority in the countryside would have been particularly nervous about alcohol's presumed effect as a solvent of the
natural judgment and the formal rules of society. Their tendency to
blame all social problems on alcohol is especially evident in homicide
trials and the 1692 Mexico City riot; it is also expressed in a more generalized fear of "the extreme insolence" of inebriated peasants and the
belief that "there is no manner of sin which will not be committed by
drunken Indians."[96] Similarly, the Indian is sometimes depicted as
docile, humble, and hardworking *except* when he is drinking.[97] Drink
"turn[ed] the hapless heads of the Indians, making them susceptible
to the most serious crimes."[98] These preconceptions were most obvious
in the sixteenth and seventeenth centuries, but in less overt ways they
continued to affect judgments about Indians and alcohol in the late colonial period, not to mention more recent times.[99] Toward the end of the
colonial period, Spanish beliefs about alcohol were also complicated by
the effect of Spanish attitudes on the attitudes and behavior of the peasants themselves.

---

the nerves and the drunkards are without vital signs except respiration for some time.
They [Indians] are sad and melancholy and they laugh less than Europeans." See also
BNM 1358 fols. 43r, 103–107.

Increasingly destructive drinking is, however, difficult to document for the early colonial period except through the general statements of Spanish priests and magistrates. Examples from the *Relaciones Geográficas* of individual and perhaps communal chronic drunkenness have already been noted, as has testimony of violent drunken acts in Mexico City. Case evidence of problem drinking is hard to find, since most rural drinking arrests and penalties were handled within the local village or by the alcalde mayor. Judicial proceedings of village councils were rarely recorded on paper and alcalde mayor proceedings are scarce. From the records for Teposcolula, we can see how the sale of Spanish wine and the movement of non-Indians in the countryside exposed native peasants to new models of drinking behavior that were sometimes rejected and at other times incorporated into local practices. One particularly destructive new model is documented for Yanhuitlán, Mixteca Alta, in 1571. A *mulata* who had moved into the community was reported to be constantly drunk, abusive, and violent, and to be encouraging a few local women to join her in drinking sprees.[100] In 1600 the Indian town council of Achiutla, also in the Mixteca Alta, took the extraordinary step of reporting a local Indian to the alcalde mayor for chronic drunkenness and abusive behavior. Apparently he had become a serious problem that the community could not resolve on its own.

A more representative type of evidence of problem drinking in the early colonial period is a daybook kept by the alcalde mayor of Yanhuitlán on individuals whom he encountered in municipal jails during his circuit of the Mixteca Alta from September 9, 1606, to November 19, 1608.[101] During this period the alcalde mayor encountered 189 individuals under arrest in their villages. Of these, 82 had committed drink-related offenses. Forty-five of the 82 drinker-offenders had been arrested for simple drunkenness; that is, solitary drinking on weekdays or making a public nuisance while drunk. Of these, 14 were reported to have been disorderly as well as drunk. Another 13 of the 82 were arrested for illegal sale of liquor. Of the remaining 24 drink-related cases, 16 were assaults, four were disrespect to community officials, one was verbal abuse against a fellow citizen, and three were wives who had deserted their husbands.

A significant characteristic of these 24 offenders is that, except for the errant wives, they represent a minority of the total cases within each category (see Table B.1, Appendix B). These figures suggest that liquor was available and that simple drunkenness in violation of community norms was a potential problem. The figures on violent crime and disrespect, however, do not indicate that alcohol was routinely associated with such behavior or that alcohol could be considered the cause of serious social problems in peasant communities in the Mixteca Alta in the early seventeenth century.

The examination of long-term changes and continuities in native farming societies' use of alcohol in central Mexico and Oaxaca implicitly questions the sharp division between pre-Hispanic abstinence and an epidemic of alcoholism in the colonial period that was apparent to many colonial officials who recorded their thoughts on peasant drinking. Evidence of pre-Hispanic abstinence is suspiciously thin and legalistic, obtained mostly from harsh penal laws. All together, it suggests that periodic mass communal and ritual drinking was common, especially outside the heart of the Aztec domain. Native commoners evidently drank more often and to excess by European standards after the conquest, and some pre-Hispanic drinking rules and beliefs fell into disuse, but not extinction. Surviving sources shortly after the conquest are, again, administrative reports, religious chronicles, and statements by the declining native elite. They, too, pose special problems of interpretation. The Spanish depiction of drunken Indians suggests cultural differences and preoccupations of rulers, as well as possible mass alcoholism in the sixteenth century. I would say that the principal difference between pre-Hispanic and postconquest drinking patterns after the initial adjustments of the sixteenth century seems to be one of shading and degree rather than radical change. A sharp increase in the scale of alcohol consumption took place, rather than a change in its use pattern. Chronic problems of individual alcoholism and drinking by women must have been greater after the conquest, but ritualized, periodically excessive drinking was common in both periods. It is ill-advised, I think, to assume that evidence of more drinking is somehow sufficient evidence of continuous, socially destructive drinking. A major qualification to the similarity of drinking patterns before and after the conquest is growth of regional differences between Oaxaca and central Mexico. Commercialization of pulque, greater consumption, and the magnetic attraction of Mexico City as a time-out setting suggest more fertile ground for the seeds of alcoholism and alcohol-related crime in central Mexico.

DRINKING IN THE LATE COLONIAL PERIOD

Written sources on drinking in the late period are more abundant and less subject to the self-conscious moralizing of colonial officials and Indian nobles. Records generated in the seventeenth and eigh-

TABLE 2. *Pulque Revenue by District, 1782 and 1792*
(Pesos)

District	1782		1792	
Valley, State of Mexico				
Texcoco	29,565		26,005	
Tacuba	25,670		31,463	
Cuauhtitlán	21,753		21,519	
Chalco	15,976		10,224	
Coyoacán	15,752		12,489	
Mexicalcingo	15,163		15,951	
Guadalupe	10,248		6,978	
Xochimilco	7,983		5,805	
Tenango del Valle	6,133		3,289	
Metepec	4,827		4,667	
Toluca	3,852		5,597	
Ixtlahuaca	3,203		1,804	
Zumpango	2,794		5,966	
Tenancingo	1,644		1,021	
Lerma	1,309		1,028	
TOTAL	165,863	45.8%	151,297	44.4%
Puebla				
Puebla city (+ Tlaxcala?)	66,724		89,807	
Tepeaca	8,444		8,983	
Huejotzingo	4,250		5,669	
Atlixco	3,852		3,171	
Cholula	2,605		3,696	
Tehuacán	2,442		2,415	
Tochimilco	1,831		1,698	
Santiago Tecali	683		619	
Tepejí de la Seda	327		179	
TOTAL	91,158	25.2%	116,237	33.7%
Hidalgo				
Tula	16,036		13,765	
Pachuca	12,177		15,431	
Huichapan	7,202		5,510	
Tulancingo	6,472		6,551	
Apam	5,079		5,290	
Tetepango	2,467		1,483	
Cadereita	2,277		2,176	
Cimapan	2,011		1,768	
Actopan	1,818		773	
Ixmiquilpan	1,360		814	
TOTAL	54,888	15.2%	53,561	15.5%
Oaxaca	36,680	10.1%	12,977	3.8%
Morelos				
Cuernavaca	7,840	2.2%	4,895	1.4%
Michoacán				
Valladolid	2,718	.8%	2,668	.8%
Guanajuato				
Guanajuato	2,025		1,154	
Salamanca	415		192	
TOTAL	2,440	.7%	1,346	.4%
GRAND TOTAL	361,587		345,030	

teenth centuries by official attempts to tax the sale of liquor, to regulate taverns, to control the use of additives in pulque, and to prohibit production of illegal beverages and clandestine trade in legal drinks provide considerable information on the technology of production, consumption, social problems, and administrative attitudes. These sources, along with trial records, are the basis of this investigation into drinks and zones of production, and drinking patterns at the community level in the late colonial period.

Drinks and Zones of Production

Tax records from 1778 to 1796 provide the most detailed picture of the relative importance of different regions engaged in the production of pulque for sale. They are standard printed forms on which monthly figures for the tax collected were entered for each of the revenue-producing districts in the viceroyalty. Tax figures obviously do not translate directly into total sales since there is much evidence of a successful contraband trade and there were probably regional differences in administration of the tax, but the records give us the best evidence we are likely to find of regional importance in the pulque trade and provide a conservative estimate of use. The tax records for 1782 and 1792 have been summarized in Table 2. The highlands of central Mexico—the principal three districts of commercial production —and Oaxaca, where the pulque maguey grows wild and can easily be transplanted in rows and cultivated, constitute the area where pulque was produced and consumed. Together, our two regions represent nearly three-fourths of the pulque revenue in 1782 and almost two-thirds in 1792.*

The records of pulque taxes by month in 1796 for the thirty-eight revenue-producing districts suggest a strong seasonal pattern of consumption (see Table 3). There is a special concentration of tax revenue in December when twenty-eight districts reported peak sales, with smaller concentrations in January, March, April, May and November. These peak periods of sale coincide with the dry months of the year

---

*The decline in Oaxaca's share of the pulque tax seems to have resulted from peasant producers choosing to produce less or stopping production for sale after the provincial tax collectors were authorized in the 1780's to collect taxes based on the number of producing magueyes rather than on actual sales, which led to greatly increased assessments, AEO *Juzgados* bundle for 1808, April 1, 1808, report of the Promotor Fiscal de la Real Hacienda, Mariano de Castillejos, CCG "Instrucción para los visitadores de magueyes de la comprehensión de la Receptoría de Teutitlán del Valle," 1806. The rise in revenue in Puebla during the same period probably resulted from production on private pulque ranchos, which were allowed to continue paying taxes on the amount of pulque taken to market.

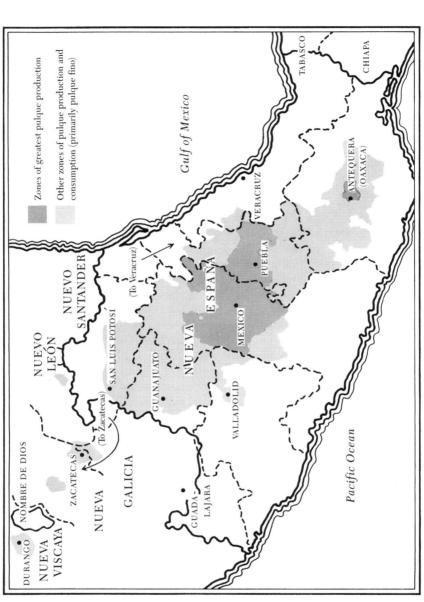

MAP 3: Pulque drink areas in the late eighteenth century. Capital cities, shown by a dot, bear the same names as the intendancies. Nombre de Dios, in the northwest corner of the map, was part of the gobierno of Nueva España

TABLE 3.   *Pulque Revenue by Month for 38 Districts, 1796*

Month	Number of districts		Month	Number of districts	
	High revenue	Low revenue		High revenue	Low revenue
January	9	4	July	3	9
February	2	6	August	—	7
March	7	3	September	1	17
April	8	3	October	6	7
May	10	1	November	9	4
June	1	9	December	28	—

SOURCE: Monthly records in AGN *Pulques* 1–12.

and the holy seasons of Christmas and Easter. The lowest sales months occur during the rainy season from June to September, which is also a period of intensive agricultural labor.

The 1784 report on districts consuming pulque blanco and *pulque tlachique* (an inferior quality produced for local consumption), together with miscellaneous information on the location of maguey fields and pulque production, is illustrated on Map 3. There is a concentration of "low-grade" pulque in the central highlands (especially in Hidalgo and Oaxaca) and, if the report is accurate, a considerable dispersion of fine pulque throughout central and north-central Mexico.

Although these tables and map provide an idea of the geographical distribution of pulque consumption and the centers of production for sale, they do not accurately portray village participation in the late-eighteenth-century pulque industry. Much—although far from all—was produced on pulque ranchos owned by Mexico City families. Since only pulque that was sold could, in principle, be taxed, the tax figures used to identify the areas of greatest production on Map 3 do not account for village production for domestic consumption or privately sold pulque.*

To describe the elusive pulque economy of villages in central Mexico and Oaxaca, we must turn to a miscellany of administrative records, wills, and passing references in judicial files. For this later period, sources allow for some precision and specificity. One of the striking patterns to emerge from the scattered sources is that the commercialization of pulque that began shortly after the conquest was most pronounced

*The role of a few great families in the pulque commerce in Mexico City is discussed in Tutino, pp. 134–41. Taxing pulque sales by villages was a chronic problem for the colonial government. In the late eighteenth century there were unsuccessful attempts to tax by the mature plant rather than the quantity sold. As one administrator said, "The consumption of this drink is . . . invisible because its sale is carried on in secret," BNM 1361 fol. 89v.

in villages within a radius of about fifteen miles from Mexico City—the maximum distance pulque could be legally transported. By the 1620's reports appear about many towns within this area specializing in pulque so intensively that it was their primary means of support.[102] In the late colonial period towns in the jurisdiction of Cuauhtitlán, San Cristóbal Ecatepec, Tejupilco, Coyoacán, Tacuba, Mexicalcingo, Texcoco, and Ixtapalapa (all in or near the Valley of Mexico) specialized in the production of pulque for sale.[103] Pulque was brought to Mexico City from as far as twenty-five leagues away (in spite of regulations permitting the transportation of pulque for sale no more than five leagues), but beyond the five-league limit it was common for only one or two towns in a regional market system to specialize in pulque for sale, while other villages produced almost exclusively for themselves.[104] In the jurisdiction of Cuernavaca, for example, only the community of Huichilac was engaged in large-scale production of pulque for sale.[105] The same holds true for Tecozautla, in the jurisdiction of Xilotepec.[106] In the Valley of Oaxaca, where pulque production reached its peak in the third quarter of the eighteenth century, the towns of San Martín Tilcajete, Santa María Coyotepec, and Tlalixtac were the primary commercial producers. Commercial production of pulque in these towns was often in the hands of a few leading local entrepreneurs who acquired large areas of land near their communities and planted their fields to maguey.[107]

Commerce in alcohol was less developed in Oaxaca. Antequera was an important provincial market, as were towns along the main roads and the periodic marketplaces in peasant areas, but there was no vast market comparable to Mexico City. There were no great private estates based on pulque production for the city. On the contrary, the pulque supply was largely in the hands of a group of villages in the Valley. On the whole, pulque, tepache, and some *aguardiente de caña* were produced in small quantities for strictly local consumption, the mature magueyes being tapped when there was a wedding or birth, or when drinking water was scarce.[108] In the Valley of Oaxaca, where commercial production was greatest in the late colonial period, many of the towns drawn into the market by the greatly increased demands of the 1770's and 1780's had limited commitments to the industry. Various records from 1806, related to a formal investigation into pulque production, state that the plantings varied greatly during the previous thirty years, declining dramatically when the tax on pulque was increased. In 1806 many towns that had produced for sale as well as for local use no longer produced for sale at all.[109]

TABLE 4. *Pulque Revenue in the Jurisdiction of Huajuapan, 1794*

Town	Revenue Pesos	Reales	Town	Revenue Pesos	Reales
Huajuapan	6		Tianguistengo	4	4
San Juan Diquiyu	1		San Juan Yolotepec	2	2
Santa María Tindu		6	San Andrés Yutatio	1	1
Guapanapa	10		Santo Domingo		
San Pedro Zapotitlán	4		Yolotepec	2	2
San Martín de la			Ygualtepec	1	4
Montaña	1	4	Santa Catarina		
San Sebastián			Chinango	6	
del Monte	1	4	Camotlan	1	4
San Miguel de			Yucuquimi	1	1
los Aguacates	6		Saltipan	10	
Silacayoapa	3		Yucuyachi	3	
Cimarronas	2	2	San Andres Dini-		
Misquistlahuaca	4		cuiti	3	
Nochistlán	3		Chazunba	6	
San Mateo del Río	2		Tequistepec	6	
Michiapa	2		San Sebastián		
Yodoino	2	2	Zapotitlán	8	
Guadalupe	5		San Pedro	1	
Nejapa	4		Tutla	2	
Suchitepec	4	4	Estefania Dominga		
Miltepec	3		de Yusuchi	1	

NOTE: 1 peso = 8 reales

Beyond the five-league radius from Mexico City, most rural communities within the zone of pulque production that encompasses our two regions produced enough for local consumption, selling their surplus from time to time.[110] This proved enormously frustrating to the eighteenth-century officials charged with collecting pulque taxes. Most villages had maguey fields and obviously were producing pulque, but because they sold it only occasionally, it was almost impossible to tax them when they did so. Pulque production fluctuated in time and place, and a number of villages in the districts of Metepec, Tula, and Oaxaca filed for relief from the pulque tax because they no longer produced for sale. Tax-collection reports for many parts of central Mexico and the Mixteca Alta in the late eighteenth century show the insignificant amounts of revenue collected from individual villages. Table 4 gives the breakdown for the jurisdiction of Huajuapan on the fringe of the Mixteca Alta in 1794 (population approximately 30,770). Pulque was taxed at 12 *reales* per *carga* (a "load," generally of about 12 *arro-*

bas, or 48 gallons) at this time, and these 36 communities averaged 39 reales in tax, so the amount of pulque sold and actually taxed was 3.25 cargas, or about 156 gallons per year per community.[111] In the Mixteca Alta district of Teposcolula, the collector in 1778 complained that so many communities produced so little for sale that the tax was not even worth collecting.[112]

In the majority of villages—with pulque produced for local consumption and occasionally for sale—the maguey fields were divided into many small holdings. Typically, a peasant family in a central Mexico village had twenty or so plants in its *solar* (house plot) as a border, plus a plot or two of land with perhaps fifty to one hundred plants. This would provide fifteen to twenty mature producing magueyes at a time. Even in the area of specialized commercial production near Mexico City, production was often distributed among many peasant families. In the jurisdictions of Teotihuacán, Cempoala, and Otumba, where pulque was produced for the Mexico City and regional markets, the tax inspector in 1716 reported that "what the individual Indian produces is extremely small."[113] More explicit evidence of this continuing pattern of small producers in a district of considerable production comes from a survey of mature, producing magueyes in the jurisdiction of Coyoacán in 1778.[114] In this document, producers in the Villa de Coyoacán and eight subject towns are listed individually with a notation of the number of magueyes each currently tapped. The results of this inspection are summarized in Table 5. The average number of mature plants harvested by each town is quite low.

There is also some evidence of pulque production on communal lands in peasant villages of central Mexico and Oaxaca.[115] This is a mode of production that would not readily find its way into colonial records unless the community was producing for sale. The few examples, found in offhand references in judicial testimony and church records, suggest that communal production of pulque was exclusively for local use. In one case, Santa María Tecajete in 1800, the record is full enough to describe the rotating system of labor that drew all able-bodied adult men into the maintenance and harvesting of the community's maguey field.[116] Most of the late colonial examples of communal rather than private production are for cofradías. This kind of evidence verifies one important type of community-owned maguey field, but it is probably not the only type, since cofradía records and periodic inspections of cofradía holdings were made in the eighteenth century, whereas records of other kinds of community property were not.

TABLE 5. *Producing Magueyes in the Jurisdiction of Coyoacán, 1778*

Town	Number of producers	Mean average, magueyes	Median, magueyes
Villa de Coyoacán	34	9.8	9
San Francisco	31	9.2	7
Chimalistaca	10	18.9	25
Santa Cruz	7	12.3	13
Xoco	8	11.6	13
San Lucas	33	15.1	13
Candelaria	10	23.5	22
San Pablo	14	20.3	19
Santa Ursula	21	20.9	21

Two striking features of the sale and distribution of pulque in peasant villages are abundantly documented in case histories. One is the important role of women in the pulque trade; the other is the informal distribution and sale of pulque within the villages. Peasant women, more often than men, took the family's pulque to Mexico City and operated stalls selling pulque in market towns. Perhaps this is related to the close association between the maguey plant and femininity. In any case, rural women seem to have been more directly involved in the commercial side of pulque than in other economic activities that brought villagers in contact with outsiders. Within the village, peasant women again were usually in charge of distribution of the drink. Most villages had few formal cantinas; pulque and other local drinks were dispensed from the doorways of homes by a woman of the household. As described in one Mixteca Alta case, local people stopping by the house would be greeted by the vendor and offered drink and sometimes food. The recipient would sometimes reimburse the vendor in cash or kind; at other times no payment would be made, but it was understood that the recipient had incurred an obligation to be settled in the future.[117] Some of the so-called taverns in peasant communities amounted to nothing more than the doorstep of a householder who was known to be tapping a few magueyes at the time. A neighbor might ask if there was any pulque. If so, he would be invited in to have some.[118] Where maguey was easily grown, most households kept a large jug filled with pulque that might be shared or sold on request.[119] This pattern of informal sale and exchange of pulque in homes probably accounts for the curious survey of taverns in the Valley of Oaxaca in 1725, which lists as many as forty-two pulquerías in a single village.

The survey was ordered by the bishop of Oaxaca and assembled from reports by parish priests. The priest of San Juan Teitipac noted in his report that none of the taverns in San Juan was "public." "Tavern" in this case apparently meant any house known to dispense pulque.[120] Nearly one hundred years later, a liquor inspector in the Valley of Oaxaca made this pattern of informal exchange explicit when he noted that there were twelve "taverns" in Tlalixtac, "if one can give this name to a small jug of pulque that is kept for sale to passersby."[121]

In addition to the itinerant wine merchants plying their trade in the countryside, true public taverns evidently were established in peasant villages by the eighteenth century. They were much more common in central Mexico than in Oaxaca. The taverns were generally owned by outside Spaniards or mestizos (in spite of the segregation laws) and in some cases were kept by owners of obrajes who depended upon local villagers as weavers in their sweatshops. Locally owned taverns often belonged to widows.[122] The development of private taverns in the countryside can sometimes be traced to the mesones that licensed villages were allowed to operate in the sixteenth century.[123]

Pulque blanco was the only legal drink during most of the colonial period, but it was certainly not the only drink that was widely consumed. Pulque served as the base for a wide variety of mixed drinks. In spite of periodic royal prohibitions against the use of additives, cuapatle was allowed to peasant traders with special licenses. In 1686, only a few months after the king had ordered that "no type of root or other ingredient that makes it [pulque] stronger, hot, or spicy" could be added to pulque, the viceroy was issuing special licenses to Indians petitioning to sell pulque with cuapatle in Mexico City.[124] Both pulque and cuapatle were prohibited after the 1692 Mexico City riot, but within a few years both were again openly marketed; cuapatle, in spite of renewed prohibitions in 1724, was permitted under special license in the eighteenth century.[125] The usual justification for these licenses was that cuapatle was a preservative that kept the pulque from spoiling in transit from village to market or that it was crucial to correct fermentation. A more important reason slipped into the testimony of one violator who argued that "without it, the pulque doesn't sell."[126] Since the pulque tax had become the main source of revenue for public works and other municipal projects, city officials were obviously concerned that the pulque sell.

Tepache, which could mean almost any mixed drink with a sour pulque and brown sugar base, was also widely consumed in rural central Mexico and Oaxaca in the late colonial period, especially on the fringes of the pulque zone where sugar cane was cultivated.[127] Also known as "pulque amarillo" (yellow pulque), it was prohibited as a "noxious beverage" in 1631 and many times thereafter, but such restrictions were impossible to enforce beyond haphazard and sporadic arrests of individuals who were caught selling it.[128]

The consumption of distilled beverages in the late colonial period seems to have been concentrated in the cities, mining areas, and zones of sugar-cane production, but it was certainly not unknown in the pulque heartland of central Mexico and Oaxaca, especially in market towns.[129] In 1778, in the mining areas alone, it was estimated that 80,000 barrels of *chinguirito* (cheap domestic cane alcohol), 20,000 barrels of Spanish brandy, 10,000 barrels of domestic anise liqueur, and 1,000 barrels of Spanish liqueur were consumed.[130] Until 1796 production of aguardiente de caña, or cane alcohol, was forbidden in Mexico, although it was legally imported in limited quantity from Cuba.[131] The 1784 inventory and various criminal trials against clandestine producers and traders in aguardiente de caña, however, suggest that it was produced as chinguirito in small illegal stills wherever sugar cane grew. Officials of the Juzgado de Bebidas Prohibidas and the Acordada claimed in the mid-eighteenth century that cane alcohol was virtually impossible to control because the distilling equipment was simple and easy to conceal. Small stills were hidden all over the rugged terrain of the jurisdictions of Xalapa and Cuernavaca; the cost was small and the profits were high.[132] Illegal "factories" producing in quantity were raided on the very outskirts of Mexico City and in the mining and manufacturing towns of Córdoba, Orizaba, Sultepec, Pachuca, Temascaltepec, Veracruz, and Puebla.[133] Cane alcohol was apparently not the favored beverage in most rural communities of central Mexico and Oaxaca, although there are clear individual examples of considerable consumption of chinguirito. The priest of San Salvador el Seco in the jurisdiction of Tepeaca (Puebla) reported in 1807 that the villagers had purchased seventy-nine barrels of aguardiente de caña in 1806 and that consumption had been growing at an alarming pace in the preceding few years.[134]

Other distilled beverages also follow a pattern of regional concentration. Mezcal, distilled juice from the baked hearts of a different species of agave, is also documented in eighteenth-century records, particularly for areas of the Bajío and northern Mexico (Querétaro, Guanajuato, Zacatecas, Michoacán, Jalisco, and San Luis Potosí), where

TABLE 6.   *Destination of Spanish Brandy Passing Through the Port of Veracruz, 1792*

Intendancy	Barrels	Intendancy	Barrels
Mexico	16,989	Zacatecas	1,562
Puebla	7,713	San Luis Potosí	825
Guanajuato	5,574	Durango	196
Oaxaca	4,436	Sonora	103
Guadalajara	4,290	TOTAL	48,432
Veracruz	4,241		
Valladolid	2,503		

TABLE 7.   *Spanish Brandy Imported into the Intendancy of Oaxaca, 1792*

Jurisdiction	Barrels	Jurisdiction	Barrels
Antequera	3,433	Nochixtlán	16
Jamiltepec	210	Villa Alta	8
Yanhuitlán	202	Tehuantepec	8
Teposcolula	176	Juchipila	8
Nativitas	87	Justlahuaca	6
Teotitlán del Camino	86	San María del Río	4
Huajuapan	70	Teutila	1
Juquila	68	TOTAL	4,436
Nopalucan	53		

agave hearts have been baked for food since aboriginal times.* Again, the beverage was prohibited, at least in principle, through much of the colonial period, with experiments in legalization being attempted in the eighteenth century in the areas of major production as revenue-producing schemes.

Imported spirits generally found their way to Mexico City, the mining centers, and provincial capitals. Customs and sales-tax records for 1792 provide specific evidence of this uneven distribution. Of the more than 48,000 barrels of Spanish brandy shipped to Veracruz in that year, more than one-third were shipped to Mexico City, where approximately 12,000 barrels were consumed and the rest transhipped to towns in the intendancy such as Toluca, Pachuca, and Querétaro.[135]

*The 1784 inventory lists a number of districts of central Mexico and Oaxaca where this distilled drink was known, although presumably not produced in quantity: Acapulco, Atlixco, Chalco, Chiautla (Puebla), Mexicalcingo, Meztitlán, Nejapa (Oaxaca), Oaxaca, Puebla, Cuauhtla, Sayula, Tacuba, Tehuantepec, Tepeaca, Teposcolula, Texcoco, Toluca, Tulancingo, Villa Alta, Xicayán, Xochimilco, Ixmiquilpan, and Yzúcar.

The remaining barrels were divided among the intendancies of Puebla, Oaxaca, Valladolid, and Guadalajara and the intendancies with mining areas in northern Mexico (see Table 6).

The urban consumption of imported brandy is exemplified by the regional breakdown of the more than 4,000 barrels that reached Oaxaca (see Table 7). More than three-fourths of this supply was consumed in Antequera, the Spanish provincial capital. The rest was divided among towns along the principal trade routes of the intendancy or towns where there were concentrations of non-Indians, such as Teposcolula, Yanhuitlán, Huajuapan, and Jamiltepec. None was reported sold in the peasant jurisdictions of the central valleys of Oaxaca or small communities of the Mixteca Alta.

Uses and Abuses of Pulque in Late Colonial Peasant Communities

The seasonal pattern of pulque consumption was related both to climate and to the religious calendar. During the months of little rainfall from October to May, pulque was widely used as a thirst-quencher. Examples of pulque replacing potable water during the dry season come from both of our regions in the eighteenth century, with some concentration in the more arid area of northern Hidalgo.[136] This extended dry period included the two great holy seasons, Christmas and Easter, which were the peak periods of festive drinking.[137] Daily use of pulque throughout the year may have been quite common in the more arid regions in Hidalgo and during drought years, which caused water shortages throughout both regions. In some areas of the Mixteca Alta and central Mexico, there is also evidence that men took jars of pulque into the fields with them to quench their thirst and "invigorate them" during the rainy months as well.[138] Water, even when it was available for drinking, was often brackish and contaminated, and pulque and aguamiel may have virtually replaced water for drinking purposes in regions where maguey was abundant. As a popular saying in central Mexico went, "Abraham cuando murió, dejó escrito en sus leyes, el pulque es para los hombres y el agua para los bueyes" ("Before he died, Abraham set down among his rules, 'Pulque is made for men, and water for mules'"). Alexander von Humboldt, in his travels through central Mexico at the end of the eighteenth century, observed that "many Indians drink no water, wine, or beer," and Pedro Carrasco reports in a study completed in 1950 that the Otomí Indians of Hidalgo have long used pulque on a daily basis as a source of nutrition and as a substitute for water.[139] There is even one colonial example of villagers in the jurisdiction of Cuauhtitlán using pulque as the cooking medium instead of water.[140] Some communities apparently drank pulque in a rather Mediterranean pattern, with meals and after work, much as is still customary in central Mexico towns such as Milpa Alta, Tecospa, and Tepetlaostoc.[141] The pattern of small-scale family production described earlier meant that the tall jar of foaming pulque was a familiar sight in village homes. Daily drinking to accompany meals at home without drunkenness is specifically noted in cases from San Martín Tilcajete (Valley of Oaxaca) in 1777, Teotihuacán (Valley of Mexico) in 1697, the jurisdiction of Cuauhtitlán (Valley of Mexico) in 1688, Actopan (Hidalgo) in 1615, and Xochimilco (Valley of Mexico) in 1590.[142]

Pulque was also associated with such rites of passage as birth, marriage, and burial, as has been mentioned, and with private parties in celebration of one's saint's day. On these occasions, the gathering often consisted of relatives and neighbors of the barrio. The cycle of regional markets also provided common occasions for peasant drinking, for example, the weekly gatherings in market towns throughout central Mexico and Oaxaca, which were accompanied by heavy drinking. Unlike the periodic drinking in the local village, which was usually restricted to pulque, in the market setting distilled drinks were also available.[143] In addition to its use as a ritual intoxicant for celebrating important events in the life cycle, pulque was periodically used domestically when illness struck. As in the early colonial period, pulque was a kind of all-purpose medicine, the medium in which most other herbal remedies were administered. It was used as a diuretic, for stomach problems in general, and as an anesthetic.[144] It was also used ceremonially in curing rites.[145] The association of female attributes with pulque in pre-Hispanic times carried over to the medicinal use of pulque by peasant women. Women who had given birth received pulque in order to regain strength and lactate. They might also be given pulque during the menstrual period to ensure that the blood would stop flowing.[146]

Peasant drinking was closely associated with Catholic celebrations: Sundays, Easter and Christmas, patron saints' days, and other special feast days such as Candlemas, Corpus Christi, and the day of the Virgin of Guadalupe. For colonial villagers, Sunday was the day of worship and release from daily labors. The Sunday holiday became virtually synonymous with popular drinking in villages, as local officials in central Mexico testified—"the day reserved for their drunkenness," "the custom of the Indians is to drink on Sundays."[147] Such observations and the many case examples of drinking on holy days are echoed in the complaints by parish priests of poor church attendance and popular drinking on Sundays.[148]

In a few cases heavy drinking on Sundays seems to have been an intensification of old rituals and part of a protest against the new religion. Sunday drinking in Huixquilucan (just outside the Valley of Mexico), for example, was associated not with Catholic fervor but with secret cave ceremonies where the liquor was consumed and offered to stone idols.[149] Drinking on holidays in the late colonial period was not, however, always a profanation, as the Catholic priests feared.[150] Pulque had been used in religious ceremonies in pre-Hispanic times, and its carryover to ceremonial occasions in the new religious practice could be an example of syncretism. Some evidence suggestive of syncretism involving pulque is its association with femininity and Catholic worship in the home. There are colonial examples from Mexicalcingo, Coyoacán, and Xochimilco of small family chapels in peasant homes with images of the Virgin Mary and offerings of pulque placed before them; and fields of maguey dedicated to the Virgin in the jurisdiction of Ecatepec.[151] Ponce described pulque offerings and heavy drinking associated with active participation in the rituals of the Church, as did the priest of Tultitlán in 1777 in his complaint that Indians were vomiting and passing out during the celebration of the Mass.[152] The fact that cofradías often owned maguey fields and produced pulque for ceremonial use also suggests some identification between liquor and religion.

Although considerable drinking did occur at intervals throughout central Mexico and Oaxaca, and daily drinking in some of the dry zones of central Mexico, sustained solitary drunkenness that impaired the individual's ability to carry out his obligations to the community and maintain his family was not sanctioned. Community rules about drinking and drunken behavior varied from place to place, and many communities could no longer enforce the old rules of behavior, but clearly there *were* rules that allowed periodic heavy drinking, especially by adult males, and condemned solitary, unsociable tippling.*

Drinking, especially during community celebrations or communal undertakings, had considerable social and ritual meaning that transcended the raw act of becoming intoxicated. The early colonial evidence gives isolated impressions of these uses. The eighteenth-century evidence is clearer and more abundant. Pulque could be used as

*AGN *Criminal* 170 fols. 90–108, 176 fols. 137–44. AEO *Juzgados* bundle for 1812, Juan Patricio Guzmán v. the priest of Santa María Tabegua, December 29, 1812, suggests that peasants who were belligerent drunkards during community fiestas were led off to the municipal jail until the celebrations ended.

a symbolic social bonding and sign of community membership, as it was in many documented cases of community drinking feasts. Such feasts were held to christen a new house or oven, to pray for abundant rainfall, to celebrate the corn harvest or the first maguey wine of the season, upon the death of a fellow villager, and on a religious holiday. One of many examples of community drinking coupled with periodic rituals is recorded in a dispute over clerical fees in Huixquilucan in 1769. In this case the priest accused the townspeople of failing to attend Mass and of keeping their newborn, their sick and dying from receiving the sacraments. Testimony by local villagers, the school-teacher, and knowledgeable Spaniards revealed that a few women attended Mass on Sunday but that the men spent the day drinking a local brew, which was sold just outside the church door. More often than not, the priest was left to worship alone. Village leaders were reported to dispense justice and to worship in carefully guarded caves. During these cave ceremonies, tepache was presented to little stone idols along with lighted candles, flowers, birds, fruit, and tamales. Public drinking feasts reached an annual peak during Easter in Huixquilucan.[153] Other feasts, such as those at Tejupilco in 1806, began at the house of the *mayordomo*, or leading native religious leader for the year, where food and drink were offered to all comers.[154] The pulque produced for these periodic feasts in Huixquilucan and elsewhere was often produced on lands held by the community and worked on a rotational basis by all adult villagers.[155] Local production, whether communal or private, was a standard part of these community drinking rituals.

Several scholars have supposed that violence must very often have been associated with such community drinking.[156] The peasant celebrations in late colonial Mexico were sometimes accompanied by extraordinary behavior such as transvestism and mock battles, but our documentation provides surprisingly few examples of notable unruliness and violence. On the whole, the community drinking feasts in eighteenth-century central and southern Mexico were convivial affairs. The main excess was in the amount of liquor consumed. The cases of community drinking about which enough information exists to allow for analysis suggest that when it occurred, violence during these celebrations was turned outward. The Huixquilucan case is exemplary and especially well documented. No witness mentioned violence against fellow members of the community during the drunken celebrations, although attacks against outsiders *are* recorded for some village drinking feasts. Of the twenty-five other examples of violence associated

with village fiestas, in fifteen cases the victim was an uninvited outsider and the violence usually took place outside town after the celebrations were over. A typical incident occurred in San Miguel Zumpahuacán, in the jurisdiction of Malinalco, during the fiesta of the patron
saint in 1784. In the evening, as the festivities were ending, three
local Indians argued with two bakers from a nearby village and two
Quevedo men from Malinalco who were relatives of the district alcalde
mayor. All were drunk. Insults led to shoves and rock-throwing, and
one of the Quevedos was killed. Probably important to this incident
was the fact that the Quevedos previously had used their privileged
political position to mistreat Indians from San Miguel.[157] In the remaining ten cases, the violence was incidental to the fiesta—a husband
finding his wife in the act of adultery—or was committed in a market
town where people from all over had congregated or in one of the
larger provincial towns, such as Toluca, where many outsiders were to
be found.

This selective pattern of violence—infrequent and directed mainly
against outsiders—suggests that rules of social behavior in the community were not dissolved by alcohol.[158] Behavior was certainly altered,
with much dancing and singing, slurred speech, and people passing
out or acting "loco," if we can believe the testimony of outsiders. The
rules may have been different in these drinking situations, but rules
there were. The explanation of this controlled disinhibition seems to
be found in the social setting of popular drinking celebrations. These
were consciously "community" celebrations, affirming the village identity; outsiders generally were not welcome. In the case of Lerma in
1733, for example, various witnesses testified that when the whole community celebrated, sometimes for five or six days at a time, no outsider
was allowed in, "not even the King's judge." *

Two other kinds of ceremonial drinking played an important part
in eighteenth-century peasant community life. One is drinking in the
context of communal or reciprocal labor. There are documented cases
in central Mexico of reciprocal labor by groups of corn farmers in
which the *milpero* whose fields were being worked supplied pulque for
the whole group.[159] Pulque was also provided for work parties in community fields or annual labor projects for maintaining village water-

---

*AGN *Criminal* 169 fols. 103–43. The extent of popular and individual drinking
sanctioned by communities was not uniform. Drunkenness was judged an offense serious
enough to require imprisonment in some communities, while in others macehuales
rebelled against local authorities who tried to arrest inebriated citizens during popular
celebrations.

works.[160] Second, in personal relationships, liquor, especially pulque, was a token of generosity, trust, and obligation. Building upon the secular uses of pulque in the early colonial period, pulque was served as an article of exchange and hospitality when neighbors called. It was offered as a sign of respect when disputes were taken to village officials, and as a seal of obligation when arranging a marriage or selling property within the community.[161] In some communities the symbolic meaning of pulque as an article of exchange was so important that refusal to share it with fellow citizens on appropriate occasions could elicit a torrent of righteous indignation and justified assault. This was the case in Teocolcingo (jurisdiction of Zacualpan) on the eve of the feast of the Virgin in September 1805 when four couples bearing flowers and candles called on a neighbor. The neighbor offered a drink of pulque to only one of the group (and refused to refill his cup). This led to a heated argument and ultimately a fatal attack on the stingy host.[162]

The ritual and social drinking described here was often restricted to adult men in the community. Women and children did drink on ceremonial occasions, as shown in many examples,[163] but there was a definite tendency to allow men more leeway to drink and participate in public ceremonies. Men performed the dances of the Moors, in reenacting the Christian reconquest of Spain, and of the *huehuenches* (old men); men held public office and presided over most of the formal affairs of the community in which pulque was served. This tendency of women to drink mostly at fiestas and then in smaller quantities is clear enough in modern studies of Mexican village life, and in the few examples of peasant norms concerning appropriate occasions for women to drink in the colonial period. In one assault case in the Mixteca Alta, a witness stated that "a wife should not drink while her husband is drunk."[164] The opposite—that husbands should not drink while their wives were drunk—apparently did not hold true. If we can judge by the behavior of peasant couples, wives who were suspected of drinking without their husbands' tacit consent could be and were punished with severity, while their husbands' periodic drunkenness in taverns as well as during community celebrations was accepted as a matter of course.[165]

Alcohol, especially pulque, was associated with periodic, peaceful rituals that expressed village solidarity, but pulque also contributed to personal disintegration and individual violence in rural areas. Alcoholism and social problems associated with drinking can be described in some detail through the case evidence of criminal and civil court records and the administration of liquor taxes. Colonial records do not usually permit a distinction between the medically diagnosed alcoholic and the excessive drinker who is not physically addicted and who has not suffered serious damage to the liver and other vital organs. Historical records bear more directly on alcoholism in social terms, identifying the solitary or chronic drinker whose ability to carry out his or her social and economic responsibilities had been seriously impaired.* Individual cases of peasant alcoholism in the form of chronic drunkenness are documented for both regions in the seventeenth and eighteenth centuries—such as an orphan boy in Mexico City, an old couple in Santa María Zocoyalco, a man from Texapa who had such a craving for liquor that his relatives had to tie him to a post (and even then he escaped and was found dead at the bottom of a ravine).[166]

Such cases of alcoholism are suggestive in themselves, but they do not provide even a rough measure of the incidence of alcoholism in the colonial period. Considered together, however, the forty or so documented cases form three patterns that may indicate general tendencies. First, the examples from central Mexico outnumber those from Oaxaca by five to one. This is not a representative sample, but a five-to-one ratio is consistent with other differences in drinking patterns in the two regions, such as greater production and commercialization of alcohol in central Mexico. Second, the evidence of alcoholism is related mostly to individual cases rather than to whole communities turning themselves over to unrelieved drinking. The consumption of seventy-nine barrels of aguardiente de caña plus local brews of tepache and pulque in the little Tepeaca town of San Salvador el Seco is impressive and suggests community-wide heavy drinking, but this is the exception rather than the rule. The payment of wages in liquor, which seems to have been so common in the late nineteenth century, was rare in the colonial period.[167] Third, and most striking, is the number of peasant officeholders who were reported to be excessive drinkers. The ritual requirements of officeholding in villages seem to have made officials more susceptible to drinking problems than other citizens. Members of the Indian cabildo received liquor on a daily basis as a sign of respect and obedience as they settled disputes and performed other community business. In their offi-

---

*There are a few examples of the physical waste associated with alcohol in individuals who had stopped eating and were reduced to a bag of bones. The root cause of this physical degeneration may or may not have been alcohol.

cial capacity as judges and community representatives, they were permitted, in fact required, to drink on weekdays and during the daytime.[168]

The relationship between alcohol and violence seems to have differed significantly in the two regions. The sample of homicide and assault cases discussed in Chapter 3 indicates that drink was incidental or absent in the Mixteca Alta. Only 14 of 81 homicides (17 per cent) and 19 of 97 assaults (19.5 per cent) were alcohol-related. The proportion of homicide and assault cases in the central Mexico sample where one or both parties had been drinking was considerably larger: 146 of 244 homicides (60 per cent), and 64 of 149 assaults (43 per cent).

These homicide and assault records also contain substantial revelations of cultural rules, attitudes, and beliefs about alcohol. Next to a husband's jealousy and his prerogative of punishing his wife, the cause of violent crime most frequently pleaded by peasant offenders in central Mexico was alcohol. Declarations of drunkenness as the cause of personal violence were both more numerous (forty-six cases) and more elaborate in the central Mexico sample than they were in the Mixteca Alta cases. Complete loss of memory was a standard claim, but alcohol was also implicated in other ways. Six of the central Mexico offenders remembered the violent scene clearly and thought that alcohol had unlocked their animal passions, making them "blind with rage," "provocative," or "hot-tempered and altered," whereas another Indian specifically maintained that there was no anger involved, "only drunkenness."[169] Alcohol was sometimes blamed only in a general way: "He did what his drunken state dictated."[170] Male offenders also quite commonly claimed temporary insanity caused by alcohol, using phrases such as "out of my mind," "confused state of mind," and "I didn't know what I was doing."[171] In the Mixteca, the range of statements about alcohol as a precipitating factor was quite narrow. In five of the twelve Mixteca cases in which the accused stated that alcohol must have caused the crimes, the offenders claimed complete loss of memory. In each of another five cases, he claimed he was "out of his mind" and had no moral control over his actions. In the last two examples, the accused said they did not know what they were doing.[172]

The courtroom setting undoubtedly affected offenders' testimony about alcohol since admissions of drunkenness usually were sympathetically received by the colonial courts. Spanish officials saw alcohol as a pervasive root cause of crime among Indians and castas, and a state of drunkenness was frequently accepted as a mitigating consideration in sentencing the offender.[173] In each of the forty-six preliminary confessions available for central Mexico, the offender had not yet been formally charged or received legal advice and presumably was offering his own justification of the crime. In eighteen other cases from the central Mexico sample, court-appointed defense attorneys first raised the drunkenness issue well after the preliminary confession and prompted clients with such glossy phrases as: "He was so drunk and so beyond himself that he behaved like a lunatic, like an automaton or a brutal machine whose movements were completely lacking in reason and free will."[174] The legal advantage of claiming drunkenness and the obvious prompting of counsel suggest that some Indian offenders who blamed alcohol were mouthing words that they did not believe. That Indians could use alcohol to advantage as an excuse for premeditated attacks was clear to one judge, who remarked that Indians often drank before they committed crimes, counting on "the security of not being punished."[175] In eight central Mexico trials of Indians, judges refused to accept drinking as a mitigating factor, arguing that alcohol was merely a pretext for a premeditated act.[176]

Although trial records can exaggerate peasant attitudes about alcohol as a cause of crime, it still appears that Indians, especially in central Mexico, were beginning to adopt the Spanish view that alcohol could dissolve one's natural judgment and good sense and could, alone, cause crime. The most persuasive evidence that this view was being incorporated into popular beliefs about alcohol comes from four central Mexico assault cases in which the victims as well as the offenders stated that the offenders' drunken state was the only possible cause of attack.[177]

Even in central Mexico, where alcohol was associated with the majority of village homicides in the eighteenth century, violence under the effect of alcohol was far from indiscriminate. One key to the situations in which alcohol was coupled with violence was the social setting. Community fiestas, harvest rites, christening of a new house, reciprocal labor, and other group rituals during which drinking occurred were rarely the settings for drunken violence among members of the village community.

One specific situation in which drinking often led to violent assault was the drinking bout between two men. The important custom of toasting was double-edged. Accepted as a sign of comradeship, it could also be used by the vengeful to lure rivals into a vulnerable position. A drink offered or requested could not easily be refused. Drinking that began on the pretext of ritual respect could become a symbolic contest between enemies rather like the wrestling bouts of Yahgan

Indians of southern Argentina, which were a substitute for war. The big drinker could gain a psychic victory without ever touching his adversary. But this was a dangerous game. Sometimes armed attack— when the opponent was in a drunken stupor—was the intention all along. As early as the 1590's cases were documented of assaults initiated by peasants who betrayed the meaning of a toast as a sign of respect, obligation, and trust by luring reluctant rivals off the street with a drink and then launching the attack.[178] Because of the imperative of accepting a drink when offered, anger and violence could also erupt inadvertently in these drinking bouts when the drinking guest refused to take any more or was not drinking as much.[179]

Drunken violence seems to have been much more common in unstructured situations in which alcohol did not signify social responsibility. This was especially true in towns that had formal taverns (as opposed to the many peasant homes with a jug of pulque) or pulquerías. Pulquería behavior, whether in Mexico City or a rural village, approached classic disinhibition, in which a person's characteristic behavior changed, often dramatically. Like many bars in American cities, the pulquería was a "time-out" setting where the rules outside did not necessarily apply.[180] The fanciful names of colonial pulquerías invited release from daily cares and responsibilities: "The Monster," "The Shrimps," "The Rooster," "The Friar," "The Louse," and "The Miraculous One."* In this setting, people expected alcohol to be a source of "alegría,"[181] or happiness, sometimes euphoric and raucous behavior. The release of emotions and words in this unstructured tavern setting could be dangerous. Leaving aside the homicides in which peasant men attacked their wives, an impressive proportion of armed attacks in central Mexico began in or near pulquerías.[182] Many were preceded by casual arguments and insults, leading to declarations of superior virility and finally to physical violence. These

---

*Naming pulquerías became a truly extravagant exercise in the nineteenth century. From Mexico City in Porfirian times come: "Los sabios sin estudio" (The Unlettered Wise Men), "El triunfo de la onda fría" (The Triumph of the Cold Wave), "Yo viajo al mas allá" (I'm on my way to oblivion), "Me siento un campeón de box" (I feel like a boxing champ), "La eterna vieja guerra" (The Old Eternal Struggle), "Las groserías de San Cristóbal" (The Gross Acts of St. Christopher), "Las batallas de la noche corrían por el mundo" (The Battles of the Night Spread Around the World), "Los Misterios del comercio" (The Mysteries of Trade), "El mercado de la carne" (The Meat Market), "La dama de la noche" (Lady of the Night), "La muchacha de los muchos besos" (The Girl of Many Kisses), "Mi único amor" (My True Love), "El vaso del olvido" (The Glass of Forgetfulness), "Mi güero" (My Blondie), "Queremos saber qué pasa" (We want to know what's up), "Me quieres aún, pequeña" (Do you still love me, sweetie), "Reír, nada más que reír" (To Laugh, Only to Laugh), "El paraíso de mis sueños" (The Paradise of My Dreams).

circumstances inviting homicide are discussed at length in Chapter 3.

Other unstructured settings that linked alcohol and violence were the meetings of diverse people from different communities on market days and at regional fiestas, in the village streets after dark, at private parties (a family setting in which the restraints of community rules for public behavior may not have applied as they did during community drinking occasions), and especially on the public roads and footpaths outside the villages. Community officials stand out as a group within communities that combined righteous violence with alcohol. Judging by the number of complaints against them, Indian officials in a drunken state were prone to use excessive force while making arrests or intervening in disputes.[183]

One reason for central Mexico's greater incidence of alcohol-related social problems was, again, proximity to the viceroyalty's primate city, Mexico. The city attracted rural traders, litigants, and supplicants with business in the capital, but equally important, Mexico City was a place of refuge, releasing them temporarily from village rules of comportment. The city's spongy foundations were almost as saturated in spirits as they were in lake water. In 1784 the consumption of pulque reached 187 gallons for every adult resident of the city—plus perhaps 3 gallons of distilled alcohol.[184] Mexico City's reputation for heavy drinking and violence was even worse than that of the notorious mining areas. In a report on the growth of taverns at Real del Monte in 1775, the liquor tax collector acknowledged that more drinking had resulted in more deaths, "but nothing like Mexico City."[185] An unknown but surely significant part of the liquor was consumed by the tens of thousands of rural people who flocked to the city for periods of a few days or weeks at a time.[186] Recurring complaints of drunken transients in the city began early in the seventeenth century and continued through the remainder of the colonial period. Drunken excesses in the cities were greatest during the Easter and Christmas seasons, as in the countryside, only on a grander scale. Indians were reported at the end of the colonial period to become drunk "in a most scandalous manner" during the Semana Santa processions.[187]

The association between drinking by rural visitors and disinhibited, sometimes violent behavior seems clear from case examples and observations of city residents. In 1692, following the urban riot, Fray Baltasar de Medina observed that rural people came to Mexico City for the markets and to transact other business and usually ended up at the pulque stalls: "The liberty of those places causes much disorder and they return from the market without money or supplies."[188] The connection between alcohol and violence committed in the city by peasants who had no record of drunken aggression at home is exemplified by an Indian of Xochitepec (jurisdiction of Xochimilco) who took his wife to the city one Sunday in 1796. From church they went out drinking and on the way home he killed her. He pleaded that he was not accustomed to drinking and had consumed so much that he blanked out and did not believe that he had killed her.[189]

The permanent Indian residents of the neighborhoods of San Juan and Santiago seemed to fall into the worst habits of the rural visitors, but in a more systematic way. In 1690 the Inquisition felt compelled to remove a cross from behind the municipal building of the Indian barrio of San Juan because dogs and revelers from a nearby Indian tavern urinated on it, and the latter showed their disrespect in other ways as well.[190] A century later, an investigation into life in the pulquerías reported the same "disorder and liberty."[191]

The Crown tried in various ways to control urban drunkenness, usually by attempts to license a limited number of pulquerías and to regulate the facilities and hours in each, to control clandestine sale and entry of liquor into the city, and to limit the number of transients in Mexico City. Most of the laws were ineffectual. Thirty-six pulquerías were licensed in the seventeenth century, twenty-four for men customers and twelve for women. In the late eighteenth century the number of legal taverns was raised to forty-eight, but there were always hundreds of stalls dispensing pulque illegally. Games, food, music, and furniture were forbidden; pulquerías were required to be open on three sides and could serve only six hours a day Monday to Saturday, and five hours on Sunday. These efforts to make pulquerías uncomfortable and unattractive were difficult to enforce and were routinely disregarded. The city's pulquerías may have been considered "caves of iniquity," "the anterooms of Hell," and "offices of Lucifer," but the city fathers were in a double bind in trying to control drinking.[192] Some of the wealthiest and most influential families in the city were pulque producers, more than five hundred shopkeepers sold wine and spirits as well as sundries, and the tax revenue from liquor was a prime source of municipal funds.

SOME CONCLUSIONS, COMPARISONS, AND IMPONDERABLES

There can be little doubt that peasant drinking did increase after the conquest—although the increase has been exaggerated by Spanish views of moderation. There is also little question that traditional drinking patterns, although by no means abandoned, underwent significant changes. The great alterations in the use of alcohol seem to have taken place in the first fifty years of the colonial period. One change was generally increased consumption (which seems to have stabilized in many communities by the eighteenth century), caused in part by the greater inclusion of macehuales in the pool of drinkers and by the introduction of new drinks, particularly cane alcohol, which supplemented and in some communities of central Mexico virtually replaced pulque as the peasants' staple drink. A second and very significant change was the adjustment of peasant ritual drinking to the many feast days of the Catholic calendar. In pre-Hispanic times, work and ritual had been deeply intertwined; work itself was ceremonially performed and was accented by ritual meaning. In colonial Christian life, the faithful were expected to labor six days a week, reserving Sunday and special holidays for service to God; in practice, they reserved it for rest, pleasure, and community activities, especially group drinking. I have the impression that social reasons for such periodic community drinking had largely replaced religious motives by the eighteenth century.* A third major change was the commercialization of pulque. Increasing trade in the drink drew many peasants into the web of urban life, perhaps giving the villages a safety valve for antisocial emotions but costing the individual peasant dearly in terms of life, health, and property. Commercialization also contributed to social stratification, as individual entrepreneurs acquired personal fortunes in the liquor trade, and may have weakened the sacred and ritual significance of the drink. Sale of pulque to some communities, establishment of privately owned pulquerías in villages, and the social problems attendant upon private production for sale worked to convert maguey into a commodity at the expense of its magical, community-oriented properties.

Nevertheless, controlled communal uses and ritual significance of alcohol continued to be evident in both central Mexico and Oaxaca in the late colonial period. Many kinds of local adjustments to colonial rule were made, and maintenance of relatively peaceful drinking pat-

*The use of drugs other than alcohol in the two regions is a separate topic—one that should shed additional light on drinking patterns. Some information on drug use is available in Aguirre Beltrán, *Medicina y magia.* I have done additional archival research on the use of peyote, which will eventually be available in a short article. The main difference between the meaning of peyote and that of alcohol in peasant communities of central Mexico in the late colonial period is that peyote was used mainly by shamans and was assigned powerful magical properties, such as predicting the future, finding lost or stolen articles, and protecting against danger; alcohol, with its milder drug effects, had little supernatural power of its own and was assigned more social uses.

terns in different places cannot be explained by any single cause. Central Mexico communities with drinking rituals associated with good feelings nevertheless shared at least two characteristics: they preferred pulque or pulque with additives to distilled beverages; and they produced most or all of what they consumed. That central Mexico seems to have had a greater incidence of alcoholism and more destructive social consequences of drinking than the Mixteca Alta may be due to the counterinfluence exerted by Mexico City against the rural villages' traditional rules governing drinking occasions and drinking behavior.

Alcohol studies have made considerable advances in the social and natural sciences during the past twenty-five years. There are now reliable studies of drinking patterns in some modern Mexico communities and elsewhere and a growing literature on the physical effects of alcoholic beverages. These studies have formed the basis of illuminating cross-cultural studies that shed some light on the main points discussed in this chapter.[193]

Alcohol has long been known to have the physical effect of depressing the central nervous system and impairing motor skills. Tests of the galvanic skin response of humans with and without alcohol in the system suggest that moderate amounts of liquor may reduce emotional tension, making alcohol a drug with some potential for anxiety reduction. Recent research comparing Eskimos, Orientals, and Caucasians suggests that alcohol may be metabolized at different rates by different groups. In particular, the smaller Eskimos as a group seem to sober up more slowly than Caucasians, although roughly equal amounts of alcohol are required to reach the same level of intoxication in both groups.[194] This issue of physical effects across populations is still hotly debated and seems a long way from experimental proof. In any case, the possibility of some differences in the physical effects of alcohol on Spaniards and on native Americans cannot be ruled out, although the historian can bring little evidence to bear on this question from written records.

Recent research into the social aspects of drinking has important implications for the role of the physical effects of alcohol on social behavior. Perhaps the most important breakthrough of a general sort is MacAndrew and Edgerton's *Drunken Comportment*, which rests on a large body of recent ethnographic work in individual communities. Their principal thesis, after consideration of the remarkable variety of drunken behavior in different groups, is that, while alcohol seems to have the physical effect of reducing anxiety and perhaps lowering the threshold of violence in individuals, alcohol's physical effects do not reach the point of breaking down restraints, releasing in a uniform way antisocial aggressions that are held in check by sobriety and social custom.[195] In a number of communities cited by MacAndrew and Edgerton, drinking is associated with social harmony rather than "uninhibited" or disruptive behavior. This conclusion that disinhibition or lack of control is not a blanket physiological effect of alcohol, even when the drinkers have consumed prodigious quantities, means that drunken behavior shades subtly but nevertheless definitely into socially variable practices in which group expectations about the effects of alcohol play a crucial part. Verbal and physical aggression *is* a common outcome of drunkenness, suggesting that alcohol may increase the probability of violent behavior, but the connection between alcohol and aggression is far from universal, and when they do occur together, the social behavior is patterned rather than random, as we have seen with the community drinking occasions in colonial Mexico, where drunken violence was directed against outsiders.

The net effect of recent research on social aspects of drinking is to call into serious question the overriding importance of the alcohol itself (especially as a disinhibitor) on the social behavior of people who have been drinking and to open up a variety of possible patterns of behavior, from random violent aggression associated with beliefs that alcohol dissolves the restraints of sobriety to peaceful communal drinking associated with beliefs that alcohol induces harmony and dissipates anger.[196] Characteristic social behavior often changes under the influence of alcohol, but these changes have much to do with what social beliefs tell the drinker about the effects of alcohol. As we have seen in the Mexican examples, social beliefs may forecast violent aggression, unpredictable behavior, or conviviality and contentment as accompaniments to drinking. Recent case studies documenting patterns of alcohol use that reduce social differences and conflict among members of the community also call into question the view that because alcohol has the physiological effect of reducing emotional tension, drinking must be a sign of escape from a world of conflict and despair.[197] In other words, there is no simple relationship between the degree of conflict in a society and the quantity of alcohol consumed. Drinking may be associated with conflict, but its use as a symbol of community membership in modern rural Mexican communities such as Tecospa and Juxtlahuaca belies the idea that periodic heavy drinking is necessarily a sterile retreat into drugged euphoria from social conflicts that the individual or the group is powerless to resolve.[198]

After weighing the written record on drinking in eighteenth-century rural central Mexico and Oaxaca and the literature on social aspects of drinking, I would emphasize that individual examples of alcoholism and violent drunken behavior, and general commentaries by colonial officials on the destruction caused by peasant drinking, are not conclusive evidence that a "plague of alcoholism" swept the Mexican countryside like the devastating *matlazáhuatl* epidemics of the sixteenth century. There *is* substantial evidence that peasants drank more—and more often—after the conquest, that the risk of alcoholism was greater, and that the religious significance of alcoholic beverages was declining. This increase in drinking usually is taken to signify "psychological unemployment," "impotence," "escape," or "psychic malaise." But the assumption that alcohol use has a direct relationship to mental health depends on oversimplified views of the physical effects of alcohol: either that it is a generalized disinhibitor and therefore causes violence and social disintegration, or that its drug and anxiety-reducing properties make it a measure of the mental illness of whole societies.[199] Moreover, such psychological explanations need to be supplemented from a perspective that allows for both the importance of social groups, villages, and subvillage units, and the possibility that drinking may have had little or nothing to do with social breakdown or social cohesion. There is little evidence that rural Indians, outside of their time in Mexico City, engaged in unrelieved drinking as an escape from depression and moral collapse. The despair of the deposed Aztec rulers is well-documented in the *Florentine Codex*, but it cannot be inferred from this evidence that peasant communities only nominally integrated into Aztec life were equally devastated by the political conquest. In fact, the discrete landholding village gained importance in the colonial period at the expense of ethnic and regional ties. Increased village drinking and the symbolic importance of pulque to community life reflect village adjustments to this change—as well as to the disasters of epidemic disease, resettlement, and colonial labor systems, and the general confusion and disorder of rural life in the early colonial period.

Chapter 3 Homicide

Records of criminal trials are one of the most useful and abundant primary sources for studying social conflict and the values, living patterns, and social behavior of Indian villagers in colonial Latin America. They contain the voices of peasants themselves speaking of the world in which they lived. Rich in information for the social history of rural Mexico, trial records nevertheless pose serious problems of interpretation: Are surviving records a representative sample of crime in the countryside? Are they even representative of the category of crime they document?

After studying the range of crimes documented for the colonial period, I have come to the conclusion that the criminal records for central Mexico and Oaxaca are not equally representative of all types of criminal behavior in the countryside. Criminal archives for rural districts rarely included detailed lists of all arrests that would permit even a rough estimate of the incidence of crime in the colonial period in the manner with which J. M. Beattie, J. B. Given, and others have dealt with the incidence of crime in English history. At best, summary arrest records, when available, provide an idea of the kinds of behavior the state identified as crimes.[1] Some categories of crime—usually the less serious from the state's perspective—were inevitably underrepresented in arrest records and were affected by changing standards of law enforcement, whereas behavior that villages considered criminal but that was not prosecuted by the state, such as witchcraft, is missing altogether. The atmosphere of suspicion and suppressed hostility documented by ethnographers among so many villages in central and southern Mexico makes it questionable to suppose that even a full picture of recorded interpersonal violence would reflect all or even the main points of tension and conflict in these communities.

Nevertheless, a few tentative statements on the incidence of crime in central Mexico and Oaxaca can be advanced in an effort to place in perspective the behavior documented as criminal in the trials, although it should be obvious even at a glance that this is not the main benefit of the surviving criminal records for peasant Mexico. On the basis of fragmentary arrest records for the seventeenth and nineteenth centuries, it seems fair to assume that rural homicide rates generally increased in the late-seventeenth and eighteenth centuries and that more homicides occurred on the average in central Mexico than in the Mixteca Alta (where they were estimated at 12 per 100,000 population annually). It *is* necessary to struggle with the relative incidence of different kinds of criminal behavior as an aid to evaluate the changing importance of personal violence in peasant social life. Even if we could establish solid estimates of the incidence of homicide at several points in the colonial period showing rising levels, this might mean an erosion in some social defenses against violence, but it would not be conclusive evidence of social breakdown. As Robert Edgerton has suggested, human societies from tribes to cities have displayed an "immense capacity for living with violence." In some societies violence is regarded as an acceptable and necessary aspect of life.[2]

Colonial trial records deal with an extraordinary variety of violations of colonial law, which incorporated the principles of formal, institutionalized social control. Documented crimes include among others homicide, assault and battery, rape, robbery, nonpayment of debts, slander, sodomy, adultery, prostitution, and child-abandonment; but can we say that the records contain a representative group of cases for any of these criminal categories? For nearly all categories the answer is no. No formal requirement demanded that rape, adultery, robbery, and the others *within* villages be brought to the colonial magistrates for trial. Village leaders usually disposed of such cases without leaving a written record. There is good reason to suppose that when minor offenses within villages reached the colonial courts it was because one of the parties to the crime was dissatisfied with the verdict, because the village officers considered the case too sensitive to settle locally, or because the parish priest took it upon himself to inform the alcalde mayor. These cases contain much suggestive information, but they cannot be treated as a representative group.*

The law and judicial practice in colonial Mexico required that three categories of crime in rural communities be reported to the colonial courts: homicides, serious cases of aggravated assault, and seditious acts.[3] We can expect colonial records to contain a fairly representative sample of these cases, even though some homicides and many armed assaults undoubtedly escaped the attention of colonial magistrates and

---

*An interesting study of when the colonial courts were used by peasants could be made, but this raises a different set of questions. The central Mexico records suggest that peasants living near Mexico City were more likely to bring domestic problems (such as adultery and wife-beating) to the attention of the colonial courts.

the records of many others, especially in central Mexico, have been lost. Acts of homicide had certain legal characteristics in colonial Mexico beyond the formal requirement that they be reported to the viceregal authorities. These aspects lead me to think that surviving trial records for homicide are more comprehensive than those for other colonial crimes. Since a crime is only a crime when a law makes it so, the peasant subjects had to accept the legal system's definition of a particular crime if we are to be reasonably sure that it was reported as a matter of course. Virtually all types of homicide were recognized as criminal by both the colonial authorities and Indian villagers. From what we know of pre-Hispanic criminal law, homicide was among the few acts generally considered criminal under Indian law as well as under the imposed Spanish law.[4]

One advantage of studying homicide is that both comparable information from other societies and established techniques for organizing evidence are available to illuminate the meaning of recorded cases.[5] Homicide has long been a favorite category of analysis by criminologists, and with good reason. It is perhaps the only social act that is almost universally regarded as a crime.[6] It is generally acknowledged to be the one type of crime that can be handled statistically for most societies.

I have therefore restricted this study to trial records for homicides and armed assault and battery cases, emphasizing the more reliable homicide sample wherever possible. Information was drawn from 564 trials in rural communities of central Mexico and the Mixteca Alta. Of these trial records, 362 were located in an area that roughly corresponds to the modern states of Mexico and Hidalgo, and 202 cases come from the Alcaldía Mayor of Teposcolula in the Mixteca Alta. More than 95 percent of the central Mexico trial records date from 1780 to 1815, and the Mixteca Alta trials are distributed quite evenly over the periods 1620 to 1650 and 1780 to 1815. Although the total number of homicide and assault cases for the Mixteca Alta is smaller, the sample is more complete than the central Mexico sample for two reasons. First, the area of the Mixteca records is roughly six times smaller in size and eight times smaller in population than the area of the central Mexico records. Second, I have examined nearly all of the extant colonial homicide and assault records for the district of Teposcolula compared to about three-fourths of the nonmilitary cases in AGN *Criminal* that pertain to rural central Mexico (380 of an estimated 500 volumes of nonmilitary criminal records). On the assumption that this selection is a heterogeneous sample of homicides and assaults in the two areas, chances are about 90 in 100 that the results will have an error of less than ±3.7 per cent.[7]

The records deal primarily with crimes that took place within Indian communities and were tried in the courts established by Spanish law at the district and provincial levels. The trials involved Spanish and Creole judges and lawyers and Indian peasant and other lower-class participants and witnesses. People classified as Indians make up 64 per cent of the central Mexico offenders and 76 per cent of the victims. The Mixteca Alta sample yields a higher proportion of Indians: 95 per cent of the offenders and 90 per cent of the victims. This difference reflects the larger proportion of non-Indians living in rural central Mexico.

Homicide and assault trial records involving Indian peasants are usually quite long, a typical case running about thirty folios (sixty pages). A reasonably fair hearing was assured by the appointment of a defense attorney without charge through the Juzgado de Indios if the defendant could not afford to hire his own counsel.[8] Administrative reforms were made in the Juzgado de Indios in 1785 to provide adequate pay for the court-appointed attorneys and competent defense work from them.[9]

These trial records usually provide four kinds of information: the criminal setting and act (time of day, location, reasons for attack, words exchanged, weapons used, and wounds inflicted); the personal and social background of offender and victim (age, marital status, race, occupation, home town, character traits, relationship between offender and victim); the legal defense; and the court's verdict. Important recurring sources of information in the records are (1) the initial one- or two-page report of the crime made by the village officials to the alcalde mayor, usually dictated within a few hours of the act; (2) the offender's declarations (usually a preliminary declaration shortly after arrest and a formal declaration made under interrogation during the trial, covering two to five pages); (3) testimony by victim, expert witnesses, eyewitnesses, and character witnesses, which comprise the bulk of most trial records; (4) the judge's summation of incriminating evidence; (5) the defense lawyer's case, including legal arguments and the testimony of additional witnesses; and (6) the judge's explanation of the verdict and sentence (the last three categories usually take up six to ten pages). Witnesses usually responded to specific questions put to them by the court, but the victim and the offender in the preliminary and formal declarations responded to a more open-ended inquiry into their views of what happened. The standard questions for the victim (even in most homicides, the victim lived long enough to make a statement) were: Who wounded you? Why? Where? With what weapon? Who witnessed the attack?

I have tried to use the trial records to show how patterns of violent crime emerging from a large body of case evidence can reveal other aspects of peasant societies. The patterns of homicide, as a social act, can illuminate basic values and points of tension within the society. At the very least, a large group of homicide trial records allows us to see the settings and relationships in which violence that could threaten life was committed in these peasant regions. Although I greatly admire the ability of Oscar Lewis and Ricardo Pozas, among others, to evoke Mexican rural life through the biographies of individual peasants like Juan Pérez Jolote and Pedro Martínez, it is primarily in the accumulation of individual coincidences that the delicate network of relationships and feelings can be made visible through written records by the social historian who has not directly experienced the time and place of the people he studies.

THE HOMICIDE SETTING

The temporal distribution of the village homicides in our two samples is summarized in Tables 8–10. Here, the points of similarity between the Mixteca Alta and central Mexico are more striking than the differences. Most homicides in both regions happened at night and only about one of ten homicides took place in the morning. Sunday stands out as the day of the week when homicides were most likely to occur in both regions, with midweek being least violent.

The seasonal pattern is less clear than the time of day and weekly distribution. What stands out most clearly for both regions is the low point in the annual cycle: June and July for the Mixteca Alta, and May, June, and July for central Mexico. The months with the highest number of homicides in the Mixteca Alta were in the spring, but in central Mexico, they were in the fall.

Together, Tables 8, 9, and 10 suggest that rural homicides generally occurred outside the normal periods of work—after returning from the fields in the evening, on Sundays (which became the day of rest and

TABLE 8.   *Distribution of Homicides Throughout the Day*

Period	Central Mexico		Mixteca Alta	
	Number	Percentage	Number	Percentage
Morning	11	11%	6	11%
Afternoon (to dusk)	36	36	12	21
Evening	55	55	38	68
TOTAL	102		56	

NOTE: Percentages in this table and others that follow do not always sum to 100 because of rounding.

TABLE 9.   *Daily Distribution of Homicides*

Day	Central Mexico		Mixteca Alta	
	Number	Percentage	Number	Percentage
Sunday	44	51%	21	44%
Monday	11	13	9	19
Tuesday	7	8	4	8
Wednesday	3	3	—	—
Thursday	8	9	4	8
Friday	4	5	4	8
Saturday	10	11	6	13
TOTAL	87		48	

TABLE 10.   *Monthly Distribution of Homicides*

Month	Central Mexico		Mixteca Alta	
	Number	Percentage	Number	Percentage
January	13	7%	11	10%
February	18	10	6	5
March	15	9	8	7
April	14	8	14	13
May	10	6	17	15
June	8	5	3	3
July	12	7	5	5
August	13	8	13	12
September	13	8	12	11
October	19	11	5	5
November	21	12	7	6
December	19	11	10	9
TOTAL	175		111	

worship in the colonial period, sometimes spilling over into Monday, which was popularly referred to as "San Lunes" from late colonial times), and before and after the peak periods of agricultural work in June and July when peasant farmers spent nearly every day in the fields. The slack periods in the farming cycle coincided with the great religious seasons of Easter and Christmas, a potentially explosive combination of leisure time and popular celebration. For the Mixteca Alta, the high point in the seasonal distribution of homicide seems to come after the Easter season and before planting, whereas the central Mexico peak seems to be after the fall harvest through Christmas. I suspect that if we had a larger sample of assaults to include with the homicides, two annual peaks would be evident in both regions—before the planting at Easter and after the harvest near Christmas. A dimension of the temporal distribution not evident in the tables, which further supports the leisure-time patterns, is the tendency of homicides to occur on holidays other than Sundays or during the Easter and Christmas seasons, for instance on Candlemas, Corpus Christi, or the feast of the village patron saint. Twenty-six of the 175 homicides in the central Mexico sample and 16 of the 111 Mixteca Alta homicides for which we have information took place on such holidays.

The location of homicides, summarized in Table 11, shows a strong contrast between our two regions. Twice as many of the central Mexico homicides were committed within the community of the offender and victim. Of the intracommunity homicides, the Mixteca cases overwhelmingly took place in the home, and the wife was nearly always the victim. In central Mexico, by contrast, homicides often happened in the local tavern or on the public streets as well as in the home.[10]

Nearly two-thirds of the Mixteca Alta homicide cases that contain information on the place of attack happened outside the community compared with fewer than a third for central Mexico. Public roads were notoriously unsafe, especially in the eighteenth century, but these figures should not be taken to mean that most homicides out-

TABLE 11. *Location of Homicides*

Location	Central Mexico		Mixteca Alta	
	Number	Percentage	Number	Percentage
Within the community				
In home of offender or victim	66	27%	17	30%
In or near pulquería	47	19	2	4
At private fandango	8	3	1	2
At community fiesta	7	3	—	—
On the street (both from same town)	40	16	—	—
On the street (offender and victim from different towns)	8	3	—	—
TOTAL	176	71	20	36
Outside the community				
On road	28	11	15	27
In campo	32	13	11	20
At rancho	6	2	—	—
In different town (usually market day)	5	2	10	18
TOTAL	71	29	36	64
GRAND TOTAL	247		56	

side the community were committed by strangers. As we shall see, most homicides in the Mixteca Alta, including those committed on the roads or in the fields outside the community, involved relatives, fellow citizens, and acquaintances.*

THE HOMICIDE ACT

Choice of weapons for deadly assault varies considerably among societies and within single societies over time. In some societies killers shoot; in others they stab; in yet others they beat.[11] For both of our regions, a knife was the usual weapon, followed by rocks, clubs, and fists—weapons used to beat the victim to death. Compared to their counterparts in central and southern Mexico today, colonial peasants rarely used firearms. In the modern Morelos community study by Lola Romanucci-Ross, more than nine out of ten homicides are committed with rifles or pistols, and in the Maya community studied by June Nash, firearms are used in half of the homicides. In both of these communities stabbings account for nearly all of the other homicides, or 7 per cent and 46 per cent, respectively. Beatings account for none of the Morelos homicides and for only 5 per cent of the Maya sample. By contrast, colonial homicides were overwhelmingly committed by stabbing and beating, with the latter representing a much larger proportion of deadly violence (Table 12). Indians were forbidden under colonial law to own firearms without special license. But the law alone is not a sufficient explanation for the infrequency of homicide by gun, since colonial citizens were also forbidden to carry *armas cortas* (short knives), the most commonly used deadly weapon. Firearms were expensive and in short supply. Most eighteenth-century peasants could not afford them, whereas today firearms are found in many village homes.

The use of firearms—and the choice of weapons generally—also bears on the important matter of premeditation. Poison is the instrument that most surely implies premeditation, but the firearm is next, since, with the exception of hunting, almost the only reason to carry a pistol or rifle is to defend against a life-endangering assault, or to commit one. Knives are more ambiguous in their connection to deadly purpose. They were certainly viewed as offensive weapons, and colonial law forbade carrying them in public. At the same time, they were used in virtually every household and by butchers, tanners, and pulque collectors, as well as farmers. Instruments used in beatings gen-

---

*In looking for relationships between time and place, I found no clear patterns.

TABLE 12.   *Homicide Weapons*

Weapon	Central Mexico		Mixteca Alta	
	Number	Percentage	Number	Percentage
Knife	91	48%	29	37%
Rocks	32	17	14	18
Fists, feet, teeth	19	10	10	13
Cudgel, club	17	9	12	15
Sword, machete	8	4	5	6
Firearms	6	3	2	3
Razor	5	3	1	1
Poison	2	1	1	1
Whip	2	1	2	3
Plow tip, scythe	2	1	2	3
Piece of iron	1	.5	1	1
Chain	1	.5	—	—
Scissors	1	.5	—	—
Pistol butt	1	.5	—	—
Chile smoke	1	.5	—	—
Rope	1	.5	—	—
TOTAL	190		79	

erally are the weapons least suggestive of premeditation. Rocks, sticks, farm implements usually were the weapons at hand—in addition to fists and feet—when an argument escalated into unplanned bodily harm. Relationships between weapons and premeditation indicate an apparent contrast between the central Mexico cases and those from the Mixteca Alta. In the Mixteca, beatings with hands and feet, rocks, farm implements and clubs account for more deaths than do stabbings; in central Mexico, stabbings were more frequent than beatings. By itself, this difference is not strong evidence of more premeditated homicides in central Mexico, but it is consistent with the patterns of institutional relations discussed later in this chapter and does seem to suggest that, for whatever purpose, more men in central Mexico villages went armed in public, even within their communities.*

Insults exchanged before an attack and later recalled by two or more witnesses provide us with a particularly important sample of authentic Indian utterances directly connected to the act. Insults are spontaneous outbursts, a form of aggression in themselves, while later declarations place the speaker in a defensive, self-conscious posture. "Fight-

*There does not seem to be a clear correlation between weapons and settings, except that knives were used more often outside the home, especially in central Mexico.

ing words" is perhaps a better term than "insult," since in each case the verbal exchange immediately preceded physical violence.[12] Such exchanges are recorded in nineteen cases from the Mixteca Alta (eleven Indians, eight non-Indians) and eighty cases from central Mexico (forty-eight Indians, thirty-two non-Indians). In the Mixteca Alta cases the fighting words ordinarily were literal accusations, sexual in content, referring to the uneasy relations between Mixtec husbands and wives, which are also evident in offender-victim relationship patterns. The most common fighting words were *puta, cornudo, alcahuete*, and *cabrón* (whore, cuckold, pimp, he-goat—one who consents to the adultery of his wife). Other stock Spanish insults such as *perro* (dog) and *borracho* (drunkard) appear in the Mixtec records only on the lips of non-Indians. Indians in the Mixteca Alta either did not use these terms often or did not take particular offense when they were used.

In the central Mexico cases Indians used a greater variety of Spanish expletives, and no clear distinction exists between fighting words used by Indians and those used by non-Indians except for aggressive, community-oriented Indian outbursts, such as "What are you doing in my neighborhood?" (¿Por qué venís' a mi barrio?).[13] Sexual allusions predominate, but they are often used figuratively. *Joto* and cornudo, for example, were used when there was no reason to believe that the person insulted was in fact a homosexual or a cuckold. These sexual allusions—cabrón, joto, cornudo, *pendejo, hijo de puta*, and *carajo*— were usually used as declarations of one male's superiority in manliness and sexual prowess over another.* The typically Spanish insult, hijo de puta (son of a whore), was commonly used by central Mexico peasants, but *hijo de la chingada* (son of a violated woman)—conveying a preoccupation with rape—which is considered so characteristic of modern Mexican insults, is missing from this sample of late colonial records.[14]

At least thirty-five of the eighty insults carry a strong *macho* tone, and twenty-one of these thirty-five were uttered by Indian peasants: for example, "If you're a man, you should come outside and fight";

---

*"Carajo" refers to the male genitals. It was considered a particularly gross obscenity, implying that the man so insulted was inferior and cowardly, Santamaría, pp. 212–13. "La chingada," which Octavio Paz considers so characteristic of modern Mexican insults and the Mexican male's preoccupation with violation by force, is missing from this sample of colonial records. One colonial example of the use of "la chingada" was a mulato named Pioquinto Ruvias who used it to insult Doña Isabel de Lorenzana in Oaxaca City, AEO *Juzgados* bundle for 1751–1755, document dated October 9, 1754. Spaniards' expletives appear in AGN *Inquisición* 430 exp. 8; *Criminal* 311 exp. 2A, and 145 fols. 324–.

"Stop if you're a man"; "You're no man"; "There are nothing but sheep here and I'm going to fight them all"; "You're a bunch of pendejos— I'm the only man"; or most often, "Now we'll see who is a man."* Only two examples of such macho insults leading to assaults appear in the Mixteca Alta cases. In one case, a Spaniard declared, "I'm as much a man as anyone"; in the other, an Indian peasant declared, "I'm a real man" (Soy mucho hombre).[15]

Indians as well as non-Indians in central Mexico employed the typically Spanish insults—perro, hijo de puta, borracho, *puerco*, and *mierda*—and made pejorative references to dark skin—(negro, mulato). The central Mexico fighting words also include direct accusations, such as "You're a gossip and a thief" and "Rapist!" or simple profanity, such as "Ave María Diablos." Generally speaking, the fighting words used by Indians in central Mexico suggest that Spanish beliefs and behavioral patterns exerted a deeper influence on peasant life there than in the Mixteca Alta at the end of the colonial period and that central Mexico peasants came closer to a standard of masculinity and a subculture of violence that seem nearly universal among the lowest socioeconomic classes in modern societies.[16]

THE OFFENDER-VICTIM RELATIONSHIP

Relations among the participants are particularly important aspects of any social situation. In societies (such as that of Indian Mexico) that hold kinship and custom in higher regard than we do, the relation between offender and victim in cases of personal violence is especially significant. When our data on personal relations for central Mexico and the Mixteca Alta are forced onto charts, several patterns emerge that are fairly consistent with the findings of sociological studies on personal violence in other societies.

An apparently universal characteristic of homicides is that the offenders are overwhelmingly young adult men.[17] According to one leading criminologist, the most typical murderers are in their twenties; many are teenagers; some are in their early thirties; and very few are over forty years old. This pattern is confirmed for one modern southern Mexican village, San Juan Chamula, where the killers are mostly men

*AGN *Criminal* 39 exp. 18, 126 exp. 2, 128 exp. 4, 129 exp. 6. Another offender-victim pattern corroborated by the ascribed motives in confessions is the property dispute. Economic relationships account for a small proportion of the offender-victim relationships, but in nearly every case where the offender in an attack stemming from an economic relationship makes a confession, he justifies his behavior on the basis of an unpaid debt, a boundary dispute, or stolen livestock.

TABLE 13.   *Female Indian Offenders and Victims*

Offense	Central Mexico	Mixteca Alta
Homicide		
All offenders	240	94
Female offenders	10	1
Percentage female	*4%*	*1%*
All victims	234	94
Female victims	42	17
Percentage female	*18%*	*18%*
Assault		
All offenders	154	91
Female offenders	11	5
Percentage female	*7%*	*6%*
All victims	179	91
Female victims	59	26
Percentage female	*33%*	*29%*

between seventeen and twenty-seven years old.[18] The distribution of our group of homicides by sex and age certainly follows the pattern of male dominance—96 per cent of the central Mexico offenders and 99 per cent of the Mixteca Alta offenders were men—but the offenders were somewhat older than might be expected. The Indian offenders average thirty-three years in central Mexico and twenty-nine years in the Mixteca Alta (mean). The average age of non-Indian offenders in central Mexico was thirty. In both regions substantial numbers of offenders were over forty (15 per cent in central Mexico and 9 per cent in the Mixteca Alta). That many of these older Indian offenders were in their fifties and sixties explains why the median age—thirty for central Mexico Indian men and twenty-five for Mixteca Alta Indian men— is substantially lower than the mean averages.*

The differences between Indian men and women both as victims and as offenders in homicides and aggravated assaults are more striking (see Table 13). In both central Mexico and the Mixteca Alta, Indian women rarely killed—they comprise only 3 per cent of homicide offenders and only 7 per cent of assault offenders. Female victims were considerably more numerous but still no more than 33 per cent of homicide or assault victims in either region. In short, the majority of assault and homicide cases involved male victims of male assailants, which, again, is the usual pattern across most societies.[19] Mixteca Alta

---

*Based on sixty Indian cases and twenty-four non-Indian cases from central Mexico; and twenty-seven Indian cases and four non-Indian cases from the Mixteca Alta.

cases depart, however, from the usual distribution by sex in the proportion of females as victims to females as offenders. Among homicide cases, for which there are comparable figures from some other societies, there were more than seventeen female Indian victims to every female killer in the Mixteca Alta cases. Figures for modern societies ranging from rural-agricultural (Ceylon) to urban-industrial (Philadelphia) yield much lower ratios: 4.8 : 1 (Israel), 3.2 : 1 (Ceylon), 2.7 : 1 (England), and 1.3 : 1 (Philadelphia).[20] The central Mexico ratio of female victims to female offenders, 4 : 1, is in the range of these lower figures.

Offender-victim relations beyond distribution by sex are summarized in Table 14. The interpersonal relations can be divided among three broad categories: kinsmen, sex partners, and sex rivals; fellow townsmen; and citizens of different communities. The distribution of homicides across these three categories of association approximates the pattern of killing within the group that sociologists also consider to be nearly universal.[21] Even where the offender and victim were from different communities, seldom was the victim a stranger to his assailant. Only in cases of deadly assaults accompanying armed robberies in the countryside were the offender and victim likely to be total strangers.

Among Indians in both regions, an important proportion of the victims were wives, sex partners, and sex rivals. These high figures are particularly remarkable because husband-wife assaults are routinely underrepresented in the criminal records of societies in which wife-beating is socially acceptable.[22] Adultery and the jealousies of villagers caught up in sexual affairs—situations intimately related to the position of women in these village societies—appear to be fundamental sources of violent conflict in both of our rural areas.* The figures for Indian spouses and sex partners contrast sharply with the proportion of wives, sex partners, and sex rivals victimized among non-Indians in the central Mexico group, where only 15 of 137 assaults and homicides were directed against wives or sex rivals.

Another pattern common to both regions is that Indians were more likely to assault or kill within the community than they were to attack outsiders. The relations in Table 14 do suggest two strong contrasts between the Mixteca Alta and central Mexico: central Mexico Indians were almost twice as likely to kill outsiders as were Indians from the Mixteca Alta; and homicides and assaults within communities were

---

* Unfortunately, the colonial documentation does not allow us to distinguish the subtle, important differences between moral and immoral adultery in these societies noted by Selby, "Study of Social Organization," p. 38.

TABLE 14. *Offender-Victim Relationships*

Relationship between victim and offender	Central Mexico				Mixteca Alta			
	Indian offenders		Non-Indian offenders		Indian offenders		Non-Indian offenders	
	No.	Pct.	No.	Pct.	No.	Pct.	No.	Pct.
HOMICIDE								
Kinsmen								
Spouse	22 ⎱ 25%		—		10 ⎱ 51%		2	
Sex partner or rival	18 ⎰		5		16 ⎰		1	
Affine other than spouse	3		3		—		—	
Sibling, cousin, parent, child	10		3		6		—	
TOTAL	53	34%	11	13%	32	63%	3	38%
From same community								
Town official offender or victim	4		—		5		—	
Other	51		26		6		—	
TOTAL	55	35%	26	31%	11	22%	—	—
From different community								
Indian victim	40		13		5		2	
Non-Indian victim	9		23		1		—	
Robber offender	—		8		2		3	
Official offender or victim	—		2		—		—	
TOTAL	49	31%	46	55%	8	16%	5	63%
GRAND TOTAL	157		83		51		8	
ASSAULT AND BATTERY								
Kinsmen								
Spouse	23 ⎱ 35%		7		17 ⎱ 42%		4	
Sex partner or rival	11 ⎰		3		18 ⎰		2	
Affine other than spouse	4		1		—		—	
Sibling, cousin, parent, child	2		—		2		—	
TOTAL	40	42%	11	20%	37	45%	6	29%
From same community								
Town official offender or victim	24		—		21		5	
Other	17		11		2		1	
TOTAL	41	43%	11	20%	23	28%	6	29%
From different community								
Indian victim	10		19		17		8	
Non-Indian victim	4		5		4		—	
Robber offender	—		7		2		1	
Spanish official victim	1		1		—		—	
TOTAL	15	16%	32	59%	23	28%	9	43%
GRAND TOTAL	97		54		83		21	

more sharply concentrated in the nuclear family in the Mixteca Alta (nearly two-thirds) than they were in central Mexico (one-third). Cases of personal violence directed against community officials are recorded for both regions, but attacks on neighbors and fellow townsmen who were not sex rivals were more frequent in central Mexico. Taken together, the figures suggest a fairly even distribution of relationships across kinsman-neighbor-outsider categories for the central Mexico homicides and a heavy concentration for the Mixteca Alta cases in the kinsman category. In this regional distinction it is important to note that the higher percentage of kinsman homicides in the Mixteca may be related to the lower total incidence of homicides and aggravated assaults there. Perhaps conflict over adult women is fundamental in peasant societies throughout Mesoamerica, and it is only when the incidence of homicide increases that a broader distribution of social relations between offenders and victims becomes evident. This is an intriguing possibility, but the historical record offers little opportunity for testing it.

If we move the information on offenders and victims from the interpersonal context to an institutional framework of domestic, intracommunity, political, and economic relationships, several more contrasts appear between the two regional societies. Homicide and aggravated assault by Mixteca Alta Indians usually took place within the domestic institution—the nuclear family household. The domestic offender was nearly always the male head of the household, and his victim, if female, was nearly always his wife. In none of the recorded cases did a wife kill or seriously injure her husband. A fairly typical case of Mixteca Alta homicide stemming from adultery took place in Santiago Yolomecal in 1743. Domingo Martín unexpectedly returned home from the fields to find his wife in the arms of another Indian of Yolomecal. Apparently without hesitation, he wounded his wife, killed her lover, and took refuge in the village church. The district judge excused Domingo from responsibility on the grounds that he was a coarse individual, totally ignorant of his legal rights, whose actions in any case were mitigated by the circumstances.[23] Similar cases are documented for central Mexico, but there are also other types of homicides related to adultery. The Indian widow Augustina María, for example, was brutally stabbed thirty-six times in her home in Xoxocotla (jurisdiction of Cuernavaca) in November 1799. Her nine-year-old son testified that his mother was murdered by Ysidro Vicente, a married man who frequently slept with her. That night Ysidro was angry because Augustina had been drinking. She retorted that it was none of his business since they were not married and she was not spending his money. Ysidro then stabbed her to death and set the hut on fire.[24]

The many instances of family violence with wives as victims and the occasions of assault by husbands on other men strongly suggest that the conjugal unit was an important source of social conflict or, at least, was the level of peasant society in which conflict was most likely to take violent forms. The idea that conjugal violence was most frequent primarily because domesticity was the level of most frequent social contact is belied by the near absence of violence between close blood relatives, such as siblings and cousins, who lived near each other.[25] The concentration of Indian women in cases of domestic violence also suggests that the woman's range of participation in institutional relationships was narrower than the man's, confirming the impressions of Spanish sources that peasant women traveled less than men, rarely worked in the fields, did not hold political or religious offices, and did not take primary responsibility for family contacts with outsiders. In fact, community norms generally brought suspicion on married women who ventured outside the home without the husband's knowledge or had any contact with other men. Married women, too, were often "outsiders" in the barrio of their husbands where they made their homes, since they usually had been reared in another village or neighborhood and had few blood relatives nearby to protect them (assuming protection would have been forthcoming) and were therefore more likely to be victims than aggressors in violent attacks within the village.[26]

Attacks on or by village officials comprise one-fourth of all armed assaults in both regions but less than 10 per cent of the homicides in the Mixteca Alta and 2.5 per cent of the homicides in central Mexico. Most homicides involving officials in both samples were supposedly unintended, if we may believe the offenders' declarations. The contrasting proportions of homicides and assaults suggest that the relation between village officials and macehuales—basically one of superordinates and subordinates in social and political terms—contained seeds of violent conflict but that, whether out of fear or respect, the conflict rarely reached the level of killing.

Although these figures are about the same for both regions, events leading up to assaults involving village officials in the two areas differed in kind. In the Mixteca Alta, most of the twenty-one assaults by macehuales on officials occurred when the latter legally attempted to make arrests (eight cases) or enforce community labor service on individual citizens (eleven cases). In most of the central Mexico cases (sixteen of twenty-four), macehuales attacked officials or complained that offi-

cials had attacked them, in circumstances that suggest official abuse of power. Central Mexico community officials in these cases were usually charged with raping local women, whipping macehuales without cause, embezzling community funds, forcing macehuales to work noble lands on feast days, and exacting other kinds of involuntary labor. Whippings and beatings inflicted by community officials seem to have been more brutal in central Mexico in the late colonial period. In Tlalmilalpa in the jurisdiction of Metepec, for example, the church *fiscal* (the community official responsible for seeing that fellow villagers attended Mass and paid their *araceles*) was charged with whipping to death a young man who had failed to attend Sunday Mass in March 1724. The fiscal, who was not a native of the community, was also charged with excessive cruelty in his treatment of other citizens.*
By contrast, in the town of Santo Tomás (jurisdiction of Teposcolula) in the Mixteca Alta in 1738, the cacique acknowledged that he had occasionally given light slaps to townspeople who failed to perform their communal service, but in defense of his villagers he lodged a formal complaint against the Spanish alcalde mayor for ordering that these same people receive fifty lashes and other harsh punishment.[27] These contrasts suggest that local officials were assuming more arbitrary and physically abusive powers in central Mexico in the late colonial period, leading to the corrupt practices of modern caciquismo, or local boss rule. The Mixteca Alta attacks on officials suggest that villagers—initiating the assaults—were inclined to oppose violently what they considered arbitrary uses of authority by local officeholders.
The near absence of reported personal violence resulting from economic strains in intracommunity relationships is another striking institutional pattern in the Mixteca Alta sample. Of the seventeen attacks by Indians that grew out of robberies or arguments over property (primarily debts, destruction of property, and land disputes), only three—or 2 per cent of all Indian homicides and assaults—were directed against members of the same community. Taken alone, these figures do not indicate that conflict over property was rare, but they do at least suggest that such conflict did not escalate into dangerous

---

*AGN *Criminal* 221 fols. 210–25. Here are other examples of the brutality of central Mexico village officials: Francisco Antonio, the Indian alcalde of San Francisco Chilpa in the jurisdiction of Tultitlán was reported in 1763 for beating the townspeople without provocation, especially when he was drunk, AGN *Criminal* 177 exp. 12; the Indian alcalde of San Pedro Xalostoc was convicted of the same abuse of office, AGN *Criminal* 120 exp. 17; the Indian municipal council of Xochimilco made a series of complaints in 1798 against the Indian jailer for excessive punishment of local prisoners. Apparently, he clubbed them without reason, AGN *Criminal* 154, fols. 536–52.

violence. Political relationships provided an important setting for personal violence within the Mixteca communities (5 homicides and 21 assaults), but attacks against members of the community who were not officeholders stretching the limits of their authority or sex rivals were comparatively few (6 homicides and 2 assaults out of 134 cases).

Institutional patterns of violent crime within Indian communities in the central Mexico sample are somewhat different. Reported violence within the domestic setting was important (77 of 194 trials), as was violence involving political officials (24 cases), but intracommunity violence not arising from a political relationship between officeholder and citizen was much more common in central Mexico than in the Mixteca Alta. Many of the intracommunity problems in the central Mexico trials can be traced to economic relationships. Twenty-five of the forty-five assaults and homicides involving members of the same community who were not officeholders grew out of arguments over unpaid debts, petty theft, land boundaries, and crop damage.

Institutional patterns for non-Indians in the central Mexico cases are described more easily in negative terms than in positive ones. Classification of cases into economic, political, and intracommunity categories is difficult because non-Indian offenders were often newcomers or transients in the communities where the crimes took place. The two institutional relationships from which non-Indian offenders in rural areas were largely absent are family and political crimes. It appears that most often the relation between offender and victim was economic (especially when the victim was an Indian) or the setting was the pulquería (tavern) and the offender and his victim were no more than casual acquaintances.

CRIMINAL TESTIMONY AND THE QUESTION OF MOTIVATION

Motivation is perhaps the most formidable of all topics in criminology. Except for inferences from the offender-victim relationship, criminologists usually decline to study motive through criminal records. With good reason, they have called into question the objective value of motives that are ascribed by arresting officers, offenders, and witnesses in the courtroom. What used to pass as "motive" in studies of crime based on the written record was little more than the criminal setting or the precipitating causes of the violent act. Although a close study of motive is beyond the compass of my sources, the motives ascribed in assaults and homicides by Indian participants and eyewitnesses are still valuable social facts, even if they cannot be taken at face value to represent the "real reasons" behind the violence. They give us clues to folk explanations and norms—how the people interpreted their situations and what was considered proper or expected social behavior in different circumstances. In other words, they can provide suggestive information on popular ideas of what was worth living and dying for, but they should not be confused with the psychic reasons for action, which are largely unknowable.

Value-laden statements on motive made in colonial courts have some serious shortcomings. First, trial records tend to overrepresent unpremeditated acts. Since premeditated crimes were punished more severely, it was in the interest of the accused to claim that his or her aggression was unintentional, unplanned, an act of self-defense, or caused by an external force such as Satan. The cultural distance between court officials and Indian peasants as well as this tendency of offenders to hide underlying motives made it difficult for the courts to establish root causes and to discern premeditation. As a result, judges frequently explained the objective cause in terms of *riña* (loosely used to mean only an argument that preceded the attack) or self-defense. Riña usually amounted to a superficial precipitating cause, such as an imagined slight or insult, an argument about whether to go on drinking, or a dispute over who should pour the pulque, rather than revealing the main source of conflict between offenders and victims. Francisco Rafael Silva, a mestizo from Tulancingo, for example, went drinking with friends at a pulquería outside of town on a Sunday in September 1804. After drinking from ten in the morning to three in the afternoon, they got into a casual argument and exchange of insults outside the pulquería with some strangers who worked at the Regla hacienda. Words led to blows and Silva killed one of the strangers with a razor.[28]

As Spanish-imposed categories that glide over the surface of motive, these arguments themselves have little analytical value. It is often difficult to separate Spanish-imposed categories of motive and peasant evaluations of colonial law from the peasant participants' conception of wrongful acts. The two inevitably blend together in the formal court setting, with the offender adjusting his statements to the expectations of the court in unpredictable ways. This was not always done out of cynicism; the trials were a learning experience for the subject population, in which law as an institution of social control was taught by the rulers. Second, Indian statements as to motive were shaped to some extent by Spanish methods of interrogation and the formal question-and-answer structure of much of the testimony. Official reports of a judicial examination also can distort oral testimony in less obvious ways. Words of witnesses were not always reproduced just as they were spoken; spontaneously, the scribe was tempted to clarify, to restore the syntax of oral statements, and sometimes to frame them in the third person. Third, words are usually insufficient to convey the complexity of reasons behind an unpremeditated act. Peasant witnesses and judges in trial proceedings were inclined to attribute homicides to categories of motive such as drink, riña, and adultery when it is clear from the patterns imbedded in the peasants' testimony that they recognized more complex motives.[29] A fourth weakness of the colonial records as evidence of perceived causes of death is their lack of at least one category of homicide that the courts considered nonculpable, but that Indians regarded as both culpable and premeditated: death by witchcraft. Cases of witchcraft enter these records only when revenge was taken on the supposed witch.[30]

If these distortions are kept in mind, the testimony in homicide and assault trials can still be useful. In some trials clear directives came from higher authorities on how the judge should proceed to examine witnesses and search out motive. In these cases riña acquires a more precise meaning. In the 1806 death of an Indian of San Simón de los Herreros at the hands of a neighbor, the local judge was instructed to consider five categories of riña as possible motives: personal hatred, private interests, gambling, women, and alcohol.[31] Although such categories rarely are mentioned in trial records, they seem to have been an unstated means for the courts to classify motive in colonial Mexico and move beyond the simple fact that an argument preceded the attack.

Apart from the "fighting words" already discussed, the least biased type of testimony in the trial records is the preliminary declaration— an unstructured, often rambling statement about the violent act made by the accused shortly after arrest. The first statements by peasant offenders normally were longer and more subjective, although not necessarily more revealing of probable motives, in the central Mexico cases. These longer declarations appear to me to be somewhat clumsy attempts by the accused to establish a legal defense for their acts rather than more earnest attempts to unburden their souls in the less formal situation. The more garrulous central Mexico offenders seem to be engaged in a more studied dialogue with the colonial judicial system. The statements on motive by offenders and victims in the central Mexico sample total 312 Indian and 36 non-Indian participants; for the

Mixteca Alta, I have the statements of 132 Indian and 19 non-Indian participants.

Motives stated by offenders are summarized in Table 15. These figures may not indicate actual motives, but they do, at least, tell us something about peasants' justifications of their violent acts. The sharpest contrast between the two regions in the reasons given is the relative importance of adultery, alcohol, and riña. More than one-fourth of all offenders in the Mixteca Alta groups claimed the cause of the assault was the adultery of their wives (and in most cases, the husband discovered his wife and her lover *in acto flagrante*), but only 9 per cent of the central Mexico assailants used this justification. Alcohol as a motive is ascribed by offenders, on the other hand, in almost reverse numbers. The psychic effects of pulque, tepache, and aguardiente de caña were cited by many more central Mexico offenders than by their Mixteca Alta counterparts. Riña—the somewhat vague ascription of dangerous acts to an argument or insult—was the motive claimed by three times as many central Mexico offenders as Mixteca Alta offenders.

Three other regional contrasts can also be inferred from Table 15: (1) a larger number of different motives came from central Mexico than from the Mixteca Alta; motives ascribed by central Mexico offenders cover twenty-three of the twenty-five categories in Table 15; the Mixteca motives cover sixteen; (2) if we may believe the central Mexico offenders, uncontrollable passions worked overtime to cause their lethal/dangerous violence; the accidental killings of third parties in a fit of rage, because of riña, under alcohol's supposed effect of releasing animal passions, and by the hand of the devil account for 49.5 per cent of the offenders' stated motives compared to 19.2 per cent for the Mixteca Alta; and (3) disputes over property seem to loom larger for Mixteca Alta offenders. This third contrast requires two important qualifications: most of the Mixteca Alta property disputes were with outsiders rather than among members of the villages (fifteen of twenty Mixteca robberies were committed against peasants on the open road by outsiders and thirteen of fourteen land disputes involved members of different communities), but nearly all of the property disputes in central Mexico involved members of the same community; and eleven of the self-defense cases were grounded in property disputes, giving an adjusted total of 21 per cent for central Mexico.

To some extent, the motives stated by offenders (the actors' point of view) fit the offender-victim patterns (our observer's point of view),

TABLE 15. *Motives Ascribed by Offenders in Homicides and Assaults*

Category	Central Mexico		Mixteca Alta	
	Number	Percentage	Number	Percentage
Alcohol	93	26.7%	19	12.6%
Riña	65	18.7	10	6.6
Sex-related and conjugal				
Rape	3	.9	2	1.3
Unwanted infant	2	.6	—	—
To protect honor of female relative	5	1.4	6	4.0
To be rid of cuckold husband	6	1.7	—	—
Wife's adultery	32	9.2	43	28.5
Domestic quarrel	10	2.9	8	5.3
TOTAL	58	16.7	59	39.1
Property disputes				
Over money	15	4.3	—	—
Over land	12	3.4	14	9.3
Over animals	14	4.0	6	4.0
Over other property	9	2.6	1	.7
Robbery	13	3.7	20	13.2
TOTAL	63	18.1	41	27.2
Related to community authority and sanctions				
Resent acts of authority	10	2.9	12	7.9
To defend community values	2	.6	1	.7
To escape arrest	2	.6	—	—
TOTAL	14	4.0	13	8.6
Personal honor				
Retaliation for gossip	—	—	2	1.3
Victim mistreated offender's parents	1	.3	—	—
Revenge	4	1.1	—	—
TOTAL	5	1.4	2	1.3
Miscellaneous				
Self-defense	22[a]	6.3	3	2.0
Accidental (victim intervened in quarrel)	11	3.2	—	—
Witchcraft	11	3.2	—	—
Devil	3	.9	—	—
To punish careless worker	3	.9	3	2.0
Hate *gachupines*[b]	—	—	1	.7
TOTAL	50	14.4	7	4.6
GRAND TOTAL	348		151	

[a] The reasons for the initial attacks in the central Mexico claims of self-defense were property disputes (11), riña (5), personal honor (3), miscellaneous (3). Alcohol was a secondary factor in thirteen of these cases.
[b] Peninsular Spaniards.

underscoring the formally subordinate position of the peasant wife and at least the myth of patriarchy. The Mixteca Alta Indian who had killed his wife or mistress usually blamed jealousy ("celos") aroused by her adultery and spoke of her infidelity as "treason" or a great "shame" she had brought upon him.[32] In one case the husband even claimed that his wife had begged him to kill her for having offended him.[33] The only other justification that Indian husbands offered for attacking their wives was the man's right to punish his partner for failing to do her work or for talking back.[34] If the wife died in these cases, the husband invariably claimed that the death was accidental. The pattern of motives ascribed by Indian husbands in central Mexico was similar, although punishment while the husband was "aflame with anger" at the wife's insolence is mentioned more often than suspicion of adultery.[35] The wife as victim in central Mexico, unlike her Mixteca Alta counterpart, consistently attributed the husband's aggression to *his* adultery. This regional difference may suggest that peasant husbands in central Mexico villages were closer to masculine attitudes common to colonial urban culture derived from Spanish examples and to modern Mexican society, which approve of extramarital relations for the husband and equate manliness with individual hermeticism, violence, sexual conquest, and physical superiority beyond the family setting.

Next to the category of the husband's jealousy, his prerogative of punishing his wife, and other sex-related reasons, the cause of crime most frequently mentioned by offenders in their preliminary declarations was alcohol. If we test the statements about alcohol as cause of violence against the documented association of drink, homicide, and assault, the regional contrast with respect to alcohol discussed in Chapter 2 is reinforced: drink-related Mixteca Alta homicides were dramatically fewer than documented central Mexico drink-related homicides. The figures for armed assaults are similar, although the central Mexico proportion is significantly less than for homicides. The fact that one or both parties to a homicide or armed assault had been

TABLE 16.   *Alcohol in Armed Assaults and Homicides*

Category	Homicides		Assaults	
	Central Mexico	Mixteca Alta	Central Mexico	Mixteca Alta
Total number	240	103	154	107
Number alcohol-related	143	13	62	17
Percentage alcohol-related	60%	13%	40%	16%
Inconclusive cases	17	14	16	2

drinking does not necessarily suggest a causal relation. As we know from modern as well as colonial evidence, peasants in Mesoamerica frequently drink before an assault in order to "get up courage" to commit an act upon which they have already resolved and in order to take advantage of the reduced responsibility under law that is associated with alcohol. Even the fairly high degree of association between alcohol and peasant homicide in central Mexico may mean that alcohol was usually a catalyst for premeditated acts rather than the sufficient cause. The fact that only 27 per cent of the central Mexico offenders claimed alcohol as the primary cause of their violence, while alcohol was actually associated with 60 per cent of central Mexico homicides and 40 per cent of assaults would seem to suggest as much.

Although alcohol was generally incidental in the colonial homicide and assault cases, it was more often the stated cause of personal violence in central Mexico than in the Mixteca Alta, where the range of statements about alcohol as a precipitating factor was quite narrow. In five of the eleven Mixteca cases in which the accused stated that alcohol must have caused the crime, the offender claimed complete loss of memory. In each of another five cases he claimed he was "out of his mind" ("fuera de mis sentidos," "sin sentido," or "sin juicio") and had no control over his actions. In the last example the accused said he did not know what he was doing ("no supo lo que hizo").[36] Declarations of drunkenness as the cause of personal violence were both more numerous (sixty-four cases) and more elaborate in the central Mexico trials. Here, too, a common defense based on alcohol was loss of memory. This was the case when Feliciano José, an Indian carpenter on the Tenextepango sugar plantation near Cuauhtla killed fellow worker Diego Martín on a Saturday night in April 1803. When arrested, Feliciano claimed that he was very drunk that night and could recall nothing of what happened to him or to Diego. In spite of Feliciano's long criminal record and the suspicious return of his memory of the events during the trial, he was eventually pardoned on grounds of riña and drunkenness.[37] Complete memory loss was a standard claim, but alcohol was also implicated in other ways, usually as the cause of temporary insanity (see Chapter 2 for additional information on drinking as a stated cause of violence).

Although trial records can exaggerate Indian ascription of crime to alcohol, it does appear that Indians, especially in central Mexico, were beginning to adopt the Spanish view that alcohol could dissolve the natural judgment and good sense of people and could, alone, cause crime. Angelina María, an india of San Francisco Tepexuxulco,

charged Pablo Ginés, mestizo, with assault one night when her husband was away. Ginés pounded on the door, demanding pulque after
she had gone to bed. When she refused to open the door, he broke it
down and attacked her, as she explained, "because of the hatefulness,
provocative manner, and stupidity of drunkards."[38] The most persuasive evidence that this negative view was working its way into
popular beliefs about alcohol comes from four other central Mexico
assault cases in which the victim as well as the assailant stated that
the offender's drunken state was the only possible cause of attack.[39]
The almost accidental quality of many of the drunken assaults in the
central Mexico group compared to those of the Mixteca Alta group suggests that the central Mexico setting may have nurtured more of the
kind of drunkard who is everybody's enemy after dark.

Enforcement of social customs by Indian officials or revenge against
violators of community norms was another motive ascribed by Indian
offenders. The punishment-for-adultery rationale of married male offenders would fit in this category, along with crimes of personal violence against other relatives who were lazy or had lost family valuables,
or against people who gossiped about fellow townsmen or who were
stingy with food and drink on ritual occasions or refused to share a ritual
drink when invited. In these cases, which occurred in both regions,
the offender sometimes went on to explain that the victim's behavior
had brought shame on him personally and thereby threatened his honor
and position in the community.[40] In other cases the offender claimed
to be acting in a more impersonal way to protect the community. Crimes
by individuals claiming to act in behalf of the community include assaults by officials on truculent citizens who had not paid community
taxes or had refused to perform communal labor; assaults by citizens on
allegedly high-handed or corrupt officials; and attacks on outsiders who
ventured into the community as paramours or exploiters.

SENTENCING

Sentences for homicide and assault and battery provide additional
information about the standards of justice applied to Indian peasants
and the purposes of criminal penalty. They also provide another opportunity to compare central Mexico and the Mixteca Alta near the end
of the colonial period. Direct comparisons, however, are frustrated
by the relatively small number of trial records that include sentences,
the different distribution of cases (taken from the *libros de reos* as well
as trial records) over time in the two regions—the central Mexico
cases are concentrated in the period 1790–1810, while the Mixteca

TABLE 17.   *Sentences for Homicide*

Sentence	Central Mexico		Mixteca Alta	
	Number	Percentage	Number	Percentage
Capital punishment	4	2.6%	10	17.9%
Labor service	49	32.2	13	23.2
Fines	14	9.2	17	30.4
Corporal punishment	4	2.6	11	19.6
Exile	2	1.3	5	8.9
Official relieved of office	1	.7	—	—
Pardon	56	36.8	—	—
No punishment	22	14.5	—	—
TOTAL	152		56	

Alta cases are grouped in the periods 1600–1630, 1730–1740, and 1780–1790[41]—and the fact that most of the central Mexico sentences were passed by the Audiencia and the Mixteca Alta judgments were made by the alcalde mayor, with only a few cases passing under formal review by the Audiencia.*

With these limitations in mind, several broad patterns of punishment are still evident in Table 17. First, capital punishment was rarely inflicted, even in homicide cases. This is especially true for central Mexico, where only 4 of the 152 homicide convictions led to death sentences.[42] Death sentences were most common for incorrigible highwaymen who had killed as well as robbed their victims and in rape-murders. A concerted effort by Viceroy Duque de Linares to reduce highway robbery in central Mexico led to 25 hangings in the three-year period 1710–1712.[43] The Acordada, a new tribunal in the eighteenth century charged with enforcing the laws against crime on the main roads of central Mexico, passed down most of the late colonial death sentences. Between December 15, 1742, and January 29, 1746, 55 death sentences were carried out under order of the Acordada.[44]

Interestingly, relatively more death sentences were handed down in the Mixteca Alta homicide cases, ten of forty-five. This has, I suspect, little to do with a higher incidence of capital crime in the Mixteca Alta. The alcaldes mayores who had to cope daily with truculent peasants and rural lawlessness were inclined to deal harshly with convicted criminals in the hope of deterring others by example, while the High Court in Mexico City had the luxury of a more Olympian view and paid

---

*The alcalde mayor and his lieutenants were not, however, free agents. They were subjected to detailed instructions as to what they were to look for and even how to report it when they found it.

greater attention to rules of evidence and other legal niceties. The alcalde mayor's preoccupations with maintaining law and order are also witnessed by the relatively larger number of whippings meted out in the Mixteca Alta. Especially in the seventeenth century, six to fifty lashes were standard sentences for most peasant crimes adjudged by the alcalde mayor of Teposcolula, including vagrancy, verbal abuse, and adultery.[45] Whippings were less common in the central Mexico sentences, in part because of the influence of the High Court in Mexico City, which considered that whippings (compared to labor service) achieved nothing "useful," but when they did occur, they shared a pattern of discrimination with the Mixteca Alta corporal punishments —only non-Spaniards were subject to this painful, occasionally deadly humiliation.[46]

The small number of death sentences given by the Audiencia is closely related to the High Court's careful attention to proof of premeditation, treachery, and assassination as the three categories of homicide for which death was the prescribed sentence. Multiple slayings, even if not premeditated, could also be considered capital crimes.[47] The homicide trial records for central Mexico in the late eighteenth century generally follow the principles and procedures prescribed in the *Libro de los principales rudimentos tocante a todos juicios, criminal, civil y ejecutivo, año de 1764.*[48] This handbook defines an assassin as "he who kills another for pay" and a treacherous murderer as "he who kills by catching the victim asleep or from behind with a knife or firearm so that the victim cannot defend himself, or [who] lures him out of his house under the guise of friendship and kills him." These two categories are clear enough, but assassinations and treacherous murders rarely occurred in our sample of colonial trials. The third category—premeditated murder, or "hecho pensado" —is more difficult to demonstrate, as was required, beyond a reasonable doubt with witnesses. With few exceptions, defendants in homicide cases were able to produce their own witnesses to counter the prosecution's efforts to prove malice aforethought.[49] The Audiencia considered the possibility of premeditation in virtually all of the homicides studied but very rarely concluded that the evidence was sufficient to warrant a verdict of premeditated murder. Even in cases where the circumstantial evidence of premeditation was overwhelming, the High Court was inclined to rule that there were extenuating circumstances that justified a reduced sentence.[50] Instead of murder, the offender usually was judged to have committed what we would now call voluntary manslaughter—homicide that was intentional but committed "in a sudden rage of passion engendered by adequate provocation"—or involuntary manslaughter—unintentional killing "perpetrated under circumstances of recognized mitigation."[51] Unlike the practice in English common law, colonial Spanish practice sometimes considered "adequate provocation" to include insulting words and gestures. That very few of the offenders had been previously arrested was also an important mitigating factor. Multiple killings were judged especially serious. Miguel Ruvias, an Indian residing on a rancho in the jurisdiction of Tulancingo, argued with Isidro Bernardo, another Indian ranch worker, over Isidro's suspected infidelity to his wife, Miguel's sister. The argument became a fight in which Miguel stabbed Isidro to death. If the violence had stopped there, Miguel would probably have received a sentence at hard labor, but he went on to kill Isidro's mother and was sentenced to die.[52]

Another reason for imposing few death sentences was the colonial government's preference for putting criminals—who were legal slaves under the Spanish system of justice—to useful work. From the first years of Spanish rule, there were legal precedents for reduced sentences even in cases of first-degree murder committed by Indians. The Mexican Audiencia in 1548 had decreed that Indians should be enslaved rather than executed for capital crimes.[53] The standard sentence for individuals convicted of what amounted to involuntary and voluntary manslaughter under Anglo-American law was a period at hard labor. The law of the *Siete Partidas*—the thirteenth-century book of laws for Castile codified under the direction of Alfonso el Sabio—was the guide to criminal justice most often followed in the trials. It prescribed a maximum sentence of ten years of service, but the colonial judges usually sentenced offenders to shorter periods after weighing the evidence of diminished responsibility and extenuating circumstances in each case.[54]

Penal servitude in colonial Mexico is a complex subject, full of inconsistencies and legal changes. Laws were issued forbidding sentences of hard labor to Indians convicted of drunkenness or adultery and to any married Indian male convicted of a minor offense; and no sentences of galley service were permitted to any Indian convict.[55] But another law included in the *Recopilación de leyes de las Indias* allowed, in principle, for sentences of service by Indians in convents and public works in their own communities.[56] Mixteca Alta records from the early seventeenth century suggest that short sentences at hard labor, along with whippings, were common for nearly all offenses at that time.

Convicts sentenced to hard labor in the first years of the seventeenth century were often sent to obrajes. Although this practice was forbidden by law in 1609, and the number of obraje sentences for homicide offenders declined thereafter, examples of obraje service extend into the eighteenth century.[57] The rationale for continuing obraje sentences for Indians after they were forbidden by royal edict is contained in a report on crime in Mexico City issued by the Sala de Crimen in 1638. The judges of the Sala offered two justifications: Indians sentenced to mine service and to the Valley of Mexico drainage project almost invariably escaped, but obrajes were self-contained and well-guarded; and obraje service (the Sala used "obraje" to refer to various kinds of "shop" labor, including the work of bakers, hatters, spinners, weavers, and tailors) would teach Indian convicts a socially useful trade they could pursue after the sentence was completed—an early example of criminal sentencing couched in terms of rehabilitation.[58] By the late eighteenth century, homicide convictions for peasant men usually carried a sentence of four to ten years of service in a presidio or one to five years in public works, especially road construction.[59] Women offenders sentenced to service spent one to eight years in a *casa de recogidas*. Fines, which were also common in both regions, were effectively sentences to labor service, since peasants rarely had the money to pay the fine. Often, the fine was paid by a hacendado or obraje owner to whom the offender was then indebted and who thereby acquired the offender's labor services until the value of the fine was worked off.

One curious side to criminal sentencing in central Mexico is that fully half of all those convicted of homicide in the late colonial trials were released without punishment or were pardoned before serving a sentence of labor service ordered by the courts. General pardons (*indultos*) were granted periodically by the Spanish Crown as a benevolent gesture to commemorate a royal marriage or birth or a great military victory.[60] Royal pardons of this sort were decreed at least five times between 1780 and 1810.[61] Homicide offenders were not automatically released by general pardons; their cases were reviewed individually, and only those convicted of unpremeditated killings were eligible, then often only if the victim's next of kin agreed to a pardon.[62] Occasional indultos were granted by the Audiencia without reference to royal decrees if the victim's family consented. Of those offenders released without pardon or punishment, several were judged to have committed "justifiable" homicides in self-defense; some assault and battery convictions were nullified because the wounds inflicted were not serious and the victim recovered fully; but most releases occurred in cases of trials and sentencing long delayed. Fourteen of the twenty-two homicide offenders in central Mexico who were released were judged to have purged their guilt with the time they spent in prison awaiting a verdict. These pardons and early releases were presented as acts of grace rather than favors to the privileged; occasional acts that sacrificed punishment to preserve belief in royal justice.

The rigors of prison should not be underestimated, even though incarceration was generally viewed as a means of detaining the accused pending trial rather than as a form of punishment or as an institution to protect society from its criminals.[63] Colonial jails were usually dank, cheerless, unsanitary places where many prisoners lost their health and some their lives. At the very least, prolonged imprisonment imposed serious hardships on the families of inmates. I have seen few formal sentences of imprisonment as distinct from labor service, but it was not uncommon for men and women accused of homicide to wait two or three years for a verdict—and one unfortunate man waited fourteen years for the court to judge him guilty.[64] Especially at the end of the eighteenth century, the Sala de Crimen was burdened with an enormous backlog of cases, mostly minor offenses, which delayed swift justice for serious crimes.[65] Some of the sentences to a year or less of labor service are deceptively light, because the convicted man received a reduced sentence for having already spent three or four years in prison awaiting a verdict.

The court's consideration of extenuating circumstances and diminished responsibility in individual cases of homicide is prescribed in the criminal codes that were consulted and cited by the attorneys and judges in these trial records. The *Siete Partidas* discusses principles of criminal justice and punishment at some length. It lists seven standard types of punishment: death or loss of limbs; hard labor; banishment to an island and deprivation of property; incarceration; banishment to an island without loss of property; public disgrace and loss of privileges; and whipping.[66] In fixing the punishment, law 7-31-8 of the *Partidas* instructs the judge to consider the social position and age of offender and victim, type of crime committed, and circumstances surrounding the criminal act (time of day, location, premeditation), with considerable leeway for the judge to exercise personal discretion:

When judges sentence anyone, they should carefully consider the station of the party against whom the sentence is pronounced, namely, whether he is a slave, a freeman, a nobleman, the resident of a town or village, and whether he is a boy, a young man, an old man, or a slave. A slave should be more severely punished than a freeman; a man of low rank than a nobleman; a young man than an old man or a boy; and although a nobleman or any other person distinguished for his scientific knowledge or for some other excellence which he possesses, may do something for which he must die, he should not be put to death in as disgraceful a manner as the others; . . . or he should be banished from the country if it should be desired to grant him his life. Where the party who has committed the offense is under the age of ten years and six months he shall not suffer any punishment. If he is more than that, and under seventeen, the punishment should be less in severity than that inflicted for the same offense on others who are older.

Judges should also take into consideration the position of those against whom an offense was committed, for a party guilty of unlawful acts against his master, his father, his lord, his superior, or his friend, deserves a more severe penalty than if he commits it against someone to whom he was under none of these obligations. The judge should also consider the time when and the place where offenses were committed, for if the crime to be punished is one of frequent occurrence in the country at that time, the penalty imposed should be severe in order that men may fear to commit it.

We also decree that judges shall consider the time in another way, as where a party commits a crime by night, he shall be liable to a greater penalty than one who commits it by day, because from its commission by night many dangers and evils may result.

The place where the unlawful act was done should also be taken into consideration, for a party who commits a crime in a church, or in the king's palace, or where judges hold court, or in the house of a friend who trusts in him, deserves a greater penalty than if he had committed it elsewhere. The manner in which the crime was committed should also be noted; as a party deserves a more severe punishment who kills another treacherously or perfidiously, than if he killed him in a fight, or under any other circumstances. . . . Judges should also consider the nature of the offense, whether it is serious or insignificant; for they should impose a greater penalty for a serious offense than for one which is trifling. . . . After the judges have diligently and carefully considered all the matters aforesaid, they can increase, diminish, or dispense with punishment, as they think proper, and they should do so.

In a separate section on homicide, the *Siete Partidas* begins with a strong statement that murder (intentional homicide) requires the death sentence (7-8-2). The next three laws, however, outline the many circumstances that may diminish the offender's responsibility and justify less severe punishment.[67]

How were these laws interpreted and applied by judges in colonial Mexico? In the formal sentencings, social station appears to have been a secondary factor. Colonial law actually reversed the meaning of the *Siete Partidas* by ordering that crimes in which the victims were Indians were to be punished more severely than similar crimes with Spanish victims, although there is little evidence that this law was followed with any consistency.[68] Although sentences to whippings in our homicide cases were meted out only to Indians and mestizos, as mentioned above, and most exiles were Spaniards, there is no clear relationship between race and sentences of capital punishment and labor service. Spaniards as well as *castas* and Indians were sentenced to death and to hard labor. None of the killers was young enough (under seventeen) to qualify for the reduced sentence based on age. The age of offenders does not appear in any of the judges' verdicts as a mitigating factor, although the age of the victim was an important consideration. When the homicide victim was a young child, the offender received particularly stiff punishment, usually execution. Antonio Loreto, husband of the *cacica* of Tetela del Volcán (jurisdiction of Yecapixtla), was executed, for example, after he had murdered a nine-year-old girl who saw him rob money and clothing from a neighbor's house during Sunday Mass in September 1812.[69]

Insufficient evidence of premeditation or some extenuating circumstance was usually found to prevent a death sentence in these homicide trials, although in a few cases the judge apparently chose to make an example of an offender who was especially unrepentant or who was unfortunate enough to have committed a murder at a time when crime prevention was on the minds of the colonial authorities. The harshest sentences depended heavily on proof of premeditation and malice aforethought, which were very difficult to demonstrate with unimpeachable witnesses. The mitigating factor most successful in reducing the sentence from death to a few years' service or a fine was passion. If the killing developed out of a heated argument or involved the passions of sexual relationships (particularly if a husband discovered that his wife was committing adultery), this was considered important evidence of an unpremeditated, if not always a justifiable or unintentional, attack.

Drunkenness was another extenuating circumstance the defense sometimes used with success, especially since Spanish officials were inclined to think of Indian peasants as natural drunkards and to blame their violence on liquor rather than other circumstances. "Excepción de ebriedad" (drunkenness as mitigator) was recognized as a principle of justice by the colonial judges. The *Siete Partidas* specifically mentions the offender's drunken state as possible evidence of diminished responsibility in homicide cases (7-8-5), prescribing a standard penalty of five years in exile. In studying the role of alcohol in crime and the sentencing procedures in cases of drunken homicide, I find that the drinking argument was considered a weak defense in comparison to self-defense or the role of spontaneous anger. In practice, drinking was not accepted as a license to kill. Alcohol, as we already know, was present in more than half of the central Mexico homicide and assault and battery cases, but in only 10 of the 143 alcohol-related homicides in central Mexico did the offender base his legal defense primarily on the "excepción de ebriedad." Drinking was usually developed secondarily as a key that unlocked the passions, and the main argument was that the offender had no previous criminal record, that he did not intend to kill the victim, that the death was accidental ("casual"), that the victim provoked the attack or attacked first, that because of rage the offender could not control himself, or that Indians were innately stupid.

Since a defense case based on the excepción de ebriedad was a risky strategy, it is not surprising to find drunkenness introduced only as a secondary argument in actual trials. In the absence of evidence to the contrary, the defense could build a circumstantial case that there was no premeditation and that the offender had no control over his actions because he was drunk. On the other hand, if the judge discovered that the offender and victim were enemies or had argued recently, he was as likely as not to conclude that the offender had gotten drunk in order to have a pretext for killing or that the offender may have been drinking but was not, in fact, drunk. The odds of success in a homicide defense based primarily on excepción de ebriedad were no better than even. Of the twenty homicide trials for central Mexico and the Mixteca Alta in which the defense case rested primarily on the excepción de ebriedad, the judge rejected the claim in nine, and sentenced the offenders to death or a long period of presidio service.[70] A second reason for not relying on the excepción de ebriedad was that even if it was accepted as a mitigating factor, the sentence was still relatively heavy —usually one to five years at hard labor plus a whipping.[71] Alcohol might reduce responsibility but it was rarely accepted by the colonial courts as an excuse for murder.

In sum, the penalties of peasant homicide offenders usually took the form of labor service or fines rather than death or mutilation, with a surprising number of pardons for convicted felons toward the end of the colonial period. Justice was slow and not altogether equal—the word of a Spaniard carried more weight in court, only non-Spaniards were whipped, Indians could not be sentenced to the galleys, and the rich often were able to avoid imprisonment pending trial—but careful attention was paid to the special circumstances of each homicide. This pattern of sentencing is especially striking when it is compared to sixteenth-century and seventeenth-century English and Puritan American justice. Elizabethan criminal law made no distinction between murder and manslaughter, and sentencing was founded on a spirit of revenge reminiscent of Hammurabi's code. English law called for the death of convicted felons and, although not all were put to the rope—many died in jail before their trials and some were pardoned—the death sentence was declared with a frequency that contrasts with the practice in colonial Mexico.[72] Even in the eighteenth century, when royal pardons were more liberally applied, the foundation of English criminal law still was the terror of capital punishment.[73] The relentless certainty of justice in the Puritan colonies paid little attention to human emotions or personal motives; it justified summary trials and rigid adherence to harsh sentencing. The whole process of Puritan justice had, as Kai Erikson says, "a flat, mechanical tone because it dealt with the laws of nature rather than the decisions of men."[74] Colonial Spanish justice, although growing out of a natural-law tradition, depended heavily on the judge's personal exercise of a kind of Solomonic discretion. This was a system in which the judge personally administered justice, the highest attribute of sovereignty from a Spanish viewpoint. Justice in this system probed the murky depths of human sentimentality and private motives, admitting much hearsay evidence and personal opinion that would have been stricken from the record in English courts. Little wonder, then, that premeditation and malice aforethought in the lengthy homicide trials were rarely proven to the court's satisfaction.

CONCLUSION

Since homicide is a social act, the patterns of behavior discussed in this chapter can help us understand aspects of life as well as death in rural Mexico, much as the anthropological analysis of kinship systems has some predictive value for economic and political behavior in peasant societies. By interpreting specific acts of homicide as evidence of social life and expected behavior, we can identify connections and regional contrasts among the acts, institutions, and ideas that have been presented separately and speculate on the meaning of some of these larger patterns.

Every society seems to have its own set of tensions that produce interpersonal violence. Violence that threatened lives in central Mexico and Oaxaca was not uniformly distributed across all types of social relations. It occurred in more or less predictable ways and at more or less predictable times. The situations in which homicides occurred furnish evidence of three levels of conflict: family, intracommunity, and intercommunity. In colonial central Mexico and the Mixteca Alta, homicides and armed assaults were concentrated at the base and at the outer limits of social relationships. The fundamental conflict that produced serious violence centered on the position of the woman as wife in the nuclear family household. When adultery by the wife was evident, or often when it was merely suspected, the husband's attack was immediate and predictable. The wife's adultery also led to more than a few cases of paramours killing husbands. A wife's laziness or her lack of humility toward her husband also often precipitated violent, sometimes fatal aggression by the husband.

Whether we view such conflict in the family as a source of cohesion in the larger society, as does Max Gluckman, or as evidence of the price paid by villagers for their primary allegiance to the community, it is clear from our regional examples that family violence cannot be accepted as the key indicator of social disorganization in these peasant societies, as Robert Redfield and others have done. The contrast between peasant violence over wives and against outsiders in a hostile countryside on the one hand and relative peace among village neighbors on the other is quite striking, especially in the Mixteca Alta cases. Even in the central Mexico sample, where the incidence of violent crime seems to have been higher and where there was more intra-village homicide outside the nuclear family, there are very few examples of violent personal conflicts transformed into political factionalism that threatened accommodation within the community (on conflict, violence, and accommodation, see Chapter 4). Intracommunity assaults in the Mixteca Alta were inflicted in the name of existing rules of conduct, not for the purpose of changing social relationships. Most intracommunity attacks involved single village officials against an irate citizen or the whole community rather than two or more groups struggling for local supremacy at the expense of community bonds. Solidarity of this kind does not imply an absence of conflict—conflict and the frustration of at least some individual desires are inherent in societies in which power and wealth are distributed unequally[75]—but rather the restriction of violent conflict to relationships from which it was least likely to spread to factionalism or new violence at other levels within the community. Wives made ideal victims in this context because community norms tended to isolate then from numerous everyday village social and political relationships and because village exogamy tended to isolate them politically in a community where they had few if any alliances based on kin or long friendship. Even more pervasive violence at all levels of social relationships within villages than we find in our eighteenth-century evidence would not necessarily be a sign of weakening community ties. Some social systems undoubtedly can tolerate more conflict than others. William F. Whyte found, for ex-

ample, that the relationship between cooperation and conflict in selected peasant communities of South America is not always one of high
conflict and low cooperation or high cooperation and low conflict.
Several of the villages Whyte discusses have high levels of both cooperation and conflict.[76]

The number of attacks on wives and the rarity of attacks by women
is consistent with other evidence of the position of women in these
societies. We lack information on many aspects of women's lives in the
eighteenth century, but in formal terms, at least, peasant villages in
central Mexico and Oaxaca seem to have been patriarchal and were
often reinforced by patrilocal residence patterns dating from pre-
Hispanic times. Men occupied the positions of high social status, such
as political office, and were accorded the deference of authority in the
home, including the prerogative of disciplining wives and children.
Men had greater freedom of movement and expression, visiting local
taverns, traveling more often to the fields, to regional markets, and to
the neighboring Spanish capital, and overindulging in drink on non-
ceremonial occasions as well as during fiestas. Agriculture, the primary
economic activity in these peasant societies, was largely in the hands
of men. Central Mexico women were actively involved in the sale of
pulque, but, generally speaking, women's mobility and contact with
life outside the home was more restricted than men's. Wives spent
much of their lives at home preparing food, maintaining the house,
and caring for children. As in modern peasant communities, unac-
companied women did not move about freely, even within the village
itself.[77]

An ideology of male dominance in a community does not, of course,
always mean that power resides in such formal roles and that women
are powerless, long-suffering victims. The sex groups in Mexican villages depended on each other, and their relative positions were often
partly submerged in the higher goal of protecting the community, as
we shall see in the matter of community uprisings (Chapter 4). Women
exercised informal power through their handling of the family's finan-
cial resources and in the rearing of children.[78] On the other hand,
an emphasis on women's informal power can lead to the conclusion,
as in Susan Rogers' work on contemporary France, that men, who oc-
cupy the formal positions of authority, are powerless because the peasant community is essentially powerless, a condition that existed only
partially in central and southern Mexico during the late colonial period.

The second concentration of homicides and assaults covers those in
which villagers attacked or were attacked by outsiders. Thirty-one per

cent of the assaults in both regions pitted peasants against outsiders; for homicides 40 per cent of the central Mexico cases and 22 per cent of the Mixteca Alta cases involved outsiders. Most of these Mixteca cases took place outside the village and were connected with robberies by groups of highway bandits or property disputes between neighboring estates and towns. Highway robbery and territorial disputes account for many of the outsider-peasant assaults and homicides in central Mexico, but a third motive, riña—those quarrels, often macho in tone—cropped up in taverns and public markets. The proportions for both regions would be even larger if we included the attacks on public officials—alcaldes mayores, tenientes, priests, tax collectors, and schoolmasters—documented in the rebellions discussed in Chapter 4.

Homicide trial records provide us with evidence of the participants' perspective and also with the basis for an observer's view of the crime. As Paul Bohannon found in studying homicide among the BaLuyia people in Kenya, there were discrepancies between the participants' and observers' views that revealed the special concerns of different social groups. The Europeans rather mechanically blamed native violence on alcohol, and the BaLuyian farmers asserted that land disputes were at the root of most homicides. Bohannon, however, found that most native homicides were neither alcohol-related nor directly attributable to property disputes. They were more closely associated with adultery and relatives' interference in one another's legitimate activities, situations that had only secondary importance in the minds of colonial Kenyans.[79] In our Mexican cases the colonial authorities were likewise disposed to explain Indian homicide in the abstract as the result of alcohol, whereas the Mixteca Alta peasants generally recognized the actual situations that led to violent death. Mixteca Alta offenders spoke feelingly about the shame of adultery. Drunkenness was more often associated with homicide in central Mexico, but even there it was rarely blamed by the people involved. Central Mexico peasants mentioned virtually everything from property disputes to adultery to alcohol. Far fewer cases of murder were attributable to drunkenness and patterns of offender-victim relationships were sharper than would be expected if these peasants killed blindly in their cups.

One important index of the degree to which Indian villagers were conscious of their own motives and acknowledged them for homicide is the "fighting words" exchanged before an attack. In the Mixteca Alta, these insults mirror the evidence of offender-victim relationships in outlining two dominant patterns of homicide: punishment of adultery and defense of community norms. The central Mexico words had less to do with concrete personal disputes between offenders and victims than with a generalized aggressive masculinity. Insults were more often figurative assertions of superior manhood and sexual conquest than direct accusations of wrongdoing. A macho tone in many of the insults—figurative sexual allusions and the use of the same obscenities by different ethnic groups—and an ambivalence about drunkenness evident in the survival of ritual drinking patterns on the one hand and the frequent use of borracho as a personal insult and attributions of violence to alcohol on the other are all clearly present in the central Mexico cases but largely absent from the Mixteca Alta records. Mixteca Indians seem to have adopted Spanish expletives more selectively, reflecting their specific preoccupation with marital relations.

The behavior and settings associated with homicides in the villages of our two regions form fewer and sharper patterns in the Mixteca Alta. Mixteca villagers killed during leisure periods—on Sundays, at night, during the dry months before and after the peak periods of agricultural labor, especially during Easter and Christmas; the homicide situation was usually connected to adultery or the abusive acts of village officials; drunkenness was not often involved; stated motives were usually consistent with the patterns obtained from the observer's viewpoint; and the "fighting words" usually were direct accusations and offer little variety. These well-defined patterns suggest that community norms were not changing rapidly in the late colonial period and were recognized and obeyed fairly consistently.

In central Mexico, the homicide situations, stated motives, and fighting words are more varied and less predictable. Most killings followed the leisure-time pattern, but there were also more homicides during the day and on weekdays; they more often involved knives and other deadly weapons that imply premeditation; the victims were strangers and neighbors more often than in the Mixteca Alta; the conflicts underlying violent aggression included many cases of property disputes within the community, others in which there was no apparent underlying dispute beyond machismo, as well as cases of adultery and political abuse; stated motives covered the gamut from alcohol to self-defense to jealousy, shame, and property disputes but tended to favor riña and alcohol, which focused attention on precipitating events and passion rather than social relationships and shame; alcohol was more likely to be present, and more homicides took place in the "time-out" setting of the tavern;

and the "fighting words" included various kinds of sexual mockery as well as true accusations.

These contrasts provide evidence of greater complexity and uncertainty in village social relations in central Mexico. The kinds of social conflict in which violent attacks occurred were less predictable in central Mexico and more often occurred without any clear reason beyond the offender's drunkenness or an untoward remark. The central Mexico offenders' declarations were longer, less precise, and more subjective, which again points to less certain norms or predictable social behavior. Finally, the settings and participants' statements point to the central Mexico area as being more influenced by the less sociable aspects of drinking and masculinity that relate to the adoption of Spanish attitudes in exaggerated forms and by more sustained and powerful outside influences on village life. All together, these regional patterns of fighting words, offenders' declarations, and offender-victim relations mark central Mexico villages as being more dependent lower-class communities—more affected by outside cultural influences and colonial power, which tended to weaken bonds of community solidarity.

Finally, the formal trials themselves were social processes that bear upon the nature of this colonial system and the relations of peasant subjects to colonial rulers in different regional settings. Two activities recorded in the trial proceedings are important in this respect: the interpretations of behavior made by the courts and the peasants; and the sentencing and its purposes. Both tell us something about how peasants participated in the system of justice.

When peasants in central Mexico committed homicides for which no easy justification supplied an excuse, they rationalized their acts on the basis of uncontrollable anger and momentary passions. These were precisely the kinds of circumstances that the colonial courts took seriously as evidence of an involuntary act. Whether the assailants resorted to such a defense because they understood that it would get them a lighter sentence or whether they had come to believe these interpretations of behavior after many generations of sustained contact with this system of colonial law (or both), central Mexico peasants, in particular, seem to have understood the standards of Spanish justice and to have communicated with the courts in ways that suggest a deeper penetration of colonial institutions.

The pattern of sentencing may seem capricious at first glance—much discretion was left to the presiding judge and crimes that seem

to be almost identical did not always receive the same punishment—
but it was a calculated blend of punishment, correction, and mercy
consistent with the methods of Spanish rule mentioned in Chapter 4.
The courts were an integral part of the colonial system's purposes
of enrichment of the home country and political control over the
natives. The apparent leniency of the courts in punishing peasant
homicide offenders and their careful attention to extenuating circumstances were in part a recognition by the state that personal violence
(especially homicide and battery that did not escape the courts' pur-
view and thereby threaten the state's control over its subjects) was
an understandable, sometimes legitimate and inescapable way to express grievances and defend individual interests.[80] This attitude toward homicide is reflected in the rare use of capital punishment and
the large number of royal pardons granted to convicted felons in the
late colonial period. Sentencing in homicide and assault and battery
cases usually took the form of utilitarian punishment—a period at hard
labor in the presidios or public works, where the supply of labor for
these poorly paid, back-breaking jobs fell far short of demand. Except
for occasional sentences to exile, few of them suggest that the courts
were greatly concerned with protecting society from its criminals by
execution or incarceration. The Crown seems to have been more concerned with protecting its colonial control. Pardons, for example,
created a bond of personal indebtedness between convict and king that
worked to preserve faith in the monarchy and to neutralize potential
political opposition in criminals who were not repeat offenders. The
Crown was sensitive to threats of insurrection and foreign encroachment (convicts were used to *defend* the colony as military conscripts
in coastal fortresses and infantry units!) but seems to have been little
concerned with the elimination of interpersonal violence. As long as
the lower classes of Indian peasants and Indian, mestizo, mulatto, and
Creole laborers lacked group consciousness and were not mobilized
in a class war or a struggle against Spanish rule, the colonial government could afford to treat homicide and aggravated assault in a utilitarian way without having to fear for its political survival.

Chapter 4 Rebellion

U prisings have been a popular topic in the study of lower-class life and change in the Latin American countryside. Modern historiography of rural uprisings goes back to the works of nineteenth-century local historians, who used examples of rural violence to inform a literate urban readership of the barbarousness of peasants and vagabonds, and to warn of the horrors awaiting Latin America's pockets of "civilized" city life. The 1920's brought a new surge of interest in the history of rural revolts in Mexico. Studies undertaken then were designed to document a tradition of peasant uprising against injustice that could presage and give added meaning to the great upheaval in Mexico from 1910 to 1920. More recently, Latin American and foreign scholars have been much interested in the study of such major insurrections as the Tupac Amaru rebellion in late-eighteenth-century Peru, the Tzeltal Revolt in Chiapas in 1712, the Indian wars of northern Mexico in the eighteenth and nineteenth centuries, and the participation of rural people in national upheavals such as the independence wars of the early nineteenth century. Sociologists and anthropologists as well as historians have shown increasing interest in the history of rural violence as a touchstone to demonstrate and explain the revolutionary potential of the rural segment of modern Latin American countries.[1]

Despite obvious differences, the forebodings of the nineteenth-century local historians, the teleologically inspired studies of the 1920's, and the more analytical, detached research of modern social scientists share a common focus: insurrections or regional revolts, in which whole zones of rural people band together in a violent assault on state authority and privileged classes. In setting out to discuss rural uprisings in colonial Oaxaca and central Mexico, I am not primarily concerned with major insurrections of this sort for the good reason that there were precious few of them. To be sure, plans for insurrection were rumored in both areas, and a few short-lived regional uprisings occurred in the jurisdictions of Tulancingo, Actopan, and Metepec, along with a number of simultaneous uprisings in villages within the same region. But there was nothing comparable to the eighteenth-century Andean insurrections or, closer to home, the regional movements in Chiapas in 1712, in the Sierra Zapoteca of Oaxaca in 1660 and 1696, and in Yucatán during the 1840's and 1850's.

That regional revolts were isolated and infrequent in Oaxaca and central Mexico does not mean that the countryside was at peace with the demands and abuses of Spanish rule, "the peace of the grave," as José Vasconcelos once put it. Nor does it mean that colonial villagers were fatalistic, long-suffering people who were content to leave their fate to God ("sea por Dios") or the patrón, rarely taking the law into their own hands. In fact, a great deal of collective violence erupted at the community level.

The numerous violent village outbursts, or local rebellions, are the main subject of this chapter. The distinction between "rebellion" and "insurrection" is crucial to understanding the kind of collective acts described here. Both are violent political acts, but rebellions are localized mass attacks, generally limited to restoring a customary equilibrium. They do not offer new ideas or a vision of a new society. Insurrections, on the other hand, are regional in scope, constitute part of a broader political struggle between various segments of society, and aim at a reorganization of relationships between communities and powerful outsiders.[2] This distinction between rebellion and insurrection may not always be so clear in practice—simultaneous rebellions in a number of villages could have the same consequences as an insurrection—but nearly all of the examples located in my search for rural uprisings qualify as rebellions.

This discussion of armed uprisings follows the approach to drinking practices in Chapter 2, which emphasized the combination of particular practices and habits into patterns reflecting adjustments to colonial pressures in the last century of Spanish rule. Translating the specific circumstances of individual uprisings into patterns of conditions and responses moves progressively, perhaps perilously, from real and in some ways unique events to abstractions. These patterns offer comparison and simplification at the expense of real-life complexity.* As explanations, they are no better than the quality of evidence that supports them. The evidence is a series of 142 judicial investigations of communities in revolt between 1680 and 1811. Of these cases, 91 are from the districts of central Mexico used in this study, 19 from the Mixteca Alta, and the remaining 32 from the Valley of Oaxaca. Rebellions and insurrections of earlier periods and in areas on the fringes

---

*Uprisings that serve as the basis of the patterns discussed here are listed under regional and district headings in Appendix A.

of our central and southern Mexican regions are included only when they suggest new developments or shed light on main points. I have grouped my questions about these uprisings into two main sections. First, speaking generally, what happened? How did the movements begin, who participated in them, what did the rebels do and say, how long did the uprisings last, and how did they end? Second, what were the causes and the results of these village rebellions? I should emphasize that I am interested primarily in identifying general patterns. Individual uprisings are discussed when they illustrate a general point especially well or provide a striking exception. Most of the evidence and specific illustrations, however, will be found in the notes.

PEASANTS IN REVOLT: GENERAL CHARACTERISTICS

Eighteenth-century rebellions were not random or limitless in variety. They reveal quite a definite structure and sequence of development. Most of the village uprisings in central Mexico, the Mixteca Alta, and the Valley of Oaxaca were alike in repertory of actions, instruments, and dramatis personae. Some features are especially striking. Nearly all were spontaneous, short-lived armed outbursts by members of a single community in reaction to threats from outside; they were "popular" uprisings in which virtually the entire community acted collectively and usually without identifiable leadership. The rebellions were highly aggressive but significantly patterned acts, punctuated by open insults, threats, attacks, and a general release of high emotion; most were directed against agents of the state and local buildings that symbolized outside authority. The rebellious behavior was controlled in the sense that there were few examples of general destruction and pillaging.

The spontaneous, collective quality of these village uprisings is repeated time and again throughout the eighteenth century. At a commonly understood signal, usually the ringing of the church bells or the sounding of a trumpet or drum, the townspeople assembled with whatever weapons were at hand.[3] The weapons—household tools, farm implements, sticks, and rocks—generally confirm the spontaneous eruption of the violence. These humble tools provided variety enough: pickaxes, hatchets, machetes, cattle bones, hoes, iron bars, clubs, cudgels, chains, sharp-tipped spindles, knives, burning sticks of pitch pine, lances, and a unique indigenous weapon, powdered chile peppers, used to blind and immobilize the enemy temporarily. Uprisings that lasted for more than a few hours usually brought into play more specialized weapons, such as bows and arrows, sabers, spears, javelins, and horses. Infrequently, eyewitnesses mention fire-arms. Only 3 cases of an old blunderbuss or flintlock pistol being used by villagers are recorded among the 142 risings. This would suggest that firearms were rarely to be found in rural villages, whether be-cause the colonial prohibitions against Indian ownership were rigor-ously enforced or because villagers could rarely afford to acquire them. Rocks, thrown by hand or hurled with slings, usually were the most damaging weapon used by villagers in revolt. In cases of serious harm to persons and property, the victims frequently spoke of "a deluge of stones" or "a shower of rocks" descending upon them.

Virtually the entire community turned out for local rebellions.[4] Militiamen called in by the Spanish authorities were likely to en-counter nasty mobs of hundreds of women brandishing spears and kitchen knives or cradling rocks in their skirts, and young children and old people carrying or throwing whatever they could manage, as well as better-armed groups of adult men. "The whole community" and "multitudes" of armed villagers of all ages are descriptions con-stantly repeated in the reports and testimony. The place of women is especially striking. Perhaps because men were more often traveling outside the community or working fields several miles from town, more women than men usually took part. In at least one-fourth of the cases, women led the attacks and were visibly more aggressive, insulting, and rebellious in their behavior toward outside authorities.

In 1719 Mariana, a tall scar-faced Indian of Santa Lucía near the city of Oaxaca, led a mob of men and women against a group of royal officials, priests, and militiamen who had come to mark the town's boundaries. After cutting the measuring rope, she took on one of the Spaniards in a hand-to-hand struggle, held up a bleeding arm to spur on her compatriots, and led the rock-throwing barrage that drove the outsiders back to the city.[5] Scenes like this have been repeated often, not just in the eighteenth century, but well into contemporary times. This open, sometimes leading role of women in the Oaxaca and central Mexico rebellions contrasts with the accounts of uprisings and Indian wars in northern Mexico, which consistently refer to adult men doing the fighting. Perhaps the difference stems from clearly defined male specialization in hunting and the use of weapons in the less sedentary native societies of the borderlands and the more active participation of women in the complex social relationships of sedentary peasant villages in central and southern Mexico.

The question of leadership in village uprisings is difficult to docu-ment. Colonial authorities were inclined to assume premeditation and leadership by a few local troublemakers, but the evidence from trials and investigations does not lend strong support to this assumption. Alcaldes mayores and higher judges usually were determined to find "cabecillas," people who led or incited others and who were singled out for punishment as examples to the rest of the community. This was a convenient way of demonstrating the firm hand of Spanish justice without encouraging the whole community to desert for fear of punishment, but I suspect that colonial Spaniards, whether Creoles or *peninsulares*, could not conceive of a political movement that did not have a leader who planned and directed it.

In spite of the assumption that movements require leaders and of the political advantages of exemplary punishment, surprisingly few of the trial records for community uprisings provide clear evidence of planned leadership. In the formal trials village rebels, in order to escape punishment themselves, sometimes willingly testified against a few of their compatriots in response to leading questions from the prosecutor. Still, of the 142 cases, only 20 offer clear evidence against one or a small group of peasant leaders (usually the village governor and other members of the hereditary nobility). Parish priests led five attacks; five more—all from central Mexico—were inspired by resident non-Indians; and in another twenty cases prosecutors alleged individual leadership but were consistently contradicted by peasant witnesses who insisted that the violence was not organized ahead of time by local leaders. The choice of everyday objects for weapons, the timing of uprisings when some adult men were away, and a lack of clustering by season, festive calendar, or days of the week lend additional weight to the conclusion that these outbursts were generally unplanned.[6]

The behavior of villagers in revolt belies the image widely held by scholars of docile, or "encogido," Indian peasants who were too attached to servitude and too alienated from society at any level to take up arms for social reasons. Thunderous shouts, whistles, obscene, mocking insults, and impudent gestures, often accompanied by the beat of a drum or the sour notes of an old trumpet, were standard accompaniments to the rebellions. Role reversal was another distinguishing mark. Village rebels could assume the arrogant manners of their colonial masters. Especially in central Mexico, peasant rebels insulted district officials in the same terms that Spaniards had heaped upon them—"dog," "nigger," and "pig." Priests and alcaldes mayores were forced to humble themselves before the village elders. Outside our regions there are examples of peasants forcing local Spaniards to hear pagan services and making Spanish women marry Indian men with the blessing of native priests.[7] Generally, such changes in roles parallel Octavio Paz's description of Mexican fiestas—an explosive suspension of everyday rules and privileges when the poor could dress like the rich and men like women, without fear of censure. The fiesta, according to Paz, is a kind of symbolic revolution, but as a symbolic act it replaces or exhausts the commitment to overturn the social circumstances that resume at the end of the fiesta. The rebellion is not identical in its result, for it is a political action more than a therapeutic expression of conflict that usually did not return the community to exactly the same position afterward. On the other hand, community rebellions usually did exhaust themselves without spreading their feelings of outrage to other communities and without creating an unflinching opposition to colonial rule. After initial success in driving out the enemy, the rebellions occasionally turned into festive celebrations with music, dancing, singing, and general "alegría" replacing the howls of anger.

Although the rebellions seem to have been unplanned and accompanied by a spontaneous and noisy release of emotions, there is pattern and direction in the way the outbursts were played out. Certain landmarks in the village were starting points for organized violence; other places were the usual targets at which the violence was aimed. The village church was usually at the heart of the action. The townspeople often gathered in the churchyard cemetery to hear the news before moving on the enemy. Since rebellions were directed against outside authority including the priesthood, it seems paradoxical that the Church, the religious arm of the colonial state, should provide a symbolic dwelling place, a home base from which to assert the community's power. The answer, I think, is that Christianity occupied an ambiguous but very important place in the adjustment of Indian villages to Spanish rule. The Church, in pursuing its own purposes—conversion, enrichment, and ministry to the souls of Indian neophytes—nurtured communal responsibilities through cofradías and new rituals.[8] Although not always displacing local popular beliefs, Christianity reinforced an Indian inclination to communal organization. The parish priest might be hated and ridiculed by villagers, but the church and its grounds were sacred places, connecting the past to the present and future.[9] Colonial parish churches often were built on the holy places of pre-Hispanic gods, sometimes with the very stones of ancient temples. Village churches were impressive in size and by the eighteenth century venerable in age, many of those in our two regions having been constructed in the sixteenth century. Their grounds often enclosed the cemetery, which further connected the community to its past. The atrium, or courtyard, facing the church (usually walled) was a sanctuary of trees and shade and a meeting place for community business, public ceremonies, and cofradía activities—a living arena of community decision-making and collective activity.

Few of the rebellions turned into general looting and burning. On the contrary, the violence was almost always focused on a particular person or place. The object of attack typically was a colonial official or a building identified with outside authority, usually the *casas reales* (government offices) or the jail. The jail was the most frequent in-animate victim of the people's wrath, villagers descending upon it to release a native son or daughter and then set it aflame. It was the most concrete and hated symbol of the rule of alien law. As one thoughtful Oaxacan priest tells us, "Because the Indians grow up in the open fields, they view imprisonment as a fate worse than death."[10] Human objects of community violence were local agents of the state: usually the alcalde mayor or his deputy assigned to the town (26 per cent); sometimes the parish priest (22 per cent) or officials who attempted to collect an unpopular or increased duty (20 per cent); and occasionally the schoolmaster (3 per cent). If the victims were not state officials, they were likely to be citizens from a rural town, or from the political head town or a subject town, and sometimes abusive native officials or local rivals in a factional dispute.

Restriction of violent action to specific targets was not accompanied by restraints on the intensity of the violence itself. Although most of the armed uprisings were short-lived, they were more than just symbolic gestures. Weapons were used to expel the offending parties. Killings and serious injuries were often the result. In at least eighteen cases colonial officials, militiamen, and other outsiders were killed.[11] In many other cases the enemies were seriously injured or fled just in time to escape alive. In one case an alcalde mayor saved his own life by hiding in a rolled-up mat in a dark corner of the casas reales.[12] Priests seem to have been the one group that was attacked but rarely injured. Unlike their martyred brothers in the northern borderlands or Chiapas and Yucatán during the regional insurrections, priests in central Mexico and Oaxaca were menaced and sometimes injured by flying rocks, but none was killed.

The violence was not often sustained for long. Unless militia forces were sent in, the attacks usually ended in a day or two, although short bursts of collective violence seem to have occurred sporadically in some villages over long periods of time.[13] Occasionally, the local priest or the alcalde mayor persuaded the villagers to lay down their arms, identify the cabecillas, and negotiate a settlement. Since priests are often considered to have had great moral suasion in their parishes, it should be noted that the voices of spiritual reason and moral authority counted for little in subduing these village outbursts. There are many more cases of priests shoved aside with cross in hand and words rebuffed than cases of priests swaying the angry mob in the heat of battle. A few rebellions were quelled in mid-course when the crowds were dispersed with firearms, and in one case an alert militiaman halted a rising by cutting the bellropes.[14] But most village rebellions simply burned themselves out without much interference from the colonial authorities. The violence usually ended with the villagers achieving their immediate goal of driving off the intruders, releasing their fellow townsmen from jail, or extracting a promise from the colonial authorities that their grievances would be acted upon. Especially if the rebellion had resulted in killings or serious injuries, the attackers, and sometimes the entire community, abandoned the town site for refuge in the mountains. Depending on the season, the town might be vacated for several months, but such an exodus rarely led to permanent desertion. Village representatives were usually quick to complain to judicial authorities in the provincial capital and enter into litigation for a formal settlement.

The Spanish response to community uprisings in central and southern Mexico, a calculated blend of punishment and mercy, generally followed the principle of "pacification without destroying the Indians." Since the colonial militias were small and often ill equipped to subdue peasants in revolt, and since the surplus produced by villagers in the form of taxes and labor drafts was an important source of revenue for the Crown, or as a Oaxacan priest put it, "La tilma del indio a todos cubre" (the Indian's cloak covers us all), colonial leaders were anxious to end revolts by negotiation and especially to prevent them from spreading. The Spaniards' fear of regional insurrections was apparently quite real. It was common for officials to think of rural uprisings in terms of dread diseases such as epidemic "contagion," "cancer," and festering wounds that would spread and consume the body politic. Such fear was strong in the minds of Mexican officials after the widespread uprisings in southern Peru and Bolivia in the early 1780's. A 1781 rebellion at Izúcar de Matamoros evoked fear of another Tupac Amaru uprising; and late colonial rebellions north of Mexico City made royal officials take precautions against spread to the "wild" Chichimec and Huaxtec Indians.[15] As long as the violence had not spread to neighboring communities, colonial magistrates were inclined to conciliatory verdicts in which village loyalty to the Crown was reaffirmed. Generally, a few local rebels were singled out by the judge as leading troublemakers subject to exemplary punishment (whippings, labor service, exile, and occasionally execution), whereas the community at large received a pardon, tempered with a threat of harsh punishment for future violence.

Sentences for presumed leaders of village revolts in central and southern Mexico ranged from the indignity and pain of the lash to fines, exile from the district (usually for two to six years), and penal servitude. The last, which was quite common in eighteenth-century sentences, took the form of service in an obraje for one to six years, in a presidio for up to ten years, or on public-works projects for shorter periods. In one extraordinary case the judge ingeniously combined penal service with the improvement of local security by sentencing the leaders to construct a sturdy jail and to clear one league of land surrounding the town in order to destroy the rebels' easy refuge.[16] Fines had the same effect as a sentence to hard labor. Since peasants were rarely able to pay in cash, their fines were often paid by employers who were allowed to claim the labor of the convict up to the value of the fine. The harshest sentences were reserved for individuals who had escaped arrest and were sentenced *in absentia*. In most cases of conviction the leaders were released before the sentence to service had been completed or were pardoned with a threat of severe punishment if they were involved in an uprising again.[17] Capital punishment or long periods of penal servitude were more common in the rare eighteenth-century regional insurrections, such as the Tzeltal revolt of 1712. Captives taken by the Spaniards in the chronic warfare with Indians in the northern borderlands were most likely to be executed or shipped south as slaves.[18]

Except for an occasional fine and a stern warning, the community as a whole was unlikely to be punished, even in cases where death or serious injuries were inflicted. The murder of a hacienda overseer by the people of Macuilxóchitl (Valley of Oaxaca) in the 1740's can serve as an example. Macuilxóchitl's bitter land dispute with a hacienda of the Bethlemite order had escalated into regular raids against the estate and retaliatory whippings by the overseer. The overseer eventually blundered into the village to vent his anger and was immediately seized by a large group of townspeople and taken to the *casa de comunidad* for trial. With the entire community vociferously present, the elders pronounced the death sentence, and the unfortunate Spaniard was hurried off to the town plaza and hanged. Several elders were arrested, but in the course of gathering evidence it became clear to the Audiencia that the entire community had passed judgment and carried out the sentence. Without individual culprits the court was at a loss. It exacted a pledge of loyalty from the town and ordered a stone gallows to be erected in the plaza as a permanent symbol of the punishment the community deserved for its crime.[19]

One major exception to this flexible, almost lenient pattern of sentencing was the verdicts handed down by Visitador José de Gálvez following the local rebellions in Michoacán and San Luis Potosí during 1767–1769. In the 1767 rebellions, which coincided with the expulsion of the Jesuits from New Spain, the colonial authority's response was swift and severe: in San Nicolás (jurisdiction of San Luis Potosí), eleven Indians were executed, the town secretary's right hand was cut off, and the village was deprived of its political rights; in El Venado (jurisdiction of San Luis Potosí), twelve Indians were executed, seven received two hundred lashes, seventy-two were exiled, and the community lost its usufruct rights to public lands; in San Francisco (jurisdiction of San Luis Potosí), eight were executed, two were whipped, seven were sentenced to life imprisonment, and twenty-six received limited prison sentences; in Pátzcuaro (jurisdiction of Michoacán), two Indians were executed, twenty received life sentences, twenty-four were subjected to two hundred lashes, and twenty-nine were exiled. In uniquely cruel fashion, these sentences amounted to punishment for the sake of punishment as the unbending response of a leading peninsular reformer who had little understanding of the delicate divide-and-rule policies that had governed the Mexican countryside for two centuries. Two years later, when a major uprising occurred at San Sebastián Agua del Venado in the jurisdiction of San Luis Potosí, the sentence was again exceptionally severe, but it followed the standard pattern of penal servitude: all three hundred Indian men arrested were sent to presidios for varying periods of service, and eleven received heavy fines—fifty pesos for ten of them, and five hundred pesos for the principal leader, which effectively meant that he would spend the rest of his life in servitude.[20]

Although the Spanish reaction to communities in revolt was usually restrained, it did not mean that the colonial authorities sympathized with or respected the peasants' reasons for resorting to arms. Little of the utopian good will that was an important strand of Spanish motivation in the sixteenth century was evident in these eighteenth-century investigations, even among the clergymen who appeared as witnesses. Occasionally, a hostile outburst was forgiven as overexuberance

on a festive occasion or the product of a legitimate grievance, but
official explanations of the risings usually seized on solemn abstractions
and innate personality traits of Indian peasants, such as their lazy,
ignorant, uncouth, vice-ridden, insolent, rebellious nature or their uncivilized way of life, "lacking God, Law, and King."[21] When the colonial officials got down to specifics, they condemned especially the
village traditions of government "in which everyone rules." In trying
to discover the cause of a major rebellion in Zimatlán (Valley of Oaxaca) in 1772, the parish priest concluded that it resulted from the
Indians' "wicked" style of government. Drawing a parallel to Spain's
archrival England, he warned that continual uprisings could be expected in Indian villages because "everyone rules," including women
and children.[22] Consensus decision-making in peasant villages received little sympathy from Spaniards, imbued with the idea of a
natural order based on highly stratified hierarchies. Occasionally, colonial authorities saw the root of rebellion in the bad example of a neighboring town or in excessive drinking. In one case we can look beyond
the rather restrained language of the Spanish magistrates and find a
local Spaniard's feelings about Indian villagers in the wake of a rebellion. The evidence comes in the form of an anonymous note tacked
to the door of the magistrate of Tlamatlán who was investigating the
uprising of two small villages against the parish priest. The note read:

The monkey, even dressed in silk, is still a monkey. Whoever speaks of Indians speaks of shit because the Indian is like the monkey. It's as simple as
that, because the Indian, like the monkey, utters a thousand stupidities which
have neither beginning nor end. This is the truth and no lie. They are also
very malicious and devilish.

This is not a very coherent statement of opinion, but it is nevertheless
a rare glimpse of feelings that are usually masked from the historian's
view, of the hatred and fear of a Spaniard living close to villagers but
sharing with them few if any affirmative beliefs.[23] Underlying this
anonymous author's hatred and fear is the knowledge that the Indian
villagers were certainly capable of mob violence if they sensed an overt
threat to their lands or to the psychic territory of their daily and seasonal routine.

For their part, villagers usually acquiesced in the conciliatory spirit
of colonial judges, tentatively returning to the village from their mountain refuges. In the end, both villagers and colonial authorities wanted
rapid resolution and return to settled village life. The villagers had
land to farm, families to feed, and a sense of community that was not
easily destroyed at one blow; they were also aware of the costs of

lengthy litigation. The Crown had taxes to collect and a political system to preserve. Considering the slow pace of much colonial administration in the eighteenth century, the judicial system dealt with most *tumultos* with remarkable speed, completing most investigations in a matter of weeks. The old leader of the little village of Coamelco in the jurisdiction of Meztitlán, which had risen up against the parish priest in 1777, knew from experience when he wrote with obvious resignation that "a poor settlement now is better than a long lawsuit that eventually turns out well." [24]

Few of the eighteenth-century uprisings in central and southern Mexico developed into regional movements with peasant villages banding together in common cause. Those exceptional movements that did submerge purely local interests in an abortive or temporarily successful regional union followed patterns familiar to peasant insurrections at other places and times. They developed as millenarian movements or formed around nonvillage leaders with whom the peasants shared a common enemy. In both cases, they were fragile movements centered on loyalty to particular leaders rather than to principles based on an identity of conditions and desires.

One impressive regional uprising of peasants occurred in the jurisdiction of Tulancingo (state of Hidalgo) in 1769, with several thousand Indian villagers from as far away as Meztitlán and Tenango joining a "New Savior" in the mountain fastnesses of Tututepec. Millenarian appeal—a retreat from the burdens of colonial life into a new theocratic utopia—seems to have been the source of regional support. The New Savior, a charismatic native messiah, was an old Indian who was accompanied by a woman venerated as the Virgin of Guadalupe. Together, they worshiped an idol-studded cross, proclaimed death to the Spaniards, and ruled above a newly created Indian priesthood that was to replace the Catholic hierarchy and end the hated clerical and state taxes. According to these spiritual leaders, the Catholic priests were true devils who should not be obeyed. The One True God of the movement was dedicated to the corn fields and chile fields, clearly an appeal to the popular fertility cults at the heart of peasant religion. [25] By calling for an end to all colonial taxes, for sparing the lives of only those Spaniards who would pay tribute to the Indians, and envisioning a world in which bishops and parish priests would line up to kiss the New Savior's hand, the movement hinted at a classlike war of poor against rich and sanctioned bloody attacks on colonial officials and nonbelievers who blundered into the believers' path.

A second short-lived regional revolt flared in the jurisdiction of Actopan, not far from Tulancingo, in 1756. The immediate cause of this uprising is clearer than the inspiration of the one at Tulancingo, and it followed a rather different, nonmillenarian course. The occasion for violence was a new labor draft in the jurisdiction for the purpose of draining the mines at Pachuca. Villagers complained that the mine labor was dangerous and that they were just beginning to harvest their corn crop. The revolt began on a Wednesday market day in the provincial center of Actopan, with as many as 2,000 Indian men and women from nearby towns joined by non-Indians who were also subject to the labor draft. They converged on the plaza, brandishing knives, rocks, and banners, closing off the roads into town, shouting "Death to the Governors," and threatening to destroy the place. In the ensuing three days, eight Spaniards were killed or wounded and there was considerable destruction of property. Priests, some of whom had supported the Indian complaints prior to the uprising, negotiated a settlement: a half-caste *lobo* was singled out for punishment as the leader, the excesses of the common people were pardoned, and the towns agreed to a reduced labor service.[26] This insurrection is more like the sort of working alliance between villagers and lower-class townspeople who shared a common grievance that might be expected to produce strong feelings and violence against Spaniards in general. In this case, the movement joined Indian villagers chafing under new mine labor levies with vagrants and mestizos and mulattoes from the head town of Actopan, who also were being forced into the mines.

A local uprising in 1762 in the town of San Andrés, jurisdiction of Tenango (state of Mexico), exposed plans for another regional movement. The incident for the local revolt was the district lieutenant's search for contraband liquor on the evening of the patron saint's fiesta. In one house he found many men and women getting drunk around a large pot of tepache. As he tried to make arrests, the church bells were rung and "a multitude" of people descended on the house. The lieutenant and his militiamen barely escaped with their lives. In the course of the investigation into these events, witnesses testified to the long history of community revolts in Tenango and the neighboring jurisdiction of Metepec: a history of colonial officials driven out of town, of villagers refusing to obey written orders, and of several unsuccessful attempts at regional movements against Spanish authority.[27] Spanish fears of regional revolts, however, rarely were justified when the movement depended upon simultaneous uprisings by villages without a millenarian leader who could connect them to other groups outside the villages.

In Oaxaca, stirrings of regional unrest in the eighteenth century did not reach such proportions, but the revival of the cochineal trade, with coercive methods used to force production in villages of the Mixteca and the Sierra Zapoteca, did give rise to several brief regional uprisings. Townspeople of San Felipe, San Mateo, and San Francisco in the jurisdiction of Teozacualco rebelled simultaneously in 1774 against the district lieutenant for interfering in local affairs, demanding cochineal, and attempting to collect tax on liquor produced for local consumption. Rebellion planned in Achiutla (Mixteca Alta) during 1785 nearly became a regional uprising. Messengers from Achiutla carried the call to arms to surrounding villages. Again, the common enemy was the district lieutenant, who was hated for harsh treatment and abuse in the collection of the tribute tax and cochineal.* In general, however, peasants in eighteenth-century central Mexico and Oaxaca were not engaged in new economic activities that could lead to new perceptions about deprivation.

No one village rebellion typifies the structure discussed here, but the events at Tlapanoya (tributary to Atotonilco in the jurisdiction of Atitalaquia, modern state of Hidalgo) in July 1690 and at Amanalco (jurisdiction of Metepec, state of Mexico) in February 1792 bring a number of characteristics into play.[28] A brief description of these two uprisings can make our composite picture more vivid.

The Tlapanoya tumulto began on a Sunday afternoon when the In-

---

*AGN *Criminal* 306 exp. 1. Additional light might be cast on the low incidence of regional revolts in the settled highlands of Mexico in the eighteenth century by comparison to the other great highland peasant societies in Peru and Bolivia, where regional revolts were more frequent. A cycle of three periods of major uprisings have been identified in eighteenth-century Peru: 1737–1740, 1750, and 1780–1782. These widespread uprisings seem to have been touched off by similar changes in tax levies and land encroachments and the reparto de efectos that we have noted in the Mexican regions. One distinctive feature of the three periods of insurrection in Peru and Bolivia absent in the rural unrest in Mexico was messianic leadership by hereditary native nobles who proclaimed a return to the rule of the Incas, with themselves as the legitimate heirs. The bases for such a series of messianic movements would appear to be the survival of a hispanicized native elite and ethnic ties among Indian peasants reinforced by rivalries among different regions, more movement of peasants outside the villages, and weaker village units. There is some disagreement about the nature of the Tupac Amaru revolt in Cuzco province in 1780. Oscar Cornblit emphasizes the role of local Creoles in launching the revolt and the participation of *forasteros* (uprooted Indians from other regions). Magnus Mörner's careful new work on the rebellion in Cuzco province returns to the importance of the community nobles, who were fighting among themselves for the control of bridges as well as against the abuse of power by local colonial officials. Forasteros, according to Mörner, played a minor role in the uprising. It was basically fought by groups of villages attached to a mutually acceptable *curaca*. By contrast, we have noted the general decline of ethnolinguistic units in Mexico and the rarity of collective action by Indian linguistic groups in the late colonial period.

dian *gobernador* and two nobles of Atotonilco arrived in the village
with an order signed by the alcalde mayor. They were to be given cus-
tody of two citizens of Atotonilco who recently had settled in Tlapanoya to avoid the personal services exacted by the gobernador and the
alcalde mayor. The Tlapanoyans who encountered the messengers refused to obey the order and, after muttering to themselves, declared
that they no longer accepted the alcalde mayor as their judge. They
began to whistle and call for the villagers—men and women—who
assembled in a menacing crowd with clubs, rocks, plows, and other
weapons to attack the Atotonilco gobernador, who fled for his life.
When word of the tumulto reached the alcalde mayor, he sent the
militia to arrest the officials of Tlapanoya. The townspeople fled to the
mountains, but two sons of the gobernador of Tlapanoya were cap-
tured. The gobernador himself was in Mexico City at the time to regis-
ter a complaint with the Audiencia against the forced labor and cash
extortions demanded by the alcalde mayor. During the investigation
of the tumulto ordered by the Audiencia, the alcalde mayor asserted
that the Tlapanoyans were insolent people who refused to perform
labor service for the king and who were his enemies because he had
arrested seventeen men and twenty-three women of the village for
producing illegal alcoholic beverages. The Audiencia was not im-
pressed. It ordered that the village be protected against arbitrary demands of the alcalde mayor and released the arrested Tlapanoyans
with a stern warning not to take up arms against the king's representative.

The occasion for the uprising in the Amanalco jurisdiction was an
attempt by the parish priest, with the aid of three Indians, to take a
census for tax purposes. Three of the villages in the parish refused to
allow the census-takers in, saying that the priest and his assistants
could not be trusted to make a proper accounting. When the priest
tried to take the census in San Lucas, the villagers, joined by knife-
wielding, rock-throwing men and women from Amanalco and San
Miguel, chased the census-takers back to the priest's lodgings in
Amanalco. Amidst a peal of church bells, shouts and whistles, and
general "alegría," a "numberless" mob (consisting mainly of women)
broke into the church, stormed the jail, and released three of their
own number. Waving his blunderbuss, the priest fought off what
amounted to a halfhearted assault on his person by the women. Gente
de razón in the district quickly came to his aid, and in the ensuing
hours of confusion one Indian died and three were seriously injured.
The rebellion died down only after the peasants seized and battered

Isidro Hernández, one of the three Indians who were in league with the priest. A few peasants were arrested, but most escaped to the mountains; and the priest was relieved of his duties. In his attempt to investigate the uprising, the *subdelegado* of Metepec was frustrated by the welter of name-calling, complaints, and counterclaims lodged by the peasants and the gente de razón. He did determine that the priest had overcharged the peasants for his services, obstructed their travel to Mexico City, whipped local people without sufficient reason, and allowed his three assistants, particularly Hernández, to usurp community lands. Hernández was also hated for supposedly perpetrating several deaths by witchcraft. In September, having noted that the peasants had returned in peace and were paying their taxes, the subdelegado released the rebels who were still in prison.

APPARENT CAUSES AND RESULTS

Given the incomplete historical record and the impressionistic quality of competing social science explanations of collective violence, the causes of these rebellions seem impossible to pinpoint. In attempting to find them, we can at least begin by identifying the circumstances surrounding village uprisings and the goals stated by the peasants themselves. Since our sample is fairly large, patterns that emerge for the occasions of village rebellions have some potential explanatory value. They provide a rough idea of apparent or proximate causes— the attitudes and conditions that stand in close association with these cases of collective violence. We can then relate the conditions surrounding the eighteenth-century rebellions to several attempts by sociologists and anthropologists to explain peasant uprisings in terms of class relationships and "ultimate" causes.

For collective violence in Latin America and generally, some of the various approaches to explanation stress single causes (although usually without denying some importance to other factors), and others emphasize "root causes" and theories of structural strain. Primary concern with root causes provides answers that can be rationalized easily enough in the abstract but are difficult to demonstrate in a full and satisfying manner and that come too close to the value judgments of the black and white legends. To say that the "system of production" is the root cause of rebellion does not advance us very far in the direction of explaining why the revolts we can document actually occurred and why they occurred at certain times. Because historical societies have all had some measure of inequality in the system of production, and therefore some "structural strain," there would seem to be potential for social violence in all of them. Historical evidence has, so far at least, resisted the convincing application of this kind of analysis, which would ascribe sequences of specific events to broad structural tensions that seem to exist in all postprimitive societies. Neil Smelser's *Theory of Collective Behavior*, for example, proposes an admirably comprehensive scheme of four great categories of factors that combine to provoke collective violence: conduciveness, strain, generalized belief, and precipitating events.[29] Yet when he begins to apply case evidence for his basic categories of conduciveness and strain, the examples, such as seventeenth-century riots in Mexico City, are squeezed into place on the basis of superficial evidence and with little attention to qualitative differences from other societies that experienced no local or regional revolts over long periods of time.

More specific conditions for revolt have been offered for Latin American examples. One explanation links collective violence with various strains in material life, such as famines and epidemics; we can test this theory by considering the chronology of eighteenth-century tumultos. If widespread material changes (such as famine or epidemic disease) were crucial to village unrest, we should find a clustering of central Mexican tumultos in the years that Enrique Florescano has identified as periods of agricultural crisis (that is, of high prices and extreme shortages of maize) in the Valley of Mexico.[30] Florescano demonstrates a close association between eighteenth-century agricultural crises and grain prices in 1709–1710, 1714, 1749–1750, 1785–1786, and 1810–1811. By decade, the major concentrations of our late colonial tumultos occur in the periods 1761–1770 and 1801–1810. There is no great bunching of rebellions and famines around a few crucial years. In fact, the chronology of the tumultos in relation to agricultural crises approaches a random distribution. Twenty-two per cent of the uprisings occurred in the years identified as times of agricultural crisis, and these years represent 21 per cent of the period 1701–1811 (see Table 18).

Another specific cause suggested by some anthropologists for Latin American revolts is religion, usually indicating resentment of imposed changes in religious practices.[31] This certainly appears in peasant testimony about incidents of collective violence, but it is an excessively narrow approach to historical explanation, which, like "folk history," relies almost exclusively for explanation on the subordinate group's perception of its past. Natalie Z. Davis has shown that peasant riots in the name of religion in sixteenth-century Europe usually were rooted, not in a simple conflict over religious practices, but in the

TABLE 18.   *Comparison of Village Uprisings and Agricultural Crises in Central Mexico, 1703–1811*

Year(s) of agricultural crises	Year of uprising(s)		Year(s) of agricultural crises	Year of uprising(s)	
	1703			1777	
1709–10	1708			1778	(2)
	1710			1779	
	1711			1780	
1714ᵃ	1714		1780–81	1782	
	1720	(2)		1783	(3)
1724–25	1721			1784	
1730–31	1727			1785	
	1730	(2)	1785–86	1786	
	1733	(4)		1787	
1741–42	1735	(2)		1789	(2)
	1743			1792	(2)
	1744			1795	
	1746			1796	
1749–50ᵃ	1749			1797	
	1756			1799	(3)
1759–60	1758			1800	
	1762	(6)		1801	
	1764	(2)	1801–2	1802	(3)
	1766	(3)		1803	(2)
	1767	(2)		1804	
	1769	(3)		1805	(4)
1771–72	1771			1807	(2)
	1772	(3)		1808	
	1773			1810	(2)
	1774		1810–11ᵃ	1811	

NOTE: The maize prices and agricultural crises projected by Florescano for eighteenth-century Mexico are based mostly on evidence for Mexico City. Since peasants were not much involved in maize production for the city, these prices and crises may not correspond exactly to the patterns of maize supply and prices in rural areas.
ᵃ Major crises.

abuse of political and economic power by the Church as landlord or tax collector.[32] Similar grievances, especially over revised schedules of clerical fees and labor drafts, as we shall see, were associated with what appear to be religious rebellions in eighteenth-century Mexico. As Davis suggests, the range of ruler-subject relationships must be considered, in addition to the people's perceptions of their conditions and their assumption of the mantle of holy mission, if we are to account for the timing and location of these revolts.

A more common explanation of Latin American peasant movements centers on "structural contradictions," especially a combination of subordinate-group, economic deprivation, and elite intransigence.[33] This explanation places the causes of revolt completely outside the villages themselves. A recent example of this approach applied to colonial Mexico is the work of Raymond Buve.[34] He sees the principal "contradiction" in the land system, which he describes in terms of landed Spanish overlords and landless Indian country folk. According to Buve, this unequal relationship on the land, plus the colonial government's oppression of peasants in defense of the landed elite, created the conditions for peasant revolts. But this hypothesis fails to fit a good deal of the evidence both for Mexico and for other parts of Latin America. Barrington Moore, among others, has noted that peasant unrest is not simply the result of massive poverty and exploitation or of the elite's commitment to mindless repression. There are too many revolts that do not seem to follow on a period of worsening material conditions and too many rural societies living through increasing poverty without showing an increase in social violence to hazard any universal statements about economic deprivation, elite intransigence, and peasant unrest. If anything, rebellions seem to have been more common in regions and communities of Latin America that are less poverty-stricken and isolated.[35] In particular, the "structural contradictions" theory does not seem promising as an explanation of rebellions in central Mexico and Oaxaca.

Certainly, landless villages existed in these regions, and perhaps some decline was felt in the peasants' material situation in the eighteenth century, especially in central Mexico, but these conditions seem to have had little to do with collective violence. Villages in possession of substantial landholdings are the ones that appear in nearly all of the tumultos we have studied.[36] Elite intransigence—rigid, usually armed oppression wielded by colonial officials—was uncommon in the events leading up to the village revolts. As I shall discuss farther on, particular abuses of power perceived by villagers touched off nearly all of the uprisings, but abuses were seen in local terms and did not usually signify a pervasive "elite intransigence" that was intent upon securing the peace by armed force alone. In fact, elite willingness to compromise apparently prevented some of the village uprisings from spreading into regional insurrections.

One fundamental assumption that has deeply affected my own analysis is that conflict is normal rather than exceptional in societies where power and wealth are not distributed evenly or to the satisfaction of all members. Therefore, what needs explanation is not social conflict itself, but how and why conflict assumes varying expressions in different societies or within the same society at different times.

The work of the nineteenth-century German sociologist Georg Simmel offers some especially useful formulations on the nature of social conflict, in particular of social violence. Simmel conceived of four forms of interaction based on the distribution of scarce resources in societies with dominant ("superordinate") and subordinate groups: *competition*—impersonal efforts of individuals or groups to maximize their share of scarce resources; *conflict*—the personalized clash of group interests where members of only one group can have the power to allocate a scarce resource; *accommodation*—temporary resolution of conflict through an uneasy truce or when a group settles for less than it wants; and *assimilation and destruction*—final resolution of conflict in which differences between interacting groups have disappeared.[37]

Without denying the possibility of cooperation and self-denial, Simmel viewed social conflict as inevitable. Accommodation, the basis of conflict resolution between dominant and subordinate groups, may work for many years, but it is inherently fragile because subordinate groups have settled for less than they want and are unlikely to be permanently satisfied. They will be especially sensitive to further adjustments that accentuate their subordination. Still, subordination may continue for long periods of time without any concerted attempts by the subordinate groups to change the relationship itself. The inevitability of conflict, or the clash of interests, in such societies does not necessarily mean there will be social *violence*.

Social violence occurs, according to Simmel, when the inherently unstable accommodative structures between rulers and subjects lose their viability. He suggests four categories of changing conditions that may threaten an existing accommodation: (1) the legitimacy of the superordinate group declines: this can result from abuse of power or intransigent material demands of the ruler in a period of rapid change, or invasion of the subjects' privacy; or from the introduction of new perspectives on legitimacy, such as anticolonialism, which can reorient the subjects' perceptions of deprivation; (2) the ruling groups lose vitality: for example, the quality of leadership may decline, leaders may begin to reside in cities and make less frequent contact with their subjects, or a police force may become weaker; (3) the subordinate groups gain power; and (4) the subordinate groups realize latent power. Obviously, these are not mutually exclusive and independent categories. A decline in the legitimacy of the rulers, whether through increasing exploitation or through new perspectives on legitimacy, contributes to a subject group's gain in power or realization of latent power.

For our purposes the special contribution of Simmel's conception of social conflict and social violence is twofold. First, it encourages us to look beyond the peasants' own beliefs and actions to the dimensions of power and interests and to the interaction of dominant and subordinate groups. This reminder of the importance of political and social contexts is especially helpful because the trial records and other written sources generated by the rulers, which are the historian's principal evidence of peasant uprisings, have a natural tendency to direct us to internal "causes." Such internal conditions are usually crucial precipitating reasons for revolt, but they tend to mask structural considerations. Second, Simmel gives us an approach that encompasses consideration of both objective changes in material conditions *and* the rebels' perceptions of their conditions and of the legitimacy of the superordinate group. It thereby avoids on the one hand the problems of a strictly materialist approach, which would emphasize a direct connection between deprivation and social violence even though many of the most oppressed groups historically have shown little inclination to revolt, and on the other hand the limitations of purely internal or functionalist explanations emphasizing the values, motivations, and will power of the subjects. By focusing on *relative* deprivation—the gap between anticipated conditions and a less agreeable actuality—it encourages us to consider perceptions as well as material conditions and distinguish precipitating circumstances from deeper causes without slighting the role of either one in creating peasant revolts. The strength of Simmel's approach is not that it provides a neat system of explanation (it does not) but that it offers a conception of social violence that considers a whole range of social relationships, economic conditions, and their political expression. It recognizes the importance of the allocation of scarce power and that of scarce resources as major variables. Written records will perhaps always fall short of accounting for all the possibilities raised by Simmel's approach to social conflict, but his approach does provide a challenging alternative to the weaknesses of simpler conceptions of social violence.

The circumstances surrounding the village uprisings in central Mexico and Oaxaca can now be described in light of these types of interaction between dominant and subordinate groups and the conditions for a breakdown in accommodation. Despite the impressive level of violence in most of the uprisings, few are examples of complete breakdown in the system of accommodation between colonial rulers and village subjects. The community's sense of outrage in an overwhelming number of cases was directed not against "the Ruler"—the king and the viceroy enjoyed unquestioned respect—but against the individuals who personally embodied the abuse of authority in specific local cases of perceived deprivation or tyranny: the alcalde mayor, his lieutenant in charge of the village, the royal tax collector, or the parish priest. Even though these individuals might be doing no more than carrying out royal orders, villagers in revolt generally did not make the connection between their grievances and the colonial system as a whole. Only in the relationship between the local overlord and the village can we speak of accommodation giving way to violent conflict. The door was nearly always open on the peasants' side for negotiation with higher authorities who were still recognized as legitimate rulers.

In what circumstances were these personal representatives of outside authority attacked? Perhaps the most common occasion for attacks on the royal or divine representative was the collection of new or higher taxes, an apparently universal reason for peasant unrest.[38] An uprising by the villagers of Pozontepec in September 1758, for example, was touched off by the parish priest's attempt to collect a new schedule of higher clerical fees authorized by the Crown (subsequent investigation revealed other, perhaps more fundamental, peasant grievances against the priest's behavior in this parish and earlier rumors of rebellion). An argument between the priest and some of the peasants escalated to insults and shoves. That night a general tumulto broke out, the priest's house was set on fire, and the priest himself narrowly escaped the flames in his underwear.[39] Of the more than thirty uprisings against parish priests, all but eight were touched off by new clerical fees, with villagers complaining of raised charges for baptism, marriage, burial, and celebration of the Mass, or of withholding of priestly services because the villagers were not performing exceptional services for the cleric.

The collection of secular taxes was an equally important occasion for touching off community violence against tax collectors and local judges. Changes in the tribute schedule frequently ignited community violence, and some state taxes, no matter what the rate, had explosive potential. Particularly galling to villagers in central Mexico were the taxes on pulque commerce and salt production. Late colonial schoolmasters who tried to supplement their incomes as tax collectors on monopoly goods, such as tobacco, also invited violence.[40] In both central Mexico and Oaxaca, the reparto de efectos—the alcalde mayor's monopoly on the sale of certain goods within his district, such as horses and mules, which were often forced upon village buyers—touched off still other rebellions.[41]

Rejection of new or unexpected taxes is part of a larger set of circumstances of economic deprivation and economic incursion. Tax increases meant the allocation of additional family and community resources to nonproducers and outsiders, principally the state and the Church. As a new demand, however, the tax increase had a greater impact on the local economy than merely that of extracting another increment of the community's production. Since taxes normally were collected in cash in the eighteenth century, higher charges usually forced villagers to look outside their community for additional sources of cash, through the sale of village produce, rental of lands, or wage labor. The effect of a tax increase was to make the village more dependent on cash-bearing employers, buyers, and trading partners, in addition to reducing the community's share of its production. In spite of these unsettling effects of taxation, it is important to note once again that eighteenth-century peasants in revolt rarely were challenging the structure of colonial relationships between themselves and the Spanish state. They were protesting *new* taxes or new levels of old taxes, not the right of the state to tax and the Indian subjects' obligation to pay tribute and other traditional levies.

Other economic threats also occasioned collective violence in peasant villages. Labor demands by local officials, the priest, or neighboring hacendados, forced sale of community stores of an essential product, such as corn, salt, or lime, and government orders to allow traders from a rival town to sell in the local market all led to mass uprisings at the village level in central Mexico and Oaxaca.[42] The most important economic incursion after the changing tax burden and labor demands was boundary encroachments. Like tax rebellions, mass invasions or occupations of land are familiar events to students of peasant uprisings in other areas of the world. Land disputes between villages or between a private landowner and a village are not especially numerous in this sample of village rebellions (30 of 142 cases), but my earlier work on land tenure in the Valley of Oaxaca suggests that control of land was a particularly tender matter because such a close relationship endured between village identity and a specific territory. As the judge in the Santa Lucía case realized, every official boundary inspection involving the borders of a peasant village was provocation enough for a collective outburst. Comprehending this potential rarely enabled the authorities to prevent an uprising. In the case of Santa Lucía, the judge was careful to prepare himself with all the trappings of royal authority—a large retinue of high Church and secular officials, militiamen, and public criers who announced the official orders for the survey. Nevertheless, the mere attempt to execute a formal measurement aroused the villagers to take matters into their own hands and send the officials running for their lives with a shower of rocks and curses. New pressures on the land in the eighteenth century—resulting from population growth and the expansion of private estates producing for urban markets—suggest that boundary questions were a chronic occasion for violence in both of our regions, but it is noteworthy that the Oaxaca examples (both from the Mixteca Alta and the Valley of Oaxaca) of boundary wars and attacks on public officials in *vistas de ojos* were especially prolonged and acrimonious. Although their fears were not always justified, Valley peasants assumed that a survey would mean a loss of land. As one sympathetic alcalde mayor understood, "What they fear most is losing the peace and tranquillity in which they live, and the lands that each individual and his community peacefully possess."[43] Menacing crowds of Indian peasants usually turned out for these inspections. Occasionally, they would throw rocks at the officials, steal the measuring rope, and mass in front of the inspectors, refusing to let them proceed with the measurement. A frightened alcalde mayor of the Cuatro Villas jurisdiction reported the following scene at a boundary survey east of the city of Oaxaca in 1720:

When we reached the boundary of a plot of land belonging to Gabriel Martín, a native of the pueblo of Santa Cruz . . . , many Indians from Santa Cruz appeared, joining others who had assembled there. Massing together in a crowd, they sought, in disobedience of the Royal Order and Royal justice, to stop the proceedings, shouting that we would not be allowed to go beyond the said boundary. At the same time, the Indians picked up stones and threw three; they aimed one at Your representative, but it struck one of the Indian officials instead.[44]

There surely were many more cases of specific economic incursions of this type (new taxes, labor drafts, boundary troubles) than there were tumultos. One additional ingredient in a number of our examples of rebellion that seems to have been a final—if not always indispensable—precipitating factor was the arrest or corporal punishment of village officers for failing to enforce the decisions of colonial officials. Many uprisings began with the storming of the local jail where the officers were being held, with an attack on the militia detachment that was removing an arrested official to the head town for trial, or with an attack at the scene of an exemplary punishment—usually a whipping —of village leaders for objecting to the new exaction. Whippings were a special form of humiliation to Indians because, as has been mentioned, by law Spaniards could not be whipped.

A second major category of occasions for village uprisings has apparently little to do with material conditions or new economic incursions but much to do with villagers' sense of autonomy and community. In these cases, of which there are thirty-four examples, villagers testified that they rose up in defense of their liberty or their way of life. Revolts against parish priests provide some well-documented examples of such symbolic affronts. In 1799 the people of Atlautla staged a violent uprising when they learned that the parish priest had sold their prized altarpiece to a nearby rival town; in a similar incident the priest of Cuauhtitlán provoked violence in 1785 by attempting to refurbish an Indian chapel without consulting the parishioners; other priests courted trouble by repairing village churches with stones from ancient ceremonial structures. In Zimatlán in 1773 the townspeople protested violently against a priest who tried to keep them from speaking their native language, Zapotec; another town, Almoloya (1787), protested the priest's refusal to preach in their language by not attending Mass and, finally, by driving him out of town. Another priest aroused the people of Chacatongo to revolt in 1674 by moving his place of residence to another town within the parish; the priest of Almoloya created a similar complaint among the subject towns in his parish in 1792 by removing their baptismal fonts and requiring them to attend the principal church to receive the sacraments. Other priests angered peasant parishioners by interrupting local celebrations, forbidding processions, and meddling in the selection of village officials.*

Attempts to quarantine villagers in order to prevent the spread of epidemic disease also represented the kind of violation of local independence that could provoke a violent response. Teotitlán del Valle, a peasant community in the Valley of Oaxaca especially hard hit by the smallpox epidemic of late 1792, was singled out for special attention by the Board of Physicians in the city of Oaxaca. At the board's request, the intendant ordered the entire community quarantined and a makeshift infirmary constructed on the outskirts of the town to separate the afflicted from the healthy. Residents of Teotitlán were not permitted to leave the village, even to tend their crops, nor could families visit or send food to their isolated relatives in the infirmary huts. To *teotitleños* this forced community isolation and separation of family members was an intolerable intervention. Their first response,

---

*In the Papantla revolt of 1768, the alcalde mayor's plan to cut down trees in the community combined material and ideological threats to the local people: "The trees gave the people shade and helped them to persevere; also, they served for tying up their animals and protected their houses from fire; also, the twigs and leaves provided fodder." AGI *Audiencia de Mexico* 1934. Sentiments of village liberty were also aroused by official attempts to force villagers to move to a new town site or, in one case, by efforts to make them stay where they were, AGN *Civil* 1599 exp. 9, 2166 exp. 5.

conditioned by three centuries of colonial experience, was to hire a lawyer in the city to petition the viceroy for relief. The leisurely legal process was not, however, a satisfactory means of coping with this kind of real emergency. The peasants soon took the issue into their own hands, storming the infirmary, retrieving sick relatives, and burying the dead in the churchyard. The attack was apparently spontaneous, beginning with a mother attempting to recover her child from the infirmary.[45] It ended, like so many rebellions, with a plan for appeasement designed to avoid permanent confrontation with communities in the region. The intendant in Antequera first ordered the urban militia to patrol the outskirts of Teotitlán (an assignment that lasted more than two weeks) but did not attempt a punitive expedition against the town or dare to punish the townspeople beyond the brief imprisonment of fifteen men and women. Colonial authorities hit upon making a scapegoat of the lawyer as a way out of direct confrontation with the peasants. In spite of the fact that the teotitleños had come to him for advice in opposing the quarantine, the lawyer was charged with stirring up innocent Indians and condemned to a stiff prison sentence and a heavy fine. The teotitleños emerged from the affair as "extremely peaceful people" who had never been rebellious until they met this city lawyer—a convenient case of Spanish amnesia, judging by the violent land disputes involving Teotitlán with Macuilxóchitl and Tlacolula throughout the eighteenth century.[46]

A third category of conditions leading to collective violence is political relationships, both within individual villages and among villages in the same political jurisdiction. The growth of the rural population in the eighteenth century contributed to new conflict between subject towns and head towns in our regions. Agitation by sujetos to acquire cabecera status—and thereby separate themselves from nominal political subordination to another town and the consequent irritating service obligations—was a common occurrence. Attempts to transfer villages from one district to another were also common. These jurisdictional tensions sometimes touched off village uprisings.[47] The Los Reyes-Xocotitlán (jurisdiction of Ixtlahuaca) tumulto of October 1767 and the Zozoquiapan (jurisdiction of Meztitlán) tumulto of May 1805 provide good examples. The sujeto village of Los Reyes rose up against the gobernador of the cabecera, Xocotitlán, after he arrested the leading citizen of Los Reyes and his wife for "lack of respect" and failure to turn over all of the tribute owed by the village. This incident brought to the surface the villagers' fears that the gobernador served only the interests of the cabecera and of the parish priest, who resided in

Xocotitlán. The Zozoquiapan tumulto occurred when Indian villagers, led by a local noblewoman, Felipa Escudero, refused to accept an order from the Audiencia transferring their community out of the jurisdiction of Meztitlán. The militia was sent in to arrest members of the local cabildo, and the townspeople drove them out. Members of the village who testified in the alcalde mayor's investigation said they were afraid that the transfer would mean the loss of their lands and the disruption of local elections. [48]

Another kind of political problem leading to uprisings was internal factionalism, which seems to have been less directly connected to population growth than were intercommunity disputes. Armed uprisings of commoners against the local nobles and officeholders, especially after a disputed election, and attacks by one barrio on another bring us back to Simmel's premise of the tensions inherent in the relationships between dominant and subordinate groups. What is important to us in a historical study of peasant life is that major violence related to factionalism does not seem to have been more prevalent in the eighteenth century than in the seventeenth. On the other hand, factionalism and the weakening of community bonds is more apparent in the mid-nineteenth century. (We will take up this change briefly in later pages.)

Crowd behavior was also an indicator of the occasions for rebellion. We have already considered the kinds of people who participated in the uprisings, the places and people attacked, and the ambiguous end to most outbursts of this sort. Another aspect of crowd behavior —the words exchanged with royal officials and the shouts that accompanied the attacks—is especially important for a consideration of precipitating causes. In sifting through the evidence, I found that the noise of village rebellions consisted of more than the terrific din of war whoops, profanity, ear-splitting whistles, church bells, horns, and drums. There were also choruses of shouts, articulate enough to find their way into the testimony of two or more eyewitnesses. These spontaneous utterances are as close as we can probably come to identifying the conscious goals of the villagers' actions. Unlike the testimony in formal investigations—which can be useful in other ways—chants and shouts are unguarded, direct declarations of feelings that are rarely expressed at other times or documented in other kinds of written records.

Many of the shouts were scornful insults and threats to the representatives who abused colonial authority, or to other outsiders who posed a threat to the community's peace, such as the owner or administrator of a neighboring estate: "We're going to kill you and drink your blood"; "Kill these dogs"; "Kill these niggers"; "Dirty pig"; "Nigger"; "Cuckold robbers"; "Now you'll see, you devil-dog alcalde mayor and your thieving cronies"; "We'll not leave a Spaniard alive in this town"; "You'll pay for this, you dog-governor"; "Now you'll see, you lying, thieving dog"; "Death to them all"; "The governor has ordered us to kill the Riveras"; "To hell with you, Rivera, you have stolen our lands and we're going to kill you"; "War, war."[49] Righteous indignation directed against outsiders who maligned the villagers, attempted to seize their lands, or imposed new taxes are contained in all of these heated words. But there is more here. "Pig," "dog," "devil-dog," and "nigger" were standard Spanish expletives, often applied to Indians.[50] In calling a peninsular subdelegado a "nigger" or the parish priest a "dog," the central Mexico villagers turned the tables on their political masters, repaying them in kind. In two of these examples, Ixmiquilpan in 1642 and Actopan in 1756—both in areas of Hidalgo where peasants were forced into service in the mines of Pachuca and Real del Monte—the sense of outrage against an individual Spaniard spilled over into a general call of "Death to them all"; "We'll not leave a Spaniard alive in this town."[51] This would seem to be a groping toward class war, but both rebellions burned themselves out in a few days, without spreading and without any mass killing of Spaniards. Nevertheless, they are early and interesting examples of a latent potential for insurrection and liberation.

A second type of common exclamation reveals what seem to be vague democratic aspirations and an instinct for self-preservation. They were not directed at anyone in particular; they were declarations of local rights and imperatives, and of strong opposition to any new infringement on local habits: "We alone are sovereign in this town"; "Now we're the masters of this land"; "We have no master"; "This boundary measurement should not be made; the King has no business here"; "We refuse to obey the alcalde mayor or to consider him our judge." One Indian alcalde declared that his staff of authority was equal to that of the king's representative, after which the villagers shouted the same.[52] Villagers regarded themselves as "free" people, but the kind of liberty that seems to have animated the rebellions was confined to the small world of the local village. It did not readily translate into a notion of shared or equal rights with other villages that could serve as the basis for regional revolts.

Community rebellions in central Mexico, the Mixteca Alta, and the Valley of Oaxaca provide little evidence that accommodation was breaking down in the eighteenth century because of new peasant perspectives on legitimacy, elite intransigence, or a significant gain in power by the subordinate villages (all in spite of the major administrative reforms made by the Bourbons at the provincial level). Real or imagined abuse of power by district officials and loss of vitality of the ruling group seem to be the political developments most closely related to village uprisings.

The new economic demands and the cultural conditions we have identified as the two types of occasions of collective violence share a common element. Both were actions taken by the state—by local judges or priests acting either in compliance with colonial orders or on their own initiative. They are the external events that explain the timing, if not the underlying causes, of the rebellions. In Simmel's terms, the legitimacy of the priests or alcaldes mayores suffered a temporary collapse because of what the villagers perceived as an abuse of their power in making new demands on the community. In a few cases it is also possible to speak of the ruling group's loss of vitality as a factor in the descent into violence. Rivalries between the parish priest and the local Spanish judge damaged the unity of state control, confused the existing structure of accommodation, and raised village sensitivity to the abuse of state power. In five cases we find parish priests intervening directly to lead village rebellions against new laws on the administration of cofradía finances or against the arbitrary acts of the alcalde mayor or his lieutenant. The growing reliance of alcaldes mayores on lieutenants (appointed deputies who bear a resemblance to the corrupt political bosses of rural Mexico today) to oversee public affairs at the local level also weakened the lines of loyalty between peasant villages and royal officials in the late colonial period.

The vitality of the rural Church was also in decline. The parish priest's ability to guide his congregation was no longer as great as we might imagine from early Church history in Spanish America. Many dedicated parish priests still commanded the blind faith of their flocks in the last colonial decades, but even more of their brethren had lost the sense of utopian mission and personal sacrifice that had animated the "spiritual conquest" in the sixteenth century and had won the neophytes' loyalty. In spite of their numbers, eighteenth-century *curas* were usually more remote from their peasant parishioners, weakening the ties between religious authority and village life.

Some priests complained that a rural assignment was like living in exile from the civilized world they had known as students.[53] Many others became permanent residents of the parish seat, where most non-Indians resided, making only infrequent visits to remote villages to administer the sacraments. At an urgent summons to the deathbed of a peasant in a village several hours walk from his home church, one indifferent Oaxacan cura declined to go, sending a message that the dying man be given a sprinkling of holy water and a hot brick for his stomach.[54] Many quibbled with their parishioners over church finances, clerical fees, and the provision of food and lodging. All parish priests lost a measure of local prestige and wealth as a result of the Bourbon confiscation of *obras pías* and control of cofradía finances in the last decades of Spanish rule. Under these circumstances, it is not surprising that rural priests and peasant villages came into conflict, and that the moral authority of priests eroded—or that both developments could translate into collective violence.

The importance of actions by colonial authorities as occasions for local rebellions exposes the peasants' primary conscious motive for collective violence: the *defense* of relationships that were threatened. The structure of relationships showed geographic variation. Some regions—even in central Mexico—had not allowed a priest or alcalde mayor into their communities for years and paid the tribute tax grudgingly. Others paid existing tax assessments without complaint and served the priest and magistrate regularly. Defensive uprisings against state actions that were perceived as *new* encroachments were common to both kinds of villages, even though the degree of real deprivation caused by the demands of the colonial authorities was relative.

Rebellions often were set off by what appear to be minor changes, but to the rebels more than only a nominal tax increase or the arrest of a common criminal was at stake. Peasant villages were reacting to what they considered an immediate threat to their way of life. As one alcalde mayor put it, they feared "losing the peace and tranquillity in which they have lived," or being "deprived of [their] liberty," or "losing [their] lands and houses."[55] Peasants' beliefs about themselves and their communities also contributed to this climate of distrust and of resistance to change from outside. As the crowd behavior suggests, new colonial rules and restraints on customary behavior were commonly seen by villagers in revolt as threats to the ideal of the independent landholding community. Eighteenth-century peasant rebels who were later called to account and whose testimony was recorded in the formal records of investigation frequently proclaimed their "natural liberty" and inveighed against "the yoke of subjection."[56] Spanish witnesses spoke of the "false pride" of the villagers and their resistance to anything the Crown's local representatives attempted to

correct. Resistance to change in dealing with colonial officials represented an understandable distrust of powerful outsiders serving their
own interests and an affirmation of the community's solidarity and
belief in its separateness.

If we accept the inherent conflict between subordinate and dominant groups over the distribution of scarce resources and scarce power
as a necessary underlying cause of social violence but as insufficient
to explain the timing and location of rebellions in peasant Mexico, and
if we reject the attractive simplicity of a material deprivation–elite
intransigence model or a climate–agricultural crisis model, what seems
to explain our village uprisings? No theory emphasizing a single factor
appears to be satisfactory, but we have identified some common external conditions and internal perceptions that combine in the special
chemistry of collective violence in landholding villages of central
Mexico and Oaxaca. Latent peasant feelings of indignation toward and
betrayal by district officials may have been widespread in the late
colonial period, reflecting weakened ties to the ruling class at the local
level, especially the parish priest and the alcalde mayor or subdelegado. Paradoxically, stronger ties remained to the more remote colonial rulers in Mexico City and Madrid. The veritable flood of peasant
litigants and supplicants from central Mexico and Oaxaca who sought
justice from the Audiencia and the viceroy in the late years of Spanish
rule suggests an undiminished respect and need for the higher levels
of the imperial system.

CONCLUSION

One interpretation of social disorders in rural societies contends that
there is little or no potential for rebellion initiated by peasants. This
interpretation usually rests on a judgment that peasants lack the sense
of common purpose needed to create an organization to serve their
mutual interests against powerful outsiders. The only enduring local
organizations are those supported by external powers—such as the
Church and the state. Edward Banfield expressed this view of weak
peasant organization above the household level in his work on rural
life in southern Italy.[57] For Mexico, George Foster developed a similar
but more elaborate explanation of social relationships in Tzintzuntzan
(Michoacán). Foster's conception of "limited good," stressing the
weakness of positively held values and of unselfish cooperation, and
the prevalence of suspicion and envy in peasant communities, is an
important rebuttal to the once widely held view that villages were
idyllic communities founded on shared values and selfless cooperation.

Yet it, too, presents us with defenseless, atomized communities, leaving little potential for collective action.[58] Going a step further, the French anthropologist Henri Favre suggests that a subservient colonial mentality was imposed on Latin American peasants, which robbed them of self-esteem and led them to a pathological acceptance of their inferiority and of oppression and exploitation, which became their condition in life.[59] Burdened with this colonial mentality, Mexican peasants would have little potential for revolt except as a thrashing last-gasp reaction to anomie—the alienation and imminent destruction of their world by powerful outside forces. To say that peasants do not or cannot initiate revolts in their own behalf is not to say that they do not participate in insurrections. Many writers on insurrection note peasant participation but emphasize that insurrections are conceived and led by outsiders from towns and cities.[60] Another view in the same vein sees banditry, not rebellion, as the characteristic violent outlet for peasants in colonial Mexico.

A second interpretation finds an "almost innate" tradition of revolt in peasant areas. This interpretation, which challenges the idea of peasant incapacity for rebellion, has become more popular since the Chinese Revolution, in which Mao Tse-tung mobilized the countryside to capture conservative cities, thus apparently demonstrating that Chinese peasants had the potential of a spontaneous revolutionary whole.[61] Gerrit Huizer, in several books and articles, has been a leading spokesman for the view that Latin American peasants have a tradition of revolt that makes for revolutionary potential.[62]

These two interpretations of peasant potential for collective violence need not be taken as mutually exclusive. Barrington Moore, among others, demonstrates in his study of the rural origins of dictatorship and revolution in China, Japan, and India that some regional peasant societies *do* have traditions of revolt that eventually contribute to revolution, as in China.[63] Other peasant societies—his main example is India—provide few examples of collective violence in their modern history.

The considerable number of community uprisings in central Mexico and Oaxaca during the eighteenth century shows quite clearly that local villages were capable of popular spontaneous violence. As we have seen, this violence did not develop in a mindless way but had structure and coherence—even if the peasants did not fully control the situation. As a collective response to collective experience, it expressed community solidarity and hope. The spontaneous massing of armed villagers in the two regions bears witness to a long history of community violence and collective action in landholding villages under certain predictable conditions: specific changes in the economic demands of powerful outsiders and other direct encroachments on the community's rights. Defense of village integrity gave these uprisings the appearance of sacred struggles against violators of the community's visible and invisible boundaries. The community's perception of its independent rights was a relative matter, but it is noteworthy that nearly all of the 142 rebellions examined here took place in communities that possessed subsistence landholdings of their own and enjoyed a measure of separation and independence from the demands of colonial authorities through relative isolation, production of a significant surplus, or militant resistance.

The ability of our peasant communities to translate disaffection into political unrest rather than to retreat or fall into masochism is evidence of the strength of localized village identity. On the other hand, the rebels' goals were usually limited to correcting particular abuses; and the strength of *village* rather than regional resistance suggests very little identity of conditions and desires among villages that might bring them together in regional uprisings. Villagers in our two regions did not see themselves as a deprived class able to unite against a common oppressor. For most, the enemies were the neighboring villages as well as the abusive local magistrate or priest, not the higher authorities who were ultimately responsible for the burden of taxes and service. This local political unity and militant myopia made villagers good rebels but poor revolutionaries.[64] Individually, they defended their community borders with some success, but, in doing so, they failed to comprehend the larger forces that threatened their independence. They did not want to take power outside the local district, and, if they had, I suspect that they would not have known what to do with it. Without question villagers accepted the existence of neighboring haciendas and plantations; certain taxes and service; and the formalities of a higher system of justice in certain kinds of crimes and disputes; the legitimacy of colonial priests and magistrates until they personally betrayed village trust; and the sanctity of that most remote figure, the king of Spain, and his personal representative in Mexico, the viceroy.

In contrast to rural unrest in colonial Mexico, the Chinese revolution made in the countryside seems to be associated with a much less cohesive village structure, one in which village peasants rarely cooperated in common tasks and felt little solidarity with the village unit.[65] Peasant insurrections, including the Chinese example, are always fragile and seem to depend on outside leaders to transform them into national revolutions; but the Chinese peasants seem to have been better able to seize power because their weak village ties allowed the political movement to reach peasant families directly.

In late colonial Mexico little village unrest was transformed into war on the rich or on the colonial system. A few of the longer-lived village rebellions came close to spilling over into class wars with shouts of "Death to the Spaniards" and "Death to the gente de razón." Some priests and colonial representatives died in the bloody outbursts, but the exalted threats to annihilate outsiders were never accomplished. There *were* regional uprisings in Chiapas (1712), Yucatán (1761), and the Petén (1775), which became limited race and anticolonial wars. For our regions, only the Tulancingo (Hidalgo) regional revolt of some 2,000 peasants in 1769 might qualify as an uprising against the colonial system.

Our examination of peasant uprisings ends rather abruptly with the beginning of Mexico's wars of independence in 1810. Are changing conditions after independence reflected in new patterns of rural collective violence? To answer this question, we need to know much more than we now do about the last 150 years of Mexico's rural history. The secondary works on socioeconomic conditions and rural violence in nineteenth-century Mexico do, however, provide us with enough material to hazard a few guesses about changing conditions and responses that highlight our evidence on the eighteenth century. The post-independence period brought massive impersonal changes to peasant life, comparable in scale to the sixteenth-century political revolution, epidemics, resettlement programs, religious conversion, and labor and tax systems that resulted from Spanish colonization. These new challenges were in part conscious programs of the state and federal governments; in part, they were the product of Mexico's expanding population and growing role in the world economy as a neocolonial exporter of primary products.

The Indian peasant's legal status in independent Mexico was altered to make him a citizen equal before the law to other Mexicans. Paternalistic colonial laws for the protection of Indian communities were abolished. Non-Indians were no longer forbidden to reside in Indian communities, special Indian courts such as the Juzgado de Indios were disbanded, and the special protection of community property afforded by the colonial judicial system and the Indians' right to legal counsel fell into disuse. We know that these colonial laws were often honored in the breach and that the institutions created to protect Indians as wards of the Crown had serious shortcomings, but the colonial state did assume moral and legal responsibility for the survival of Christian tax-paying rural communities.

The weight of moral and legal authority in the colonial period did not sanction the dismemberment of rural communities and the seizure of their lands. This moral commitment was cold comfort to communities that lost their lands and their means of subsistence, but the survival of peasant villages was placed in greater jeopardy when the state became a moral enemy.

Equality of individual Mexicans before the law in independent Mexico would lead to careful scrutiny of the Church and other groups that had had special rights and held corporate property under colonial law. As early as 1833 the State of Mexico, a new political jurisdiction that included most of our central Mexico region, enacted a law against communal property that opened the way to alienation of village lands.[66] The process of dismemberment began in the late 1820's and reached its peak during the reform period, 1854–1876, when the Liberals attempted to integrate Indians into national society by dissolving their communal life. The national laws of the reform period against corporate property were not uniformly enforced, but illegal seizures as well as sale of village lands became more common. Village lands that were set aside for the support of the Church or that were rented out were especially vulnerable to sale by the state. Finally, during the Porfirian dictatorship of the late nineteenth century, land survey laws allowed the alienation of more lands for which the peasant occupants could not produce formal titles. This final assault on village integrity affected our regions much less than it did the northern states of Sonora and San Luis Potosí and the semitropical areas of Veracruz and Yucatán.

At the same time that state and federal governments were expropriating corporate property, other pressures were being exerted on village lands: an expanding rural population throughout central and southern Mexico, and the growth of commercial farming in such lucrative export crops as sugar cane, henequen, and coffee. Commercial farming of sugar cane expanded dramatically in Yucatán and Morelos in the nineteenth century, henequen plantations opened in Yucatán, coffee fincas developed in Veracruz, and ranching expanded in the Bajío. These expanding enterprises competed for the peasants' means of livelihood—their farm land, water sources, common pasture lands, wood lands, salt deposits, and equally important, their labor. Whole zones of rural communities that had previously enjoyed a measure of local control and placed a high value on village independence were threatened with displacement and the total subservience of unorganized landless wage laborers. The assault on peasant lands was one of a variety of incursions against rural villages that intensified in the nineteenth century: peasant labor was the object of an expanding system of debt peonage and captive labor on the plantations; and the value placed on modernization by Mexico's ruling Liberals and positivists led to a view of peasant villages as hard lumps of backwardness that had to be separated from their traditional ways if they were to become Mexican.

Central Mexico and Oaxaca were less affected by the changes in land tenure than many other regions because neither had great potential for producing the new export crops, and capital investment in the countryside of both regions was relatively weak. The central valleys of Oaxaca continued in the old pattern of strong landholding villages. Valley peasants were increasingly integrated into the regional economy and the urban marketplace of Oaxaca city, but largely on a voluntary, part-time basis. Other parts of Oaxaca were experiencing competition among peasants, politicians, and entrepreneurs for salt, farm land, grazing land, and the labor needed for weaving cotton textiles, but these new conditions did not resemble the engulfing commercial economies of Yucatán, Morelos, and Chiapas.

In the central Mexico region, pressure on village lands in the nineteenth century usually reinforced the colonial land and labor system rather than transforming land tenure and land use by new kinds of commercial agriculture. Demand for central Mexico's lumber increased in the late nineteenth century (especially for construction materials in the mines and railroad ties) and some commercial crops, such as zacatón (a native plant whose root is processed for broomstraw and brushes), blossomed; but the expansion of private lands happened more gradually, was mainly fostered by the Liberal politics of free enterprise, and pitted villages against their old foes, the pulque, ranching, and grain-producing haciendas that had their beginnings in the colonial period.* An estimated 40 per cent of the central Mexico villages retained their lands throughout the nineteenth century.[67] Other politically unsettling circumstances of the nineteenth century were the weakness of the national government and the periodic foreign invasions that threw local politics into turmoil and destroyed the legitimacy

---

*In the eighteenth century some haciendas in the future State of Mexico had added textile workshops to process estate wool. If these weaving activities had been expanded in the nineteenth century, the expansion would have increased competition for local labor and perhaps fueled more land pressure.

of central authority enjoyed during the colonial period by the Spanish monarchy.

Accompanying these economic and political changes, which threatened the semi-independent position of rural villages, were more regional revolts and leagues of peasant communities, or community factionalism and resort to political homicide, which were barely evident in the eighteenth century. Nineteenth-century regional peasant movements were especially impressive in places that had waged earlier major insurrections, such as Chiapas (1712 and 1869), Yucatán (1761 and 1847–1855), and Papantla (1743, 1767, 1847–1848, and 1891). In each case, however, the level of resistance was greater and the reasons for armed resistance more radical. The Caste War of Yucatán in the late 1840's was, for a time, a war to the death between Indians and whites; the Papantla rebels in 1848 spoke of the traditional grievances of heavy taxes, forced labor, and abuse of community freedoms, but they also called for the abolition of debt peonage and the destruction of haciendas and distribution of their lands to the villages.[68] Regional uprisings over land control were also occurring sporadically in central Mexico and the mountains of Oaxaca. The concentration of these insurrections in the late 1840's, 1860's, and early 1870's is illuminated by the weakness of elites, which was noted by Simmel as one of several changes in elite behavior that can bring on political violence. The Mexican-American War of 1846–1848 not only took the federal government's attention away from internal affairs, but also exposed the weakness of the government in defending Mexican territory. During this period, rural insurrections were mounted in Yucatán, the Isthmus of Tehuantepec, the Huaxteca region of Papantla, Veracruz, and the Sierra Gorda region of San Luis Potosí.[69] Also, attacks by leagues of rural villagers were made on neighboring haciendas in central Mexico at this time, which the Mexican historian Jan Bazant identifies as an important break with the past.* Crises in the national government in the late 1860's and early 1870's were also accompanied by insurrections over land and community rights in Jalisco, Nayarit, Zacatecas, Michoacán, and Chiapas. The legitimacy of the national government was endangered in the 1850's and 1860's, not only by its weakness in the

---

* Bazant, p. 59. Political homicide and factionalism in communities seem to replace insurrection as a response to these political and economic changes in some areas. Hidalgo's high homicide rate in the nineteenth century may well reflect increased political homicide. A similar change from insurrection to political homicide is recorded by Friedrich for a community in Michoacán, "Political Homicide," pp. 269–82.

face of civil war and French occupation, but also by its attack on the Church, which had been the state's traditional ally. A number of the rural uprisings after 1855 were led by disaffected parish priests who made common cause with villagers against the "sacrilegious" reform laws.

The catalyst in transforming local disaffection and loss of faith in national rulers into regional political movements was often an ambitious provincial chieftain who articulated the common fears and grievances of uprooted villagers and incorporated them into a wider political insurrection against the national government. Whether or not they had the gift of charisma, such leaders emerged from the shadows of earlier leaderless movements as instruments, rather than guiding forces, of the growing conflicts that accompanied the pervasive changes in the Mexican countryside during the nineteenth century. Some regional leaders, such as Manuel Lozada, maintained an impressive hold over their bands of country people clamoring for land and village autonomy. Most would-be leaders, like Miguel Hidalgo in the independence movement in the Bajío in 1810 and Colonel José Cetina in Yucatán in the 1840's, unleashed forces of hatred and despair they could not control. Among leaders of rural insurrections, Emiliano Zapata stands out as uniquely successful—a leader who gained the fellowship of campesinos in Morelos, not because of charisma or personal ambition, but because he understood their cause and was true to it.

The challenge to village boundaries and to the psychic territory of daily and seasonal routine that derived from government support of private estates and new opportunities for commercial agriculture grew in intensity in the last decades of the nineteenth century. But under a strong personalist national government there were few serious insurrections. Rural unrest became a regional and national force once again in 1910, when the legitimacy of the aged Díaz government was challenged by urban and provincial people outside of the government who sought the aid of rural groups that shared their perception of worsening conditions. Madero found potential allies in the rural communities of Morelos that were rapidly losing their lands and their very existence under the Porfirian political system and the expansion of the sugar plantations. But even in Morelos in 1910–1911, the village leaders were demanding little more than the right to exist alongside the big estates and the return of the lands that had been taken from them. The rural movement in Morelos spread and became truly revolutionary in goals and methods under the leadership of Emiliano Zapata and less powerful but still independent chieftains; but as Octavio Paz says, "Zapata would have been an obscure figure lost in the solitudes of the south if his insurgency had not coincided with the nation's general insurrection and the fall of the Díaz regime in the capital." [70]

By comparing them with the eighteenth-century peasant rebellions, the nineteenth-century regional insurrections shed some additional light on the earlier uprisings. Regional movements after independence were more frequent and less scattered than the colonial insurrections. Since peasant subordination and perceived abuses of power by district authorities were sources of local conflict and violence in both periods, we should look to changing conditions in the nineteenth century for explanation. The nineteenth-century revolts seem to have occurred in areas of major new economic incursions during periods of ineffectual national and state government. The national crisis was crucial to rural insurrection in 1910, just as it had been in 1810 and 1846. Such crises at the top were lacking in the eighteenth century. A coincidence of regional peasant movements and national political crises suggests a rupture of trust between villages and the remote high authorities, which began with the overthrow of the Spanish monarchy by Napoleon in 1808. Furthermore, the eighteenth-century villages of central Mexico and Oaxaca were more secure, integrated units in comparison to their late nineteenth-century counterparts, which apparently were experiencing more factionalism, outmigration, and loss of lands. New taxes on land, the laws against communal property, the pressure of expanding cash crop enterprises, and the spread of debt peonage threatened the very existence of some nineteenth-century villages and were perceived as terminal threats by others, raising the latent potential for revolt. Late colonial villages suffered material distress, but it was not the kind of pervasive, dislocating threat to their existence that might have promoted a concept of struggle between classes or orders and united villages in regional insurrections.

Conclusion

Drinking, homicide, and rebellion are set out separately and on their own terms in the preceding chapters, with only passing comparisons among them. In each case, however, the same basic questions underlie the presentation: How did peasants actually behave in situations that can be specified? What do their patterns of behavior reveal about peasant values and the place of the village in colonial society? My answers in general stress the village as a fundamental unit of peasant society in central and southern Mexico. In this final chapter, the separate patterns of drinking, homicide, and rebellion are brought to bear on the subject of peasant village life in the eighteenth century and its place in the colonial system during the last years of Spanish rule.

PEASANT VILLAGES

Peasant villages in central Mexico and Oaxaca emerge from this study as more than mere categories imposed by colonial rulers on degraded rural descendants of Indian societies. In the peasants' intimations of beliefs and values and in the patterns of social comportment derived from hundreds of individual cases of homicide, drinking, and collective violence, peasant villages appear as concrete, relatively enduring groups whose boundaries were defined by the villagers' shared views of the colonial world and by the administrative convenience of the Spanish rulers, as well as by the visible landmarks of buildings, pastures, and cultivated fields. Ideally, villagers believed they should live together in peace. As Eric Wolf says, "The peasant Utopia is the free village, untrammelled by tax collectors, labour recruiters, large landowners, officials."[1] The political solidarity of villages is not to be mistaken for independence or the absence of conflict; it is rather their ability either to survive conflict or to transcend it.[2] As James C. Scott observed:

It is all too easy, and a serious mistake, to romanticize these social arrangements that distinguish much of peasant society. They are not radically egalitarian. Rather, they imply only that all are entitled to a *living* out of the resources within the village, and that living is attained often at the cost of a loss of status and autonomy. They work, moreover, in large measure through the abrasive force of gossip and envy and the knowledge that the abandoned poor are likely to be a real and present danger to better-off villagers.[3]

The rebellions provide the most obvious evidence of village consciousness and feelings of social distance from the world beyond. Villages furnished the social basis for rebel organization, and nearly all of these collective outbursts were confined to single villages. Village uprisings expressed a defiant isolationism in reaction to change imposed from outside. Crowd behavior in them acted out strong peasant resentment of new colonial rules and restraints on customary behavior as threats to the ideal of the ancient and independent landholding community. Autonomy was an important social ideal; eighteenth-century peasant rebels frequently proclaimed their "natural liberty" and inveighed against "the yoke of subjection." Village independence was usually more fantasy than reality, but as Norman Cohn suggests, such fantasies can work as dynamic social myths, promoting collective action and giving unity, energy, and direction to a community.[4] External threats to the way of life of landholding villages in both central Mexico and Oaxaca in the eighteenth century seem to have encouraged village solidarity by channeling some of the potential aggression within the community outward, against those powers that made demands on it.[5]

The forms and settings of homicides committed by villagers, especially in the Mixteca Alta, repeat the overt expressions of village solidarity made in the peasant rebellions. Lethal violence by peasants in the Mixteca Alta was concentrated within the nuclear family and in relations with outsiders. There were surprisingly few intracommunity homicides that might have threatened the political peace of the village. Mixteca Alta villagers killed in restricted and fairly predictable situations, particularly in cases of adultery or insolence by married women, abuse of power by village officials, and violation of village territory by outsiders. Homicides committed by central Mexico peasants follow more random patterns of social relationships with a more even distribution across family, intracommunity, and intercommunity relationships. The more ambiguous and unpredictable circumstances surrounding homicide in central Mexico also appear in the offenders' declarations, which so often attributed the lethal attacks to alcohol or to uncontrollable animal passions. Such attributions are rare in the Mixteca Alta.

The Mixteca Alta pattern—violent households and relatively peaceful (although not conflict-free) communities—is not a peasant universal. It contrasts sharply with the distribution of interpersonal hostility in well-documented rural societies of late medieval England and colonial New England. John Demos, who has examined criminal court records for a number of small New England towns in the seventeenth century, suggests "an extraordinary degree of contentiousness among neighbors" but an apparent absence of intrafamily conflict.[6] Demos's work offers a tantalizing but imprecise contrast to our investigation of Mexico communities because he treats conflict in general, without special reference to violence, and does not deal specifically with homicide. James Given's detailed work on homicides in thirteenth-century England provides a more promising comparison, since he deals directly with homicide and rural groups. His study of eyreroll homicide records shows that many rural killings were committed by groups of people—either members of the same family or villagers in company with outsiders—rather than by individuals acting alone (the usual case in colonial Mexico). Given traces this configuration to relatively weak community bonds.[7]

These contrasting patterns of violence underscore the fundamental importance of the villages in Mexican peasant life. For their Anglo-American societies, Given and Demos posit the family as the primary unit in virtually all phases of life. Given further stresses the extraordinary horizontal mobility of the rural population; families might live in several villages and towns in a lifetime. Family solidarity in these societies was to be maintained even at the expense of the community. In much of Indian-peasant Mexico at the end of the colonial period, the family still seems to have been mainly a conjugal arrangement— a productive and reproductive unit—rather than the primary locus of social allegiance. This harks back to the Indian concept of the individual, which, in contrast to Hispanic concepts, stressed responsibility to the community over self-realization. The landholding village remained the crucial level of social identity for its members, and fighting with one's neighbors was a serious breach of community rules.[8] Village continuity and the maintenance of peaceful intravillage relationships against a hostile countryside were placed above household harmony, individual rights, and the loyalties of extended families.

Two paradoxes, however, are discernible in our Mexican cases. One is that the difference we have noted in the nature of homicides in the Mixteca Alta and central Mexico is not repeated in the character of rebellions in the two regions (which are largely similar). The second is that women assumed an active role in rebellions generally, whereas in homicides their role was nearly always that of the passive victim.

The fact that the level of intracommunity homicide was greater in central Mexico than in the Mixteca Alta, although the character of village rebellions remained about the same, suggests to me that personal violence in the community did not generate much factional strife to weaken community bonds. Although schisms are documented in eighteenth-century central Mexico as well as in the Mixteca Alta, relatively few of the killings clearly indicate a genesis in political rivalries or revenge. More of the intracommunity homicides in central Mexico were related to economic disputes (over debts, land, destruction of property, and the value of moveable goods) than in the Mixteca Alta, but in both regions these crimes were largely unrelated to partisan conflict and clan rivalries. This may suggest the decline of *calpulli*-type multifamily groups in colonial villages. In spite of changing patterns of homicide and sharper violent clashes within central Mexico communities, village solidarity appears often to have been strong enough to contain factions.

In formal respects, women were systematically subordinated to men. Men held the public offices, were patriarchs in the home, and assumed the responsibility for farming, the usual basis of village subsistence. The continuity of the village was traced through men by means of a preference for patrilocal residence and the formation of extended families and neighborhoods around male relatives. Wives in these circumstances were outsiders—reared either in other villages or in different barrios of the same community. They could be victimized with less danger to the political peace of the community than would be produced by open attacks on local men.

The formal status of peasant women, however, is insufficient to explain their active participation in drinking celebrations and village rebellions. Although women played a less active role than men in public affairs, in these collective acts they clearly participated as members of the community. Women were expected to drink less on ceremonial occasions than men in order to protect and care for their inebriated husbands or fathers or brothers, but they did take part. In those more spontaneous collective acts, village rebellions, women were often in the vanguard and were consistently mentioned as active participants. Women may have spent much of their time at home as the bearers and guardians of children, but they were probably engaged in more social contact than is generally recognized. There was apparently no ideal—much less any real possibility—of privacy at home that could shut out the community. The ubiquitous "pulquerías"—virtually every home in central Mexico villages had a jar of pulque for domestic use, sale, and hospitality—kept wives in public contact with other members of the community. Informally, then, women were recognized by the men as members (albeit junior members) of the village. If we extend Charles Tilly's argument that "the forms of violent action any particular group carried on bear strong marks of that group's day-to-day organization,"[9] women's participation in the collective violence of the village may more truly reflect their real place in the community than the formal political documentation in which they rarely appear.

In its relationships to village life, drinking is the most ambiguous of our three examples of peasant behavior. Especially in central Mexico, drinking in formal taverns was common, drinking and fatal violence often went together, and production of alcohol was becoming a commercialized, impersonal activity in the late colonial period. But Indian drinking could also express the underlying ethos of village solidarity. Much heavy drinking in late colonial villages was associated with recurring community celebrations of seasons and patron saints, in feasts, ceremonies, enactments of myth and history, and public manifestations of all kinds, which broke the monotonous rhythm of repetitious work and the flat sequence of days and months. The periodic drinking occasions, like the rebellions, brought the villagers together in a collective act that reaffirmed community membership. This convivial meaning of collective drinking can be traced also in the patterns of violence associated with drinking bouts. Few homicides or dangerous assaults by one villager upon another took place during these drunken celebrations, whereas attacks against outsiders on these occasions are more common than those against fellow townsmen.

That social breakdown was not an inevitable partner of drinking in peasant villages may surprise some colonial historians. The historical record for colonial societies and preindustrial Europe has generally been read by such superb historians as Fernand Braudel, Charles Gibson, Mario Góngora, and John Phelan to indicate that heavy drinking has been a natural partner of famine, disease, escape, personal violence, and moral degradation.[10] To be sure, alcohol in the Mixteca Alta and central Mexico was not an unequivocal boon to the peasant population. Examples of alcoholism and antisocial drunken behavior emerge from all places and periods. On the other hand, little solid evidence supports the view of peasants succumbing to a "plague of mass alcoholism," a view that pervades the literature on colonial America. Drinking problems were on the rise in the eighteenth and nineteenth centuries and seem to have increased dramatically in the decades preceding the Revolution of 1910, but the epidemic metaphor fails to do justice to the social history of drinking after the conquest. The type of liquor consumed and the location of its production were important influences on the social meaning of alcohol. Where distilled beverages were purchased, as they were in many parts of rural Mexico, more solitary drinking and more disruption and violence were associated with the drunken state. Controlled social uses of alcohol evident in central and southern Mexico in the late colonial period will seem less peculiar to anthropologists, whose literature provides many examples of peasant communities ascribing fraternal, peaceable significance to alcohol and behaving under the influence of alcohol in ways that approximate these views.[11]

Beyond signifying village continuity, the patterns of drinking, homicide, and rebellion do not seem to be closely related to one another at many points. Seasonal variations of drinking and homicide roughly coincide in two crests, preceding and following the rainy season overlapping the Easter and Christmas holidays, but it appears from the homicide and rebellion trials that alcohol was not a crucial ingredient in many of the cases of violence. Drinking certainly enters the legal literature and statements of colonial officials as a cause of unruly behavior, including rebellion and homicide, but these judgments proceed rather from a Spanish folk conception of violence than from an unprejudiced consideration of case evidence. Uprisings, which seemed to be disinhibition *par excellence*, sometimes were attributed to alcohol by colonial authorities; again, however, the case evidence indicates that drinking rarely was definitely associated with such violent outbursts. Although "alegría"—a festive mood—was shared by many of the participants in drinking celebrations and community uprisings, alcohol cannot be said to have caused the mood. In fact, the opposite seems closer to the mark. In some of the better documented communal drinking celebrations towns closed themselves off from outsiders, and the infrequent violence that erupted on these occasions was provoked by intruders.

In emphasizing the strength of community ties reflected in peasant social behavior, I am not endorsing an exclusive concentration on the integrative functions of social conflict. Conflict can be integrative, especially in periods of little fundamental social change such as the eighteenth century in New Spain, but it can also reflect disintegration and even dissolution (or it might have little or nothing to do with integration or destruction of the community over the long pull). Village conflict was often contained within bounds that minimized violence because of the community's need to maintain a solid front against concrete outside threats.[12] Our "reactive" rebellions were temporary holding operations against such threats in conditions where peaceful means of conflict resolution did not work. It is possible, too, that the growing number of festive drinking occasions in peasant communities reflects—as Mona Ozouf suggests for the festivals of revolutionary France—"a collective climate of curious and searching uneasiness."[13] On the other hand, there is little evidence that the state in eighteenth-century Mexico successfully controlled these celebrations, transforming them into occasions for affirming loyalty to the king, and draining them of meaning as acts of communal repetition and renewal.[14] In the absence of convincing data on the incidence of homicide, we cannot determine the relationship between homicide rates and community survival.

This ideology of the village as an autonomous, self-perpetuating society seems to have accompanied reduced regional and ethnic ties among peasants in the colonial period. Strong community bonds helped individual villages to protect themselves against the disruptive effects of epidemics, forced labor, and pressure on the land, but they also contributed to increased tensions with neighboring villages and a breakdown of regional identities. In a word, villages seem to have drawn in upon themselves to survive in the colonial period.

Emphasis on strong elements of community solidarity must be tempered by our evidence of regional variation. The variation is a matter of degree, but it is clear that central Mexico and the Mixteca Alta traced somewhat different patterns, especially in the use of alcohol and in homicide situations. Regional differences are especially important to note because many studies of "Indian" life in Mexico and theoreticians of peasant societies who use Mexican examples have generalized about both Indian-mestizo relations and peasant society on the basis of community studies in Oaxaca, Chiapas, and Yucatán—all in southern Mexico. The comparison with central Mexico provides an important check on this tendency to generalize from areas remote from Mexico's greatest colonial and modern urban center, Mexico City.

The drinking pattern of community rituals and the local production of pulque for local consumption were both stronger in the Mixteca Alta than in central Mexico. In eighteenth-century central Mexico, peaceful communal drinking occasions and villages producing pulque for themselves existed side by side with commercialization of pulque and the wider use of distilled beverages. True taverns in the countryside, "lost weekends" in Mexico City, individual cases of alcoholism, and sensitivity to the shamefulness and personal vulnerability of being drunk in public are all more characteristic of central Mexico than they are of the Mixteca Alta.

Regional differences are also evident in the homicide trials. In almost every aspect of offender-victim relations and crime settings documented in homicide trials, the central Mexico cases reveal a richer variety of patterns. This is especially true of the levels of social relationships (crossing family-intracommunity-intercommunity levels almost evenly in central Mexico); of the types of social relationships in homicides involving members of the same community (familial, political, and significant economic conflicts taking this lethal form in central Mexico); and of the motives ascribed in the offenders' confessions (often vague statements about passions and uncontrollable forces without clear reference to norms of social relationships among members of the community).

Two characteristics of central Mexico killings are particularly distinctive: the "fighting words"—a common trait within the considerable variety of central Mexico insults being a macho tone, pungent with the intent to defame and humble through verbal combat; and the weapons used—in central Mexico more often deadly by design (firearms and knives), whereas Mixteca Alta villagers tended to use whatever was at hand at the time of attack. Although the figures that might offer some insight into the incidence of homicide are sketchy and inconclusive, I have the impression that availability of deadly weapons in central Mexico made for a somewhat higher incidence of homicide there than in the Mixteca Alta. The habit of carrying knives, mentioned so often in the central Mexico trials, rendered fatal many quarrels that would otherwise have resulted only in bruises or superficial wounds—especially in a time and place of poor medical care; homicide victims in eighteenth-century Mexico frequently died from infection and other complications several days or weeks after deep stab wounds had been inflicted.

These regional variations suggest some subtle differences in the social characteristics of villages and in the effects of subordination within the colonial system. Patriarchy and male dominance were, at least in the formal sense, common to both regions, but the homicide evidence suggests that self-assertive and less sociable forms of manliness so characteristic of lower-class life in modern societies were diluting community-oriented values in central Mexico in the late eighteenth century. Accompanying this complication of social values in central Mexico—a mixture of an older emphasis on individual responsibility to the community with self-expression and self-interest—were a modern form of *caciquismo*, in which small groups of local strongmen, sometimes serving as *tenientes* for the district alcalde mayor, exercised grossly abusive and arbitrary power over the labor and lives of peasants,[15] and the magnetic attraction of Mexico City as a "New Jerusalem" (religious center and chief pilgrimage site) and a "New Rome" (locus of extravagance and moral decay) for rural Mexicans.[16] The political tensions evident in the homicide records of both regions appear to spring from rather different sources: in the Mixteca Alta, macehuales seem to have been fairly sensitive to the legitimacy and responsibilities of village officials; in central Mexico, coercion seems closer to the roots of political authority. Actually, these are not mutually exclusive tendencies in the exercise of political authority, for even in cases of blatant caciquismo in central Mexico, a kind of paternalistic relationship between the political chief and local people existed, a feeling that he protected them against abuse by other exploiters, such as alcaldes mayores, creditors, and priests.

THE COLONIAL ORDER

How did the social identity and durability of peasant villages in central and southern Mexico function in the larger colonial system? This is a natural question to ask in any study of peasant societies because of the peasants' subordinate relation to powerful outsiders. The durability of peasant villages in parts of colonial Mexico is a product, not simply of peasant will or Spanish consent, but of the interplay of viceregal and local conditions, the balance between village interests and the political and economic pressures of a particular type of colonial system.

The economic basis of colonial rule in our two regions in the eighteenth century was certainly exploitation—the appropriation by nonproducers of a portion of the total product of direct producers[17]—but it did not generally work to destroy the village or its subsistence base in landholding. On the contrary, the Spanish colonial system was less interested in usurping the ancestral lands of Indian peasants and, as a by-product, absorbing the captive labor force onto colonial estates than it was in exploiting the productive capacity of existing villages through taxation and coerced labor. From the beginning of the colonial period, control of labor was always more important to Spaniards as a means of exploitation than ownership of land.

This is a crucial point, for the Spanish colonial system is often interpreted in the light of European feudalism, in which landownership was the means of rural exploitation and landless or land-starved villagers were the classic peasants. The European evidence led political and social thinkers such as Antonio Gramsci to dichotomize urban and rural conflict: the country struggles over control of land, the city over control of labor.[18] This tendency to perceive rural exploitation in terms of landownership and manipulation of the labor of landless farmers has inclined students of colonial Spanish America to identify the hacienda as the "classic" land system and debt peonage as "the classic Spanish American labor device." In this view, the colonial hacienda monopolized good lands and thrust landless peasants under the wing of the paternalistic master.[19]

Growth of large estates and competition for land in central Mexico and Oaxaca certainly took place in the late colonial period; and they were exacerbated by population increase and the new economic opportunities in the regional, viceregal, and world markets. But we can hardly speak of Spanish monopolies of land and generalized peonization of village peasants. They did not develop largely as the result of two conditions: conflict and rural exploitation had at stake the control of labor and taxes as well as land; and landlessness was not a necessary precondition for the exploitation of rural labor. Colonial officials and regional hacendados found a number of ways to appropriate actual or potential peasant surpluses: royal tax payments and other cash contributions, forced sales of food at artificially low cost to urban centers, the reparto de efectos, which enriched alcaldes mayores, contracted production of textiles and raw materials at low cost, coerced labor, and encouragement of peasant purchases of high-priced goods, such as imported wines and textiles.

That peasant villages retained land is not surprising when the nature of this colonial exploitation is considered. The form of peasant villages in our regions in the seventeenth and eighteenth centuries was closely related to the role they were assigned in the colonial state's economy —its accumulation of revenue and encouragement of commercial capitalism through labor demands, direct taxes, and market opportunities. The kinds of behavior discussed in this book derive as much from adjustments to new conditions—the adaptation of one culture to the coercive demands of another—as they do from attempts to preserve communal pre-Hispanic forms of property and production—or more. The emphasis on the village and the elimination of the politically and socially stratified pre-Hispanic superstructure were encouraged by a colonial system that benefited politically and economically from this kind of adjustment.

Obviously, there were bound to be regional differences in the penetration of the colonial economy into local affairs. Pierre Chaunu's quadripartite model of economic communication for rural villages can clarify some of the economic differences between our regions.[20] Chaunu's first circle of production and consumption is formed by the rural collectivities themselves, with a radius of about five kilometers; the second circle, with a radius of about fifty kilometers, is composed of local markets, which are largely price-based if the third circle is present; the third circle is a regional price-based economy; and the fourth circle is a world market economy. In both of our regions, circles one and two account for much of the distribution of market wealth. Circle three is stronger in central Mexico with the influence of Mexico City; and circle four is present in both areas, though again stronger in central Mexico, with the exception of the cochineal and cotton textile districts of the Mixteca Alta. This model of market communications is, of course, complicated by the direct intervention of the state in the redistribution of peasant surplus through taxes and labor exactions. The chief difference between central Mexico and Oaxaca suggested by the Chaunu model—the relative weakness of outside influence in the Mixteca Alta—is, however, repeated in the social behavior I have discussed, especially in the greater number of factional disputes and of homicides related to economic disputes and machismo in central Mexico.

In neither region did the villages' independent spirit and ideal of separatism reflect economic reality. This disjunction suggests an important distinction in colonial life between village *culture* and colonial *society*. In making this distinction, I am thinking of culture as the distinctive manner of life of a group of people based on a shared way of living and looking at the world, a world view based on group-learned definitions and interpretations of behavior. Society, a looser and more inclusive concept, signifies people who interact and therefore live in some degree of interdependence. Society cannot be neatly divided into separate component cultures since groups that interact are likely to acquire at least some similar interpretations of behavior, as we saw with masculinity and drinking patterns in central Mexico. On the other hand, society and culture rarely encompass exactly the same groups of people. Indian peasants' patterns of drinking and homicide, as well as their corporate behavior in rebellions, reflect their culture's emphasis on internal village harmony that parallels the social values of "humility," "trust," and "respect" described by many ethnographers for modern villages of central and southern Mexico. This emphasis, perhaps based on the economic necessity for some cooperation in a subsistence economy, encourages a preference for self-control over self-expression and in general the assimilation of the individual into the life of the community.

At the same time, the villages formed part of an interdependent colonial society and, to a lesser extent, part of a world economic system. This interdependence and contact among groups did not necessarily contribute to understanding or affection. Villages were linked to the larger society in a hundred ways—through taxes, labor systems, the court system, commerce, cash economy, travel, disease, private property, material culture, vagrants, among others—which tended to place villagers in a subordinate, classlike position even though there was little class-consciousness among colonial peasants.[21]

Corporate values were not everywhere consistent with peasant behavior, as witnessed by the corrupting effects on community life of factionalism, conflict between nobles and macehuales, caciquismo, conflict over property, social mobility of individuals, growing class distinctions in the late colonial period, and a lack of cooperation in many aspects of daily life. Where values and behavior coincided in village life, as they did to a greater extent in the Mixteca Alta, their correspondence was supported by the emigration of marginal and dissident individuals and some personal violence (especially within the family), as well as by the operation of norms promoting peace within the village.

In short, the villages in this study were generally poor and subordinate in varying degrees to the colonial system, but still viable peasant communities. It goes too far to say that Spanish colonization brought virtually total control and transformation of villages by omnipotent Spaniards. Conflict, whether over abusive officials or factional interests, was common in late colonial villages, but to recognize conflicts of interests within communities is not to say that the life of the colonial village was a constant open battle. Forms changed, but the social obligations of the individual defined at the village and perhaps at the altepetl levels continued. Adjustments were made at the village level that, while not pre-Hispanic in form, in conception spun out the thread of village integrity and local values and were well woven into community life.[22]

Before we can really begin to explain the endurance of village culture, we need to know a great deal more about political and social relationships within villages, the role of parish priests, the effects of taxation, and a hundred other topics. Even with reasonably full descriptions of village life and the relations of villages to their natural settings and to powerful outsiders, patterned tendencies are as close as we shall come to causes in the social history of rural Mexico. At this stage of our knowledge, the "refuge region" hypothesis, which posits maintenance of "traditional" village life only in isolated or economically marginal zones to which communities retreated under the pressure of expanding Spanish colonization, does not seem particularly promising as an explanation of the perpetuation of village culture in central Mexico and Oaxaca during the late colonial period.[23] In both regions most colonial villages were heirs of pre-Hispanic settlements modified by congregación and depopulation rather than new communities of peasants in retreat. In both areas at the time of the conquest dense native settlements were producing an agricultural surplus on marginal to excellent farm lands. Distant from the main Spanish cities and colonial markets, the Mixteca Alta is more "marginal" than the central Mexico region; but the marginality is relative, for the Mixteca Alta and the central valleys of Oaxaca supported large agricultural populations, attracted a considerable non-Indian population in the eighteenth century, and bordered on a major trade route supporting non-Indian merchants, craftsmen, and state officials. Both were "marginal," however, to the world economic system—a very important point. Neither region produced cash crops for export, a situation that protected them from the pressures on rural society that the sugar-producing state of Morelos would feel in the nineteenth century;* nor were these regions integrated into a mining economy that placed heavy year-round demands on the local labor force.

Village culture in central Mexico and Oaxaca endured for a variety of reasons, not the least of which was the nature of the colonial system and the integration of villages into it. Benign paternalism by the Crown toward law-abiding Indians was less important than the fact that the traditional economy of these villages, modified to extract more labor for the service of the state or the export sector, was indispensable to the functioning of the entire colonial society. As Stanley Diamond has noted for local peasant groups in general, "So long as the central power depended upon them for support, in the absence of any alternative mode or source of production, their integrity could be substantially preserved."[24] The surplus produced by peasant villagers in central Mexico and Oaxaca in the form of taxes and services was a major contribution to the state's colonial economy and to the support of the parish priesthood, the private means of alcaldes mayores, and the maintenance of a private sector of estate-owners and merchants trading in textiles, dyestuffs, and everyday utensils. In view of the self-

---

*Cochineal and cotton textiles, which were produced by peasant villages in cottage-industry fashion, represent a different technology that did not demand the adjustments made in the sugar-cane industry.

interest of the state and the commercial elite, it is not so surprising that communities and strong village ties survived longer in areas where tributaries regularly produced a surplus. By imposing collective responsibility on villagers for taxes, labor, and obedience to royal law (even more than by legally incorporating and segregating villages), the Crown was also encouraging village identity and collective action. Competition for control of village land and labor among the various state and private interests further ensured the economic survival of the villages. The legitimate but relatively weak state control over village life was also a contributing factor. The colonial regime governed the countryside largely by not governing. The colonial bureaucracy was impressively large for its day and peasants generally acknowledged its legitimacy by flooding the high courts with petitions and complaints, protesting abuse of power rather than questioning the legitimacy of colonial sovereignty. On the other hand, the state machinery was spread thinly over the vast expanse of central and southern Mexico and it did not possess the means to coerce obedience everywhere at once. As a result, rural communities were allowed to make many of their own decisions in local matters.

The success of the Regular clergy in evangelizing the rural population also contributed to communal attitudes and organization. Both regions were centers of missionary zeal in the very early postconquest period—on the part of the Franciscans in Hidalgo and the state of Mexico, and of the Dominicans in Oaxaca. Again, the nurturing of communal ties was not simply, or perhaps even largely, the product of paternalistic gestures. A focal point of formal group identity and a source of leadership in defense of the community was often the cofradía, which was also an instrument of exploitation set up by the Church to channel village wealth into support of the clergy. In the late colonial period, Christianity was often set up *against* the parish priest by village disciples—who denounced the clergy as immoral backsliders—and acquired a life of its own, separate to some extent from the formal institutions of the Church hierarchy. As Charles Gibson has suggested, "Christianity appears as a cohesive force, not always displacing but repeatedly implementing and abetting Indian preferences for communal organization."[25] If anything, this localized practice of Christianity was encouraged by the Bourbon reforms of the late eighteenth century, which challenged priests' authority over cofradías and obras pías and their informal influence in local politics.

The exploitation of peasant villages through coercive labor systems, taxes, and low prices paid for the fruits of village labor squared with certain internal conditions in villages that also contributed to village continuity. Most important was land retention. Land was the basis of the villagers' territorial identity and fertility-based folk religions, as well as of their economy. Sufficient land provided a buffer against outside control over the daily lives of villagers and against village factionalism rooted in competition over an essential scarce or externally controlled resource.[26] The connection between peasant landholding and village resistance to outsiders has been noted by Barrington Moore and Robert Ardrey, among others.[27] The landholding Mexican village seems to fit the "castle-and-border" interpretation of territory proposed by Ardrey: "There is the castle or nest or lair to provide security, and, just as important, the border region, where the fun goes on." The dwellings of the village, often clustered around a plaza with its church, cemetery, municipal offices, and marketplace are the castle or heartland, while the community and family landholdings (farming plots, pastures, woodlands) provide an important means of livelihood for rural cultivators and also serve as a border where territorial identity is tested.

But connecting landholding to social cohesion does not explain how or why lands were retained by villages in the colonial period. To attribute colonial land retention by villages to community cohesiveness against outsiders traps us in circular reasoning that, by itself, explains nothing. Where it occurred outside refuge regions, land retention was, I think, based on a symbiosis between the early colonial political and economic system, based on encomienda and tribute tax, and village needs and desires. The early colonial state, supported by its rivals the *encomenderos*, looked upon the Indian peasants mainly as producers of revenue. It willingly confirmed villages as legal corporations entitled to their arable lands and water and an ejido of pasture land. Land provided the villages with the means of supplying the Spanish towns with food and producing the surpluses that the state and the encomenderos skimmed off from their corporate subjects in the form of taxation and labor service. On the Indian side, adjustment was surprisingly rapid to the Spanish civil law that based land rights on written documentary evidence. Villages and individual nobles frequently petitioned the viceroy for formal titles and forged titles when their rights to unentitled lands were challenged in the seventeenth and eighteenth centuries; the apparently close link between land tenure and pre-Hispanic writing systems in Oaxaca and central Mexico meant that at least some Indian societies had had experience with written entitlement before the conquest.[28]

By the late colonial period, we can also point to structural flexibility and political solidarity against outsiders as sources of strength in village culture. Flexibility and solidarity are typical of villages—even some that were miserably poor—that had successfully established claims to lands and defended them against encroachment when haciendas and ranches were developing in the seventeenth and eighteenth centuries. The people of landholding villages lived under conditions of oppression and stratification that were markedly different from those of resident laboring groups on haciendas or of rural villages that were tightly incorporated into urban, mining, or plantation economies. John Womack has summarized these differences in his discussion of rural Morelos before the Revolution of 1910:

The social difference between the old and the new oppression was as profound as the difference between a manor and a factory. Before, various communities and economic enterprises had coexisted without question in Morelos. Sugar plantations, traditional villages, small-farm settlements, single, independent farms, day laborers' hamlets, country towns, provincial cities—not all these different kinds of societies flourished, but they were all grudgingly able to survive. Oppression took place, but the individual cases lacked real momentum or coordination.[29]

The established villages outside the plantation zones, whose land rights had long histories of public recognition and legal protection, adapted most creatively to the pressures of the larger social and economic systems. Their ways of adapting sometimes took the form of new rituals, such as those evident in the drinking patterns discussed in Chapter 2, or of the ready adoption of Catholic forms—a sign of peasant desire not so much for redemption as for protection from new misfortunes.[30] Whether they were new adaptations or older patterns, we have seen evidence of the channeling of collective resistance and interpersonal violence into courses that did not threaten the community with self-destruction. Such adjustments suggest that at least some of these landed villages had, or developed, the social controls to keep drinking within bounds and to institutionalize conflict. As Lewis Coser has suggested, the flexibility of a social structure can be measured not by its ability to eliminate conflict but by its ability to keep hostilities from accumulating or being "channeled along one major line of cleavage once they break out in conflict."[31] The level of peasant society where this flexibility seems to be most evident, again, is the discrete landholding village. As in so many cases described by ethnographers, when threatened by unstable local conditions and new exploitative institutions, our peasants tended to withdraw as far as possible from outside contact in a posture of outward hostility.[32] Withdrawal, however, meant modification of existing social and political ties—giving increased importance to membership in a landed village and reduced importance to old ethnic and political ties—rather than the physical exodus of whole communities to more isolated areas.

The documentation on rebellion, homicide, and drinking provides some hints about the operation of this colonial system in areas of dense peasant settlement. It was not a society that used total subjection and degradation of the peasant majority to prevent violent overthrow.[33] Spanish absolutism was less authoritarian and, above all, less efficient than is often supposed. No colonial power has ever ruled solely by command, but the heavy emphasis of colonial Latin American scholarship on the institutions of Spanish rule (encomiendas, viceregal government, audiencias, and great estates) and coercive labor systems (slavery, encomiendas, repartimientos, and debt peonage) gives the impression that Spaniards maintained their position of authority by direct command and economic monopolies. In fact, Spanish rulers in our peasant regions relied on close control and force primarily in cases of regional uprisings, and even then preferred a show of force to open confrontation. New Spain was without a standing army through most of the colonial period, and what passed for rural police—the Acordada (which operated almost exclusively on main highways and near Mexico City) and the tenientes de los alcaldes mayores, with the support of militias organized in the nearest Spanish town—were hardly effective or sustained instruments of political repression.

Colonial government in both regions usually operated by appeasement, no doubt a conscious policy especially suited to the strength of peasant villages in some regions and the colonial motives of economic exploitation, but also an option exercised by Spanish rulers in many parts of America in the late colonial period. Unamuno's aphorism to the effect that the Spaniard has much of the mandarin about him but little of the *mandón* is suggestive of Spanish attitudes toward the exercise of political power in colonial America. The position of authority, especially in matters of justice—the highest attribute of sovereignty to the colonial Spaniards—was more important than its comprehensive exercise. It seems to me that the judicial system, more than any other social institution, made it possible for the Spanish Crown to govern eighteenth-century Mexico without a large army or police force.

The Spaniards' special problem was how to incorporate peasant villages into the colonial economic and political organization without pushing them into revolt. In pursuing this goal, they recognized Indian municipalities as corporate entities with rights as well as duties. We saw this dual policy of appeasement and exploitation in action in the sentencing of homicide offenders and village rebels. Colonial officials moved quickly to negotiate settlements of village uprisings before they could spread to other communities. Villages usually gained some redress of immediate grievances, and punishment was usually limited to exemplary sentences for one or a few supposed leaders. In homicide cases, too, punishment was relatively lenient—sentences at hard labor rather than long prison terms or capital punishment—and recognized mitigating circumstances. The Crown, in fact, seemed more interested in augmenting the labor force than in protecting society from its criminals. This attitude was a luxury afforded by the fact that village homicides posed little threat to the political control of the colonial elite. In uprisings as well as homicides, violence was tolerated, almost condoned, by the courts in their lenient sentences. Although not the only means by which common people could deal with conflict, violence was a widespread way of resolving differences that, within obvious limits, was permitted by the state as a legitimate expression of grievance when the routine ways of reminding the powerful of their obligations had failed.

We have seen how villages preserved some safeguards against colonial coercion not simply by isolation but also by a genuine capacity to express shared grievance by violent as well as peaceful means. Through village uprisings—localized protests that Charles Tilly calls "reactive types of collective action"—peasants proved themselves an active political force. But just how effective were they? In the short run, villagers could count many successes—tax payments were reduced or suspended, offensive colonial officials were reprimanded or removed, and corrupt labor practices were reformed. But since the colonial authorities were primarily concerned with specific problems of control, such victories did not improve the lot of peasant communities generally. The authorities did not correct abuses of power in other communities unless they, too, disrupted peaceful colonial relations by resorting to violence. In the long run, the most that was achieved by reactive revolts was to delay further erosion of peasant rights at the village level, reaffirm village unity, and give peasants some tactical experience.[34]

A central ingredient in the endurance of this colonial system was the peasants' attitude to state power and their ignorance of the political stakes outside their region. Once the main outlines of adjustment were made at the village and subprovince levels in the prolonged, painful aftermath of the conquest and the sixteenth-century pandemics, peasants' relationship to the state and to the colonial city was, in significant respects, fixed. In general, peasant villages in our regions in the eighteenth century accepted the Spanish Crown as a remote but legitimate sovereign, even though they might oppose the Crown's local representatives; what Alfonso Reyes called "a miracle of respect for the monarchic idea." The flood of peasant litigants to the viceregal court in Mexico City in the eighteenth century is tangible evidence of this acceptance of the Crown as legitimate arbiter of peasant grievances and a direct link between peasant and king that deflected peasants from potential insurrection.[35] None of the peasant revolts studied here had as its paramount purpose displacement of the central government.

The authorities' success in negotiating with individual villages and the low incidence of regional uprisings suggest how the Spaniards were able to rule and exploit dense Indian areas without a large standing army. Spanish control, as Stanley and Barbara Stein have said, "was predicated upon separation not integration."[36] It was a divide-and-rule system that depended upon limited cooperation among villages and the willingness of communities to negotiate individually with the colonial authorities, thereby legitimizing the formal channels of colonial justice and forestalling the decisive step beyond local success in rebellion.

The patterns of social behavior that emerge from colonial documentation on drinking, homicide, and rebellion make it clear that European colonization did not bring about a sweeping transformation of peasant to peon in densely settled areas of rural Indian Mexico. On the contrary, many villages preserved old social boundaries or established new ones and maintained a strong sense of group identity in their adjustments to the new dependency relationships imposed by colonial conditions. As an adaptation to a preindustrial colonial system, this concentration of energy and identity in the village was reasonably successful. Ironically, however, the crystallization of these adjustments in durable relationships with state and city made the same villages easy prey to greater exploitation after independence in new conditions of industrialization, commercial agriculture, laissez-faire economics, and population pressure on the land. They were also subject to greater manipulation of their discontent by the more extensive power and more sophisticated methods of modern Mexican governments.

APPENDIXES

Valley of Mexico

Mexicalcingo jurisdiction
　Mexicalcingo, 1802, AGN Criminal 138 exp. 2, 217 exp. 4
　Santa Marta, 1721, AGN Criminal 155, fols. 111–133
　Huitzilopochco, 18th century, Navarro de Vargas, p. 599
Tacuba jurisdiction
　San Pedro Excapusaltongo, 1760's, AGN Criminal 177 exp. 4
　Huixquilucan, 1769, AGN Criminal 120 exp. 25
　Tepetitlán, 1743, AGN Criminal 177 exp. 23
Xochimilco jurisdiction
　Milpa Alta, 1720, AGN Criminal 232 exp. 2
　Xochitepec, 1796, AGN Criminal 29 exp. 6
Ecatepec jurisdiction
　Tulpetlac, 1780, AGN Civil 2114 exp. 8
　Ecatepec, 1782, AGN Policía 23
Texcoco jurisdiction
　Atengo, 1688, AGN Criminal 193 exp. 226
　Acolman, 1774, AGN Criminal 145, fols. 235–
Otumba jurisdiction
　Betlén, 1749, AGN Criminal 162, fols. 94–104
　Ozumbilla, 1783, AGN Criminal 162, fols. 187–223
Cuauhtitlán jurisdiction
　Cuauhtitlán, 1785, AGN Clero regular y secular 103
Mexico City
　1692, Biblioteca Nacional MS 1358; Cavo II, 82–83; Di Tella, p. 96;
　　Rubio Mañé, II, 44–61
　1696, parcialidad de Santa María de la Redonda, Bancroft Mexican
　　MS 135
　1715, AGN General de Parte 21 exp. 165

State of Mexico, fringes of Morelos and Guerrero

Metepec jurisdiction
　Tarasquillo, 1720, AGN Criminal 168
　　　　　　　1730, AGN Criminal 168

Yolotepec, 1733, AGN Criminal 168
San Felipe, district of Ixtlahuaca, 1730, AGN Criminal 93, exp. 10
Almoloya, 1792, AGN Criminal 148 exp. 2
Metepec, 1733, AGN Criminal 168, fols. 538–
   1735, AGN Criminal 151 exp. 1, Indios 54, exp. 85
   1772, AGN Criminal 168, fols. 283–
   1801, AGN Criminal 152, fols. 270–
Ocuioaca, district of Tenango, 1807, AGN Civil 1599 exp. 1, Civil
   1505 exp. 7, Criminal 207 exp. 12
Ixtlahuaca, 1727, AGN Civil 1508 exp. 6
   1769, University of Texas Mexican MS G 205
Atlacomulco, 1733, AGN Civil 2292 exps. 10–11
   1810, AGN Criminal 229, fols. 263–
   1811, AGN Criminal 231 exp. 1
   1814, AGN Criminal 230 exp. 15
San Andrés Mexicalcingo, 1703, AGN Criminal 217 exp. 4
San Antonio, 1735, AGN Indios 54 exp. 85
Los Reyes, district of Xocotitlán, 1767, AGN Criminal 92 exp. 5
San Mateo Atengo, 1638, AGN Criminal 219
Amanalco, 1792, AGN Criminal 243 exp. 1
San Lorenzo and Santa María Guisisilapa, 1710, AGN Criminal 218,
   fols. 1–19
Zacualpa jurisdiction
   Yzcateopan, 1808, AGN Criminal 166, fols. 134–136
   Ostumac, 1810, AGN Criminal 166, fols. 274–294
   Alahuistlán, 1795, AGN Criminal 166, fols. 354–
   Apastla, 1783, AGN Criminal 167 exp. 1
      1807, AGN Criminal 168, fols. 1–13
      no date, AGN Criminal 166, fols. 185–
   Yztapa, 1800, AGN Criminal 181, fols. 201–
Tenango del Valle (see also Ocuioaca under Metepec)
   Quintana, district of Ozolotepec, 1783, AGN Criminal 123 exp. 3
   Calimaya, 1803, AGN Criminal 123 exp. 28
   Tenango, 1762, AGN Criminal 123 exp. 21 (six tumultos mentioned)
   Ozolotepec, 1799, AGN Indios 70 exp. 69
Lerma jurisdiction
   San Miguel Amealco, 1733, AGN Criminal 169, fols. 103–143
Temascaltepec and Sultepec jurisdiction
   Tescaticlán, 1714, AGN Criminal 180, fols. 50–61
   Sultepec, 1764, AGN Criminal 210, fols. 243r
   Pozontepec, 1758, AGN Criminal 210, fols. 189–205
Ichcateopan jurisdiction
   Yzcatepec, 1787, AGN Criminal 81, fols. 238–300
   Aclahuistlán, 1711, AGN Criminal 166, fols. 320–353

Malinalco jurisdiction
  Malinalco, 1803, AGN Criminal 191 exp. 1
    1818, AGN Civil 2292 exps. 7–8
  Azingo, 1786, AGN Civil 865 exp. 8
  Ocuila, 1772, AGN Civil 865 exp. 9
  Tenancingo, 1797, AGN Criminal 15 exps. 2–3
  Zumpahuacán, 1808, AGN Criminal 17 exp. 11
Cuernavaca jurisdiction
  Tepoztlán, 1778, AGN Criminal 203 exp. 4
  Achichipilco, 1802, AGN Criminal 202 last expediente
Cuauhtla jurisdiction
  Thetelzingo, 1778, AGN Criminal 507 exp. 17
Chalco jurisdiction
  Tlayacapan, 1784, AGN Criminal 1 exp. 11
  Atlautla, 1799, AGN Criminal 157, fols. 93–132
  Amecameca, barrio Tlailotlacan, 1799, AGN Criminal 226, fols. 401–
  Tlalmanalco, 1693, AGN Criminal 227 exp. 9
    1773, AGN Criminal 90
  Chimalhuacán, 1802, AGN Criminal 255 exp. 13

State of Hidalgo

Tetepango jurisdiction
  Misquiaguala, 1681, AGN Criminal 115 exp. 1
  Axacuba, 1744, AGN Criminal 53 exp. 20
  Tlapanaloya, district of Atitalaquia, 1690, AGN Criminal 54 exp. 14
Actopan jurisdiction
  Tetitlan, 1764, AGN Criminal 117 exp. 7
  Actopan, 1756, AGN Civil 241 exp. 1
Meztitlán jurisdiction
  Meztitlán, 1772, AGN Criminal 102, 104, 107
  Zozoquiapam, 1805, AGN Criminal 180, fols. 361–
  San Juan Meztitlán, 1805, AGN Criminal 180, fols. 430–
  Coamelco, 1777, AGN Criminal 79 exp. 1
Pachuca jurisdiction
  Real del Monte, 1805, AGN Criminal 115 exp. 7
  Pachuca, 1771, AGN Criminal 303 exps. 1, 305, 306, 308
Ixmiquilpan jurisdiction
  Sabanilla, 1746, AGN Criminal 57 exp. 1
  Donicha, 1779, AGN Criminal 75 exps. 3–4
Tulancingo jurisdiction
  1769, AGN Criminal 308
Xilotepec-Huichapan jurisdiction
  San Francisco Soyalmiquilpa, 1818, AGN Criminal 26 exp. 9
  San Pedro Donicaá, 1766, AGN Criminal 178 exp. 1

Santa María Tixmadeje, 1789, AGN Criminal 202 exp. 1
Alfajayuca, 1766, AGN Civil 2166 exp. 5
Zimapan jurisdiction
    Zimapatongo, 1807, AGN Criminal 178 exp. 23
Tumultos in central Mexico unidentified by jurisdiction:
    La Milpa, 1766, AGN Criminal 155, fols. 358–
    Dayonthe, 1805, AGN Criminal 179, fols. 455–

State of Puebla

San Andrés Chalchicomula, 1768, AGN Criminal 307 exp. 2
Tetela de Xonotla, 1798, AGN Historia 334 exp. 5
San Gabriel Chilac, 1801, AGN Historia 413
Soquitlán, 1708, AGN Criminal 660
Izúcar de Matamoros, 1781, Calderón Quijano, II, 163–75

State of Oaxaca

Valley of Oaxaca
    Cuilapan, 1725, AGN Hospital de Jesús 307 exp. 4
    San Pablo Etla, 1755, AGN Hospital de Jesús 308 exp. 18
    Sant Cruz Amilpas, 1710, AGN Indios 37 exp. 190
        1720, AGN Tierras 381 exp. 5
    Zaachila, 1710, AGN Indios 6 primera parte exp. 473
        1776, AGN Intendencias 12
        1784 AGI Audiencia de Mexico 2588
        1806 AEO Juzgados 1806
    Guelavía, 1690, AGN Tierras 148 exp. 3
        1705, AGN Tierras 223 exp. 4
    Ocotlán, 1788, AGN Tierras 867 exp. 2
    Soledad Etla, 1797, AGN Tierras 1877 exp. 2
    San Miguel Tilquiapan, AGN Tierras 1363 exp. 8
    Zimatlán, 1740, AGN Tierras 1460 exp. 7
        1773, AGN Criminal 306 exp. 5
        1774, AGI Audiencia de Mexico 2588
    San Antonio de la Cal, AGN Tierras 2259 exp. 4 (1730–1787)
        1754, AGN Tierras 2386 exp. 1
    Teotitlán del Valle, 1792, AGN Epidemias 15
        1793, AGN Indios 101 exp. 8
    Santa Lucía, 1717, AGN Criminal 283 exp. 3
    Various towns, 1784, AGI Audiencia de Mexico 2588
    Abasolo, 1800, AEO Juzgados 1800
    Tlalixtac, 1804, AEO Juzgados 1804
    Trinidad de la Huertas, 1808, AEO Juzgados 1808
    Macuilxóchitl, 1757, CCG Hacienda Buenavista papers
    Tlapacoya, 1785, AGI Audiencia de Mexico 2588

Lachixijo, 1804, AEO Juzgados 1804
San Pablo, district of Cuatro Villas, 1689, AGN Indios 30 exp. 244
Ayoquesco, 1742, AGN Indios 55 exp. 91
Mixteca Alta (1629–1823)
    Achiutla, 1629, CDCh roll 6, exp. 209
    Petalcingo, 1631, CDCh roll 6, exp. 227
    Sujeto of Teposcolula, 1639, CDCh roll 8, exp. 286
    Xinastla, 1680, CDCh roll 8, exp. 475
    Santiago Tillo, 1683, CDCh roll 9, exp. 502
    Tamazulapa, 1686, CDCh roll 9, exp. 520
    Xaltepetongo, 1688, CDCh roll 9, exp. 529
    Tiltepec, 1692, CDCh roll 10, exp. 551
    Usila, 1702, AGN Indios 35 exp. 123
    Yanhuitlán, 1775, CDCh roll 15, exp. 410
    Chalcatongo, 1779–80, CDCh roll 15, exps. 428, 430
        1674, CDCh roll 21, exp. 107
    Achiutla, 1785, CDCh roll 15, exp. 469
    Yolomecatl, 1743, CDCh roll 14, exp. 209
        1744, CDCh roll 14, exp. 222
    Santo Domingo Yodoino, 1753, CDCh roll 14, exp. 251
    San Andrés Xinastla, 1737, CDCh roll 12, exp. 172
    Teozacualco, 1774, AGN Criminal 306 exps. 1, 3
    San Miguel Malinaltepec, 1806, AEO Juzgados 1806
    Theotila, 1754, AGN Inquisicion 960, fols. 263–89
    Teposcolula, 1777, CDCh roll 15
        1785, CDCh roll 15
    San Miguel el Grande, 1780, CDCh roll 15
    Coixtlahuaca, 1822, 1823, CDCh roll 20, exps. 32, 196
    San Pedro Añañe, 1823, CDCh roll 21

Incidence of Crime with
Special Reference to Homicide

T he criminal records I have examined for rural central Mexico
and Oaxaca do not permit a systematic study of the incidence
of crime. They are primarily full records of individual trials;
certainly they do not include all trials, much less all crimes committed
in these two regions over any considerable length of time. Except for
homicide, criminal records—even summary lists of all arrests in modern societies—are notorious for underreporting most types of crime.
For the colonial period of Latin American history, the surviving criminal records are distorted not only by crimes that went undiscovered
but also by the fact that most crimes committed within Indian communities did not have to be reported to the colonial authorities. Generally
speaking, for crimes other than homicide and rebellion, the surviving
trials and summary reports for rural districts present seemingly in-
surmountable obstacles to estimating the incidence of criminal acts.
Recognizing the inadequacy of these records for estimating the incidence of crime, we can, however, make cautious use of the few summary accounts of crime that are available for these two regions in the
seventeenth and nineteenth centuries to suggest some comparisons
and contrasts between the two regions and some possible long-term
changes in the frequency of homicide, the one criminal act that is usually well represented in criminal records and which is the center of
attention in Chapter 3.

The only colonial document I have located that summarizes criminal
arrests in the Mixteca Alta dates from September 9, 1606, to November 19, 1608. It is a daybook kept by the alcalde mayor of Yanhuitlán
to record the cases he decided while on circuit in the district or that
were brought to him in Yanhuitlán by Indian *alguaciles* from communities in his jurisdiction. Entries include the crime committed; the
name, sex, racial designation if non-Indian, and hometown of the
offender; and whether alcohol was involved. Of the 189 arrests, all but
one of the offenders were Indians; only 42 were women (see Table
B.1). Perhaps the most notable feature of the alcalde mayor's book
is the absence of homicides. The Mixteca Alta was not free of homicides in the early seventeenth century—we have trial records of hom-

TABLE B.1.   *Summary of the Alcalde Mayor's Daybook, Yanhuitlán, 1606–1608*

Type of crime	No.	Alcohol-related	Female offenders	Type of crime	No.	Alcohol-related	Female offenders
Simple drunkenness	45	45	11	Husband abandoned	3	3	3
Assaults[a]	35	16	2	Attempt to seduce a			
Adultery	23		11	married woman	3		
Debts	20		1	Tax evasion at mesón	2		
Operation of illegal				Prostitution	1		1
tavern	13	13	6	Advising son to			
Disrespect to public				commit murder	1		
officials	15	4		Vagrancy	1		
Robbery	10			Wife abandoned	1		
Verbal abuse	10	1	5	Disobedient son	1		
Promiscuity of				Fled jail	1		
single adults	3		2	Fled service	1		

[a] Includes 22 cases of wife-beating and 6 cases involving other female victims.

icides earlier in 1606 and in 1609—but it is quite possible that no homicides were reported during the period covered by this record. We may cautiously infer a low incidence of homicide in the district in the early seventeenth century. Judging by the number of homicide trials in the same area during the 1730's, 1740's, 1790's, and 1800's (ranging from one to eight per year), the homicide rate probably increased in the late colonial period. Another outstanding feature of crime in the Mixteca Alta in the early seventeenth century is the relative importance of arrests involving strained and illicit relations between men and women. Of the 189 arrests, 69 were cases of assaults on women, adultery, promiscuity, solicitation, and marital abandonment. All but 7 of the 35 assault arrests were cases of men beating women, usually their wives.

Another source bearing on the incidence of crime and the relative importance of homicides is the annual reports of state governors of Oaxaca, Hidalgo, and Mexico in the middle to late years of the nineteenth century. These reports occasionally contain detailed tables summarizing arrests for different crimes over specified periods of time. Obviously, we cannot assume that the patterns suggested by these nineteenth-century data are valid for the eighteenth century, but in the absence of summary records for the late colonial period, they are our best source of information on regional differences in the rate of homicide. The governor's reports from which I have tabulated crime statistics are: Hidalgo, 1869, 1871–1872; Mexico, 1877, 1878, 1879, 1889–1893; and Oaxaca, 1869–1870, 1871–1872, 1874–1875, 1881–1882, 1897–1898.

In all three states, assaults with injury, robbery, and homicide consistently were the leading categories of arrests. Unless modern Mexico is an exception to the rule that violent crimes represent less than half of all crime—a rule based on many national studies of crime—nonviolent crimes are probably greatly underreported in these summaries. Although assaults topped the lists in each state report, followed by robbery and homicide, the state of Hidalgo stands somewhat apart from Oaxaca and Mexico in the relative importance of homicide in comparison to assault. In the Oaxaca and Estado de Mexico evidence, more than six assaults were reported for every homicide (7.3:1 for Oaxaca and 6.2:1 for Mexico). In Hidalgo, there were fewer than three assaults for every homicide (2.9:1). These regional patterns are repeated in the proportion of reported crime represented by homicides: 17 per cent of all crimes reported in Hidalgo were homicides, compared to 7 per cent in Mexico and 6 per cent in Oaxaca.* Not only did homicides represent a larger part of all crime in Hidalgo, the incidence of homicides there was apparently much higher than in Oaxaca or Mexico. Hidalgo averaged 237 homicides a year between 1869 and 1872, or roughly 58.6 homicides per 100,000 inhabitants (1869 population: 404,207). The state of Mexico (1877 population: 683,323) averaged 207 homicides a year or 30.2 homicides per 100,000. And Oaxaca, with the fewest number of homicides (179.6 per year) averaged 27.6 per 100,000 (1869 population: 650,564). Comparing the nineteenth-century central Mexico and Oaxaca figures with European countries at roughly the same time (ranging from .94 to 12.67 per 100,000 population), the incidence of homicide in Mexico was very high.†

Our colonial homicide trials are scattered all over the modern states of Hidalgo and Mexico, so there is no reason to break down these state figures for local districts. The one possibly important regional pattern within the state of Mexico that is evident in a distribution by district is that districts nearest Mexico City recorded the largest number of homicides (the districts of Chalco, Tenango, Tlalnepantla, and Texcoco). Toluca also ranked among the leading districts in number of homicides. This may suggest a somewhat higher incidence of homicide in and near the urban centers of central Mexico.

Colonial trials for Oaxaca are concentrated in the Mixteca Alta, and it is of some interest to compare the rate of homicide arrests in this region with other parts of the state (see Table B.2). Of the twenty-five districts of Oaxaca, the three Mixteca Alta districts of Nochixtlán, Teposcolula, and Coixtlahuaca (encompassed by the colonial alcaldía mayor of Teposcolula) ranked ninth, nineteenth, and twenty-fourth in number of homicides reported. Combined, these Mixteca Alta districts

---

*Assaults, robberies, and homicides probably were the main categories of crime in the nineteenth century, but they were also categories in which the judicial system took special interest and may therefore be overrepresented in the crime statistics.

†Quiroz et al., p. 111.

TABLE B.2.   *Homicides in Oaxaca,*
1869–1870, 1871–1872, 1874–1875,
1881–1882, 1897–1898

District	Number reported	Average per 100,000
Oaxaca City	85	17
Villa Alvarez	84[a]	16.8
Tlaxiaco	65	13
Huajuapan	52	10.4
Etla	52	10.4
Miahuatlán	52	10.4
Ejutla	51	10.2
Silacayoapan	48[a]	9.6
Nochixtlán[b]	41	8.2
Tlacolula	37	7.4
Ocotlán	37	7.4
Jamiltepec	34	6.8
Juxtlahuaca	31[a]	6.2
Villa Juárez	31	6.2
Tehuantepec	28	5.6
Juchitán	25[a]	5
Pochutla	23	4.6
Yautepec	22	4.4
Teposcolula[b]	22	4.4
Villa Alta	21	4.2
Juquila	18[a]	3.6
Cuicatlán	14	2.8
Teotitlán del Camino	11[a]	2.2
Coixtlahuaca[b]	8	1.6
Choapam	6	1.2

[a] Based on figures for four years with the fifth year represented by the average of these four.
[b] Mixteca Alta districts of the Alcaldía Mayor of Teposcolula.

had a lower homicide rate than the state as a whole, with 15.5 per 100,000 population, compared to the state average of 25 per 100,000 for 1877 (179.6 homicides for the year in a population of 718,197).

These summary figures offer some hints of the incidence of homicide. Judging by the Mixteca Alta figures, homicides probably increased in both regions in the late colonial and early national periods. The early seventeenth-century daybook suggests a lower incidence of homicide at that time compared to later periods, perhaps one or two violent deaths a year. Adjusting for population increase, there were four to eight homicides a year in the district (judging by the trial records) in the late eighteenth century and by the 1870's about fourteen. Mexico in recent times has had one of the highest homicide rates per 100,000 population in the world (29.4). Only Guatemala (141.7 per

100,000), Colombia (33.5 per 100,000), and Costa Rica (32 per 100,000) reported higher rates in the 1960's. These figures are considerably higher than the rates for European nations, which ranged from 0.4 to 2.4 per 100,000 during the 1960's. The historical record suggests a slightly lower homicide rate in the nineteenth century and probably still lower rates in the eighteenth and seventeenth centuries, although any attempt to describe a slow, smooth upward trend is confounded by periods of political unrest and accompanying political assassinations, which are unrelated to the kinds of homicides studied here for the eighteenth century. Political homicides seem to have been especially important for Hidalgo in the nineteenth and twentieth centuries. In comparing our two regions over time, I think it can be said that there was a somewhat lower incidence of homicide in the Mixteca Alta in the late colonial period. Certainly, rates of homicide in the late nineteenth century were substantially lower in the Mixteca Alta than in either Hidalgo or Mexico.

NOTES

NOTES

Complete authors' names, titles, and publication data for works cited in short forms are given in the Bibliography, pp. 207–33. I have used the following abbreviations in the citations:

AEO   Archivo del Estado de Oaxaca
AGI   Archivo General de las Indias
AGN   Archivo General de la Nación (Mexico)
BGVV Biblioteca Genaro V. Vásquez (Oaxaca, Oaxaca)
BNM   Biblioteca Nacional (Mexico City)
BNMa Biblioteca Nacional (Madrid)
CCG   Colección Luis Castañeda Guzmán (Oaxaca, Oaxaca)
CDCh Centro de Documentación del Museo Nacional (Chapultepec Park, Mexico City), Serie Oaxaca
DII   *Colección de documentos inéditos relativos al descubrimiento, conquista y organización de las antiguas posesiones españolas de América y Oceanía, sacados de los archivos del reino, y muy especialmente del de Indias.* 42 vols. Madrid, 1864–84.
DIU   *Colección de documentos inéditos relativos al descubrimiento, conquista y organización de las antiguas posesiones españolas de ultramar.* 25 vols., Madrid, 1885–1932.
PNE   *Papeles de Nueva España.* 9 vols., Madrid and Mexico, 1905–48.
UT   University of Texas, Austin, Latin American Collection

Introduction
1. Midgal, pp. 184–207; Isaac, pp. 251–57; Rogers, pp. 733, 745. The village is more visible but not necessarily more important than the peasant family; but the nuclear family is not equally important in all peasant societies and perhaps has a special significance in twentieth-century Europe and in other areas of the world presently undergoing rapid modernization.

2. Carr, p. 57.

3. Bohannon, *Law and Warfare*, p. 45. Bohannon, *African Homicide*, is an important application of criminal records to this purpose. For a historian's approach, see Martínez-Alier, *Marriage, Class and Colour*.

Chapter One

1. Katz, pp. 123–49.
2. Gibson, *Aztecs*, p. 405.
3. Spores, pp. 90–97.
4. Butterworth, *Tilantongo*, p. 42.
5. Bray, p. 165; Berdan, p. 242.
6. Berdan, pp. 28–29; C. N. B. Davies, p. 218: "In speaking of the Aztec Empire, one has had a tendency to use lines of demarcation to separate states or provinces like the modern divisions of the USSR or the USA. This leaves the misleading impression that even the most remote mountain villages of these provinces could be controlled by the central government through its local representatives.

"But in such a mountainous territory as Mesoamerica, at a time when there were no horses and mules, not to mention jeeps and radios, such control was impossible."

7. Berdan, pp. 28–29, 120, 246–47. For a list of the areas paying tribute to the Triple Alliance see Barlow, *Extent of the Empire*.

8. Carrasco, "Transformación," p. 197.

9. Chimalpahín Cuauhtlehuanitzin, p. 259.

10. From 25 million in 1519, the population decreased sharply: 16.8 million in 1523; 6.3 million in 1548; 2.6 million in 1568; 1.9 million in 1580—to the lowest point of one million in the early seventeenth century, Sánchez-Albornoz, p. 41, based on Cook and Borah, *Indian Population* and *Aboriginal Population*. Even during this demographic catastrophe, no firm evidence exists of declining birth rates that might be taken to indicate a dimming of the will to live, Cook and Borah, *Essays*, II, 9.

11. Miranda, p. 143.

12. Gibson, *Aztecs*, p. 335; Carrasco, "Transformación," p. 192.

13. Kubler, *Mexican Architecture*, I, 157, coined the phrase "psychological unemployment" for Indian mentality in the sixteenth century.

14. Calnek, "Internal Structure of Tenochtitlán," p. 291; Lockhart, pp. 102–103.

15. *Recopilación*, Book 4, Title 12, laws 16, 17. Provisions of the same type appeared regularly in the viceregal laws of the seventeenth and eighteenth centuries as well, AGN *Reales Cédulas Originales* 1 exp. 1, 2 exps. 43, 189, 8 exp. 29, 10 exp. 74, 16 exp. 49, 24 exp. 9.

16. *Recopilación* 6-3-21 to 25. These laws provided that non-Indians not be allowed to live in the pueblos or visit them for more than two days or lodge with Indian families.

17. *Recopilación* 6-1-18.

18. *Recopilación* 6-1-21 and 23.

19. Calderón Quijano et al., II, 251, III, 166, 167, 169; AGN *Criminal* 156 fols. 1–17, 165 exp. 5.

20. Kubler, *Mexican Architecture*; Phelan, *Millennial Kingdom*.

21. Borah, "Latin America," p. 724.

22. Sánchez-Albornoz, p. 89; López Sarrelangue, "Población indígena," p. 521.

23. The notion of conceptual habits is developed in an original and suggestive way by Weismann.

24. Carrasco, "Transformación," pp. 199–200; Gibson, *Aztecs*, p. 335; AGN *Criminal* 210 fol. 193r; Arthur Anderson et al., p. 7.

25. Borah, "Race and Class," p. 338; Foster, *Culture and Conquest*.

26. Carrasco, "Civil-Religious Hierarchy," pp. 483–97.

27. Carrasco, "Central Mexican Highlands," p. 597.

28. AGN *Intendencias* 12 witness number 14, Juan Carlos Barberena.

29. Carrasco, "Central Mexican Highlands," pp. 593–94.

30. Gerhard, *Guide*, p. 270.

31. Gibson, *Aztecs*, pp. 366–67; Colín, *Atlacomulco*, documents the disappearance of a number of small ranchos and hamlets.

32. AGN *Criminal* 203 exp. 3 fol. 98r; Bancroft Library Mexican Manuscript 135 item 18 fol. 11r.

33. Butterworth, *Tilantongo*, p. 52; AGN *Criminal* 630 exp. 4, fol. 10r.

34. Colín, *Atlacomulco*.

35. A good example of this development is found in University of Texas Latin American Collection, Mexican Manuscript G 205 (1769 Hacienda de Tepetitlán in the jurisdiction of Ixtlahuaca).

36. Florescano and Gil, pp. 50–57.

37. Miranda, p. 138; López Sarrelangue, "Población indígena," pp. 521–26.

38. AGN *Civil* 1599 exp. 9 (jurisdiction of Metepec, 1708).

Chapter Two

1. One of ma..y examples of this interpretation is Braudel, p. 177: "The Indian peoples suffered tremendously from the alcoholism in which they were encouraged to indulge. It would really seem as if the civilisation of the Mexican plateau, losing its ancient framework and taboos, abandoned itself to a temptation which wrought havoc with it after 1600."

2. Other important published sources that deal directly with pre-Hispanic drinking are Chimalpahín Cuauhtlehuanitzin, Clavijero, Emmart, Gonçalves de Lima, and Guerra.

3. AGN *Inquisición* 37 primera parte exps. 6, 7, 8, 9; *Inquisición* 30 exp. 9.

4. Guerra, p. 241; Gonçalves de Lima, pp. 113, 146, 228; *Codex Mendoza*, fol. 71r-v; *Florentine Codex*, Book 10, pp. 20, 37, 56; *Chronicles of Michoacan*, p. 160; PNE IV p. 31.

5. Chimalpahín Cuauhtlehuanitzin, p. 209.

6. López Austin, pp. 125–321; *Chronicles of Michoacan*, p. 136; *Badianus Manuscript*, pp. 312, 316, 317, 319; *Florentine Codex*, Book 11, p. 179; Gonçalves de Lima, pp. 28, 30, 111, 119; Carrasco, *Otomíes*, p. 51; PNE IV pp. 44, 98, 124, 172, 181, 201, 247, 300, 310.

7. Toor, pp. 16–17. AGN *Impresos Oficiales* 48 (*Mercurio Volante* Nos. 8–10, 1772).

8. PNE IV pp. 13, 62, 171, 297, 318, VI pp. 17, 21, 112, 142, 179.

9. Steck, p. 331.

10. PNE IV pp. 13, 62; AGN *Criminal* 132 exp. 18; AGN *Ordenanzas* 9 fol. 315.

11. Bruman, "Aboriginal Drink Areas," p. 239.

12. Gonçalves de Lima, pp. 27, 142, 146.

13. Octavio Paz in foreword to Jacques La Faye, p. xix; La Faye, p. 244.

14. Guerra pp. 245–56; Gonçalves de Lima, p. 170; Carrasco, *Otomíes*, p. 71; Barlow, "Códice," pp. 5–8; Bernal, p. 5; *Codex Mendoza*, fol. 27; Rendón, p. 253; AGN *Indios* 23 exp. 297, fols. 266v–267r; PNE VI p. 202, 213, 300, 309.

15. Gibson, *Aztecs*, p. 318; PNE IV pp. 13, 76, 103, 112, 149, 171, 209, 297, 318, VI pp. 2, 3, 10, 16, 19, 21, 26, 31, 37, 172, 181, 201, 202, 218, 225, 227, 236, 247, 261, 278, 287, 300, 301, 309, 310.

16. Martín del Campo, pp. 12–16.

17. *Codex Mendoza*, fol. 27r; Gonçalves de Lima, p. 170.

18. Guerra, pp. 245–46.

19. PNE VI p. 202.

20. PNE VI p. 300; Díaz del Castillo, p. 413.

21. Reyes Valerio, pp. 13–18.

22. Rendón reported that in the post-Classic period of the fourteenth and fifteenth centuries Cuauhtitlán and Metepec were producing vessels shaped like Toltec pulque cups, p. 253. According to Barlow, "Códice," the pottery industry at Cuauhtitlán began in the mid-fourteenth century. Barlow's edition of the códice de los alfareros of 1564 provides evidence of pulque jars being produced at Cuauhtitlán in the early colonial period.

23. PNE IV p. 244 (Guatulco), VI pp. 15, 29 (Ueipuchtla), 57 (Coatepec), 90 (Ichcateopan), 107 (Ostuma); AGN *Civil* 822, fols. 220–23 (Tlacolula); *Codex Vindobonensis* (western Oaxaca); Burgoa, II, p. 125 (Mitla); Price, p. 19.

24. *Codex Mendoza*, fol. 71r-v; PNE VI pp. 15, 29, 57, 90, 91, 111, 277; AGN *Civil* 822, fols. 220–23; AGN *Inquisición* 30 exp. 9.

25. PNE VI pp. 15, 29, 57, 90, 91, 146, 278; *Codex Mendoza*, fol. 71r-v; Keen, pp. 101, 121; Zorita, pp. 131–32.

26. PNE IV pp. 166–67.

27. Zorita, pp. 123, 131; Keen, pp. 101, 111, 121; Wolf, *Sons*, p. 66; Guerra, pp. 245–46; *Codex Mendoza*, fol. 71r-v.

28. PNE IV pp. 91 ("todos en general bevian un brevaje en lugar de vino con que se enbriagavan, que sacan de un arbol o yerva que se dize maguey o metl lo qual al presente no an dexado ni se les puede quitar": "instead of wine, all [the Indians] used to drink an intoxicating beverage which they extracted from a tree or bush called maguey or metl which, to date, they have not given up and which cannot be taken from them"), 145, 186, 261, 265; Guerra, p. 261; Serna, p. 174.

29. DII 4 p. 537; PNE IV pp. 48, 61, 217, VI p. 215.

30. PNE IV pp. 95–96, 101, 104, 145, 149, 151, 166; Caso, p. 188.

31. Serna, pp. 172–74. Other examples are described in Roys, pp. 28–29, and *Chronicles of Michoacan*, p. 136.

32. The fullest example is from Yanhuitlán, Oaxaca (1544), where drink was a part of harvest rituals and rain-making ceremonies, in AGN *Inquisición* 37 exp. 8. For weddings see PNE IV p. 198, VI pp. 9, 139; AGN *Inquisición* 37 primera parte exp. 9 fol. 18v; Clavijero, p. 196, *Codex Mendoza*, fol. 61r; Zorita, p. 132. For funerals see PNE VI p. 96; AGN *Inquisición* 37 primera parte exp. 9, fol. 18v; Gonçalves de Lima, p. 180. For birth ceremonies see PNE IV pp. 95–96, VI p. 146; Gonçalves de Lima, p. 170. For warrior's rites see PNE IV p. 79.

33. AGN *Inquisición* 30, exp. 9, *Civil* 822; PNE VI pp. 146–47, IV p. 244;

Guerra, p. 246; Gonçalves de Lima, p. 177; Burgoa, II, p. 125; Bunzel, "Chichicastenango," p. 73; Keen, pp. 27, 129.

34. DII 4 pp. 537, 545; PNE VI pp. 215–18, IV p. 18.

35. Martín del Campo, p. 15.

36. For example, Luis de Velasco (hijo)'s edict against uncontrolled use of pulque, August 16, 1608, was based on his observations of drinking in Mexico City, AGN *Indios* 17 exp. 1, fol. 1v.

37. PNE IV p. 221, VI pp. 111, 146, 179, 185, 224, 227, 255; Burgoa, II, p. 125.

38. Drinking: PNE IV pp. 179, 244, VI pp. 16, 29, 227. Eating and dress: PNE IV pp. 91, 106, 118, 141, 179, 240, 244, VI pp. 90, 111, 135, 141, 217, 224, 227, 244, 259, 278, 318.

39. Steck, p. 96; PNE IV p. 171, VI pp. 147, 179, 224, 255; AGN *Ordenanzas* 3 fol. 5r.

40. Gibson, *Aztecs*, p. 318.

41. PNE VI pp. 2, 16, 19, 26, 31, 37, 172, 181, 201, 218, 225, 227, 236, 261, 287, 300–301, 307, 310.

42. PNE IV pp. 103, 171.

43. PNE IV pp. 13, 76, 121, 149, 209 , 297, VI pp. 10, 21, 236, 247, 278.

44. AGN *Indios* 4 exp. 145 (1589), 10 exps. 28, 40, 137 (1628), 11 exps. 108, 170 (1639), 13 exps. 103, 224, 325, 329 (1641), 15 exp. 129 (1649), 16 exp. 135 (1651), 17 exp. 2 (1654), 18 exps. 12, 116 (1655), 19 exps. 20, 49 (1660), 20 exps. 61, 63, 139 (1656), 21 exps. 162, 253 (1657), 23 exps. 154, 287, 298, 314 (1658), 24 exps. 117, 224, 232, 234, 240 (1667), 25 exps. 159, 189 (1676), 27 exp. 160 (1681), 29 exps. 131, 179, 30 exps. 193, 379, 422 (1689). The provision of pulque was not regulated in the early sixteenth century.

45. The 1692 revolt brought a temporary reversal of policy, AGN *Indios* 3 exp. 967; *Historia* 573 fols. 1–53 (June 3, 1697); Paynó, pp. 487–88. A rough measure of rising sales in the city is the value of the contract (*asiento*) for collecting the pulque tax after this system was begun in 1668. The first asiento was valued at 66,000 pesos per year; by 1674, it had risen to 92,000 pesos, Paynó, p. 506; AGN *Civil* 2285 exp. 8; *Reales Cédulas* 10 exp. 113; *Mercedes* 60 fols. 120v–122r.

46. AGN *Indios* 10 exp. 111.

47. See pp. 47–51.

48. AGN *Tierras* 2956 exp. 184 (1706), *Indios* 12 segunda parte exp. 134 (1640), 19 exp. 125 (1653), 17 exp. 316 (1654), 65 exp. 189 (1776), 25 exp. 73 (1675), 25 exp. 300 (1678), 25 exp. 356 (1678).

49. CDCh *Oaxaca*, roll 1, Yanhuitlán, February 5, 1571.

50. For example, AGN *Indios* 9 exp. 108 (1618): Indians of Jalapa rented their mesón to a Spaniard.

51. BNM 1358, fol. 45v; AGN *Ordenanzas* 2, fol. 208v.

52. Medina, "Tratado."

53. AGN *Indios* 19 exp. 239 (1660).

54. Canónigo Lope Cornejo de Contreras, informe to viceroy, July 4, 1692, in AGI *Audiencia de México* 333.

55. AGN *Policía* 19, fols. 116r–119r.

56. AGN *General de Parte* 21 exp. 165 (1715). This was equally true in the late eighteenth century, AGN *Policía* 19, fols. 116r–119r.

57. BNM 1358, fol. 147v. Another example is AGN *Criminal* 670 exp. 2.

58. AGN *Ordenanzas* 1, fols. 87v–89r, 2 fol. 294, 4 fols. 85r–86r.
59. AGN *Indios* 17 exp. 1; *Ordenanzas* 2 fol. 208v.
60. AGN *Indios* 17 exp. 1.
61. AEO *Juzgados* bundles for 1767–1770, 1805, 1807. Another prosperous Indian pulque merchant, Rafael Romero of La Milpa (jurisdiction of Xochimilco), complained of the envy and hatred his neighbors felt toward him because of his success, AGN *Criminal* 138 exp. 13 (1785).
62. BNMa MS 6743 exp. 8 (1662) Tlalixtac (Valley of Oaxaca): example of an alcalde mayor forcing Indians to buy imported wine.
63. CDCh *Oaxaca*, roll 1, May 26, 1568; Zavala *Fuentes* III, p. 42 (1587).
64. AGN *Ordenanzas* 1 exp. 80; *Recopilación* 6-1-36; AGN *Indios* 6 primera parte exp. 334, *General de Parte* 5 exp. 51.
65. *Epistolario* 15 doc. 867.
66. AGN *Ordenanzas* 2 fol. 303v, 3 fol. 5r.
67. PNE IV pp. 131, 142, 158.
68. PNE IV p. 179.
69. BNM 1361 fol. 28.
70. "Relación de Tequisquiac," p. 293.
71. AGN *Indios* 3 exp. 78, 7 fol. 99r.
72. AGN *Inquisición* 37 exp. 6 (Xuchitepec, 1554), 30 exp. 9 (Ocuytuco, 1539); *Civil* 822 (Tlacolula, 1571); *Criminal* 148 fols. 263– (Ocuyoacac, 1634); PNE IV p. 131 (Miahuatlán, 1576).
73. PNE VI pp. 9, 19.
74. PNE IV p. 131; AGN *Inquisición* 30 exp. 9.
75. AGN *Inquisición* 37 primera parte exp. 6, fol. 23r–v; Ricard, p. 270; *Procesos*, p. 7.
76. BNM 1358 fol. 42r; AGN *Inquisición* 37 primera parte exp. 9, fol. 18v.
77. "Relación de Tequisquiac," p. 293.
78. AEO *Juzgados*, bundle for 1767–1770.
79. Medina, "Tratado."
80. AGN *Inquisición* 839 exp. 9 fols. 241–49.
81. AGI *Audiencia de México* 1088 libro 2 fol. 66v.
82. BNM 1358 fol. 163v.
83. Fray Diego González, "Acerca del pulque en México," (ca. 1683), 17 pp. (manuscript in Condumex archive), fol. numbered 314r. For the trial of a priest for drunkenness see University of Texas Mexican Manuscript G-358, Taxco, 1814.
84. AGI *Mexico* 333, informe de Fr. Francisco Sánchez, July 26, 1692.
85. AGN *Criminal* 193 fols. 377r, 141 fols. 376–; *Inquisición* 176 exp. 16, 311 exp. 2a, 322 fol. 301, 430 exp. 8. Ideals and reality rarely coincide. There are documented cases of excessive drinking by Spaniards in colonial Mexico: AGN *Inquisición* 318 exp. 8; *Criminal* 111 exp. 3, 120 exps. 2, 17, 159 fols. 163–, 179 fols. 137–, 195 fols. 37–, 47–.
86. AGN *Criminal* 187 fols. 266– (1785). Peasants referred to pulque as "heaven's water," a gift of the gods, BNM 1358 fol. 42r.
87. PNE IV p. 31.
88. PNE IV p. 55, VI p. 20; AGN *Indios* 32 exp. 184; *Ordenanzas* 2 fol. 203v, 4 fol. 17r; BNM 1358 fols. 42r–43r; Guerra, pp. 237–38.
89. *Recopilación* 6-1-37; *Tratado de las idolatrías* I, 412.

90. Velásquez, I, 16–17. What Spaniards expected from Indian drinkers is described by the subdelegado of Amecameca in 1810: "And everyone knows that for them [Indians] drinking stimulates gaiety and, in general, they do not drink with appropriate moderation. From this, undignified acts, prostitution, and crime result" AGN *Criminal* 71 exp. 6, fol. 228r–v.

91. PNE IV pp. 13, 32, VI pp. 3, 15, 20, 23, 265; AGN *Criminal* 17 exp. 8 fol. 18or. See Keen, passim, for extensive treatment of this subject.

92. AGI *Mexico* 333, informe del Dr. Francisco Castellanos, July 7, 1692.

93. PNE IV pp. 13, 32, VI pp. 3, 20. There are outstanding exceptions to this general Spanish view of Indians and alcohol. Juan de Palafox, Bishop of Puebla, 1640–1655, emphasized Indian virtues and downplayed their vice of drunkenness in a pastoral letter to his parish priests: "It is true and I do confess that these unfortunates get drunk and lose their senses with drinks from their native plants. . . . On the other hand, not all Indians have this vice, and few [get drunk] with great frequency; and women rarely, and many not at all. And while this is an ugly vice, they have many agreeable and good habits. If we should see a Spaniard living like an Indian who does not get drunk—and there are many of them—we would take him for a saint" *Tratados Mejicanos*, I, 80–81.

94. AGN *Inquisición* 946 exp. 14 fols. 159–62, 818 exp. 41 fols. 528r, 531r; Medina; González, "Acerca del pulque" (Condumex).

95. AGN *Civil* 2126 fol. 2r.

96. BNM 1358 fol. 120; "Relacion de Tequisquiac," III, 293.

97. AGN *Inquisición* 1170, fols. 139–43.

98. AGN *Criminal* 17 exp. 8, fol. 18or.

99. Askinasy, p. 73; Rafael Ramírez, pp. 197–99.

100. CDCh *Oaxaca*, roll 1, February 5, 1571.

101. CDCh *Oaxaca*, roll 3.

102. AGN *Indios* 10 exp. 111; Gibson, *Aztecs*, p. 318.

103. AGN *Indios* 30 exp. 193. See note 44.

104. BNM 1361, 1775 informe.

105. AGN *Pulques* 2 fol. 133; *Policía* 32 fols. 187–89 (example of Culhuacán, 1800).

106. AGN *Criminal* 127 exp. 4, 25 exp. 1.

107. This is especially true in central Mexico, AGN *Indios* 10 exp. 137, 11 exp. 170, 13 exp. 329, 19 exp. 297, 21 exp. 52, 23 exp. 314, 24 exp. 117; *Criminal* 50 exp. 11, 27 exp. 9, 138 exp. 13, 730 numbered expedientes concerning the jurisdiction of Cuauhtitlán.

108. AGN *Pulques* 1 fols. 197–201.

109. AEO *Juzgados* bundle for 1806 (1806 adjustment of rates), 1808 (April 1, 1808, report of Mariano Castillejos); CCG "Instrucción para los visitadores."

110. There are a few clear examples of peasant villages buying regularly from pulque ranchos, but these are exceptional cases: AGN *Criminal* 124 exp. 5; *Intendentes* 22 fol. 199r; AEO *Juzgados* bundle for 1806 (Zaachila).

111. AGN *Pulques* 1, fol. 6v.

112. AGN *Pulques* 3 fols. 193–5, 4 fol. 339; *Intendentes* 22 fol. 69r–v (Huajuapan, 1794).

113. AGN *Criminal* 193 fol. 356.

114. AGN *Pulques* 2 fols. 165–72.

TABLE FOR NOTE 120. *"Taverns" in Valley of Oaxaca Villages, 1725–1726*

Community	Number of tributaries	Number of pulquerías	Community	Number of tributaries	Number of pulquerías
Xalatlaco	—	25	Santa Cruz	36	7
Guajolotitlán	140	8	San Juan	12	3
San Francisco	128	8	San Mateo	89	11
Santiago	150	2	San Miguel	53	8
Cuilapan	—	29	San Bernardo	18	8
Zaachila	320[a]	31	Asunción	15	3
Santísima Trinidad	65[a]	8	Santa Catalina	4	2
San Martín Tilcajete	271[a]	42	Santiago	37	3
Santa Catalina Quiane	65[a]	20	Santa Inés	24	7
Santo Tomás Jalieza	24[a]	11	La Magdalena	36	12
San Pedro Guegorexe	12[a]	4	Teitipac		
San Cristóbal	6[a]	3	San Juan	114	13
Santa Catarina Minas	28[a]	3	San Lucas	83	6
Ocotlán	80	19	San Bartolomé	32	3
San Antonino	180	26	San Marcos	66	7
San Jacinto	70	6	Magdalena	43	3
San Lucas	43	8	Santa Cecilia	17	2
Santiago	160	20	Santo Domingo	16	2
Asunción	120	20	San Sebastián	95	14
San Pedro Apóstol	160	16	Santa Cruz Papalutla	42	4
San Pedro Mártir	80	11	Guelacé	40	3
San Dionicio	20	3			
Santa Lucía	60	8			
Magdalena	75	13			
San Martín	28	3			

[a]Original figures for these towns are given in total population rather than tributaries: Zaachila, 1,602; Santísima Trinidad, 326; San Martín Tilcajete, 800 over the age of 12; Santa Catalina Quiane, 120; Santo Tomás Jalieza, 120; San Pedro Guegorexe, 60; San Cristóbal, 32; Santa Catarina Minas, 140.

115. AGN *Criminal* 39 exp. 26 (1714, San Salvador Ocotepec, jurisdiction of Cuernavaca), 98 exp. 6 (1800, Santa María Tecajete, jurisdiction of Cempoala), 140 exp. 5 (1804, Zumpahuacán), 730 (June 9, 1781, San Pedro Escapusaltongo), 730 (May 21, 1725, Barrio San José, jurisdiction of Cuauhtitlán); *Indios* 13 exp. 282 (1641, Quechula, jurisdiction of Tepeaca), 30 exp. 73 (1686, Otumba); CDCh *Oaxaca*, roll 9, exp. 510 (1684, Xinastla); CCG visita de Nochistlán (1803, Huautlilla).

116. AGN *Criminal* 98 exp. 6.

117. CDCh *Oaxaca*, roll 5, exp. 180.

118. CDCh *Oaxaca*, roll 9, exp. 528 (1688, San Pedro Añañe); AGN *Civil* 2291 exp. 11 (1724, Xochimilco). This would explain the statement in a 1778 report on pulque in the jurisdiction of Teposcolula that the drink was given, not sold, AGN *Pulques* 3, fols. 193–95.

119. AGN *Civil* 2291 exp. 11.

120. AGI *Audiencia de Mexico* 877 (1725–1726 reports commissioned by the bishop of Oaxaca) (see table).

121. AEO *Juzgados* bundle for 1808, Castillejos report, fol. 3v.

122. AGN *Criminal* 117 exp. 11.

123. AGN *Criminal* 177 exp. 12, 190 fols. 308–; *Indios* 3 exp. 79, 7 fol. 99r, 9 exp. 108; *Policía* 32 fols. 173–83.

124. AGN *Indios* 29 exp. 201, 30 exps. 193, 272, 281, 305.

125. AGN *Civil* 1599 exp. 13 (1714 license); *Ordenanzas* 9, fols. 445v–446v (1720 license); *Reales Cédulas* 44 exp. 65 (February 17, 1724).

126. AGN *Criminal* 49 exp. 30, fol. 551r.

127. AGN *Pulques* 4 fol. 4r. The contents are described in AGN *Criminal* 120 exp. 7. The following places consumed tepache according to a 1784 report on drink areas, AGN *Aguardiente de Caña* 1: Acayucan, Atrixco, Chiautla, Bolaños, Chilapa, Córdoba, Cosamaluapan, Guadalajara, Guadalcázar, Guadalupe, Guanajuato, Guauhchinango, San Juan de los Llanos, Malinalco, Mexicalcingo, Nejapa, Oaxaca, Pátzcuaro, Puebla, Cuauhtla, Salamanca, Tacuba, Taxco, Teposcolula, Teutila, Teotitlán del Camino, Texcoco, Tlalpujahua, Tulancingo, Tuxtla, Xalapa, Xicayán, Yzúcar, Zacatecas, Zacatlán, and San Miguel el Grande.

128. Many arrests are recorded in AGN *Criminal*; for example, vol. 138 exp. 17 (1647).

129. AGN *Criminal* 127 exp. 4 (Tecozautla, 1799).

130. BNM 1361 fols. 96–97.

131. Records of the legalization appear in AGN *Aguardiente de Caña* vols. 1–13 and BNM 1358, 1359.

132. AGN *Aguardiente de Caña* 12 fol. 144r, 13 unnumbered expediente: "Sobre creación de dos plazas de guarda en Cuernavaca para resguardo de este ramo."

133. AGN *Criminal* 129 exp. 6; *Aguardiente de Caña* 1 exp. 2, 2 exp. 1, 10 exp. 1, 12 exp. 1; BNM 1358 fol. 29v, 1361 fol. 10v.

134. AGN *Aguardiente de Caña* 7 (January 16, 1807).

135. AGN *Historia* 75 exp. 5.

136. AGN *Civil* 1741 exp. 2; *Pulques* 2 fol. 88r; *Criminal* 140 exp. 4, 103 exp. 2, 50 exp. 3; *Indios* 32 fol. 48v.

137. AGN *Pulques* 9 (production tables); *Criminal* 71 exp. 6; UT Mexican

MS WBS-537 (1773, Xaltocan); CDCh *Oaxaca*, roll 5 exp. 186, roll 14 exp. 238.

138. AGN *Criminal* 140 exps. 4 & 5, 180 fols. 476–; *Inquisición* 1170 fols. 139–43; *Pulques* 3 fols. 193–95; CDCh *Oaxaca*, roll 8 exp. 484.

139. Carrasco, *Otomíes*, p. 55.

140. AGN *Indios* 32 fol. 48v.

141. Van Zantwijk, p. 40; García Alcaraz, pp. 460–74; William and Claudia Madsen, pp. 701–18.

142. AGN *Indios* 3 exp. 260, 30 exp. 262; *Intendentes* 22 fol. 199r; AGI *Audiencia de Mexico* 333, testimony of Manuel Gómez Beltrán; BNMa 2449–2450, relación de San Martín Tilcajete.

143. AGN *Criminal* 127 exp. 4 (Tecozautla, 1799), 193 exp. 3 (1738, Cuauhtitlán); *Pulques* 3 fol. 82.

144. AGN *Criminal* 103 exp. 2 (for headaches), 120 exp. 7 (for stomach aches); *Impresos Oficiales* 48 (*Mercurio Volante*, December 30, 1772, for diarrhea); *Inquisición* 1170 fols. 139–43; Emmart, pp. 312, 316, 317, 319 (diuretic, to prevent lice, to promote lactation, to dry up menstrual flow); PNE VI p. 3 (purgative), 172 (for wounds), 300, 310 (good for any illness); BNM 1358 fols. 36v, 42r (diarrhea); Ruiz de Alarcón, p. 175 (for pain).

145. Ponce, p. 374.

146. Emmart, pp. 312, 316, 317, 319.

147. AGN *Criminal* 129 exp. 5, 170 fols. 134–.

148. AGN *Criminal* 49 exp. 2, 120 exp. 25, 203 exp. 4, 166 fols. 185–, 200 exp. 4, 202 exp. 1, 306 exp. 5.

149. AGN *Criminal* 120 exp. 25, fols. 271r, 352r.

150. Burgoa, II, 61; AGI *Audiencia de Mexico* 333, informe de Fr. Francisco Sánchez, July 26, 1692.

151. AGN *Civil* 2114 exp. 8; *Criminal* 29 exp. 2, 41 exp. 1, 49 exp. 30. A report on pulque published in the *Mercurio Volante*, December 23, 1772, suggests that the rays of light around the Virgin in the famous painting of the Virgin of Guadalupe are maguey spines, AGN *Impresos Oficiales* 48.

152. Ponce, pp. 375–78; AGN *Criminal* 111 exp. 3.

153. AGN *Criminal* 120 exp. 25, fols. 28off; Ramírez Tovar, pp. 35–49, describes Easter celebrations in the 1920's where dancers went from house to house receiving pulque from the villagers.

154. AGN *Criminal* 129 exp. 4.

155. See citations in note 115 and AGN *Criminal* 39 exp. 26, 140 exp. 5, 148 fols. 263–; *Indios* 30 exp. 258.

156. Carvalho Franco (pp. 37–38) goes so far as to see such drunken fiestas in nineteenth-century Brazil as the cause of antagonism as well as the occasion for it.

157. AGN *Criminal* 15 exp. 18.

158. This point has been made in a different context by MacAndrew and Edgerton, p. 88.

159. AGN *Criminal* 140 exp. 4 (1626, jurisdiction of Malinalco).

160. AGN *Criminal* 140 exp. 5, 180 fols. 476–; *Indios* 30 exp. 262; CDCh *Oaxaca*, roll 12, exp. 158.

161. AGN *Criminal* 113 exp. 1, 155 fols. 247–; CDCh *Oaxaca* roll 5, exp. 158, 186; roll 6, exp. 202.

Snatches of information from colonial trials suggest that social drinking of this sort was associated with polite formality in speech and posture much as it is described in recent field studies in southern Mexico. Gossen provides a detailed description of such drinking rituals for Chamula in the highlands of Chiapas (pp. 172–74): "This kind of speech is commonly called . . . 'nice talk,' for it pleases men and deities alike. Like most other forms of language for rendering holy, it is fixed in style, syntax, and rhythm, but allows for slight variations in setting by means of 'open slots' in the rote sequences. . . . An example comes from part of a drinking ceremony after a baptism, when the parents, the child, and the godparents have just left the church, where the child was baptized by the priest. . . . The drinking ceremony itself uses a separate set of formulas, which are related to the words of ritual gratitude, thanks, presentation, and petition. The drinking ceremony occurs in nearly all of the countless public and private ritual settings in Chamula. Symbolically, the drinking ritual achieves at least four objectives. It emphasizes the principle of equality, for each participant receives an equal amount. It emphasizes the principle of rank, for equal portions are served according to rank order, with high-prestige cargo positions, age, and masculinity generally taking precedence over low-prestige cargo positions, youth, and femininity, although there are many exceptions. It literally produces and also symbolizes the heat that is considered desirable for human interaction with deities and with each other. Finally, it symbolizes solidarity among the participants, for the liquor has been given and received by members of a group that has a common objective or common interest."

162. AGN *Criminal* 3 exp. 10, 26 exp. 25.

163. For example, AGN *Criminal* 159 fols. 163–, 176 fols. 266–; CDCh *Oaxaca*, roll 11, exp. 575.

164. CDCh *Oaxaca*, roll 11, exp. 575.

165. Especially AGN *Criminal* 176 fols. 266–.

166. AGN *Criminal* 176, fols. 224–.

167. AGN *Criminal* 39 exp. 18 (1818 *acequia* worker, Cuernavaca).

168. AGN *Criminal* 17 exp. 9, 41 exp. 33, 54 exp. 1, 67 exp. 6, 120 exp. 17, 148 fols. 263–, 154 fols. 536–, 111 exps. 3 & 10, 207 exp. 1; AEO *Juzgados* bundle for 1767; CDCh *Oaxaca*, roll 14 exp. 259; AGI *Audiencia de México* 2588, February 19, 1784, report by the bishop of Oaxaca on corporal punishment of Indians, fol. 14v: "So that even the Indian who is good and the few, the extremely few, who abstain from liquor take up drinking when they become community officials. To ruin an Indian, make him an alcalde"; 877 (report by the parish priest of Cuilapan).

169. AGN *Criminal* 198 exp. 2, 171 fol. 16r, 186 fol. 297, 179 exp. 1.

170. AGN *Criminal* 103 exp. 2, 137 exp. 6, 139 exp. 17, 155 fols. 148–51, 168 fols. 1–13, 170 fols. 90–108, 200 exp. 1, 111 exp. 10, 123 exp. 13.

171. AGN *Criminal* 15 exp. 22, 173 fols. 196–302, 633 exp. 1, 103 exp. 13, 129 exp. 6, 180 fols. 476–541.

172. CDCh *Oaxaca*, roll 2, 1598, Tiltepec, 1600, San Francisco, sujeto de Yolotepec, 1601, Yanhuitlán, 1602, Teposcolula; roll 3, 1605, Santa María Gatlasclauaca; roll 4, exp. 108; roll 5, exp. 186; roll 6, exp. 199; roll 8, exps. 299, 302; roll 10, exps. 553, 556; roll 14 exp. 210.

173. AGN *Criminal* 187 fols. 276–288; *Recopilación* 6-1-37.

174. AGN *Criminal* 171 fols. 429–46, 183 fol. 373.

175. AGN *Criminal* 159 fols. 163–80.

176. AGN *Criminal* 2 exp. 2, 17 exp. 8, 129 exp. 6, 132 exp. 15, 148 fols. 366–70, 159 fols. 163–80, 170 fols. 246–83, 201 fols. 179–88, 306 exp. 1. The anthropologist Henri Favre has noted this same pattern of drinking and violence among the modern Chamulas of Chiapas: "Generally the assassin drinks after having resolved to kill, in order 'to take courage,'" "Notas," p. 318.

177. AGN *Criminal* 111 exp. 10, 123 exp. 13, 139 exp. 17, 155 fols. 148–51.

178. CDCh *Oaxaca*, roll 2, November 7, 1598; roll 5, exp. 186.

179. AGN *Criminal* 186 fols. 201–, 119 exp. 11; CDCh *Oaxaca*, roll 11, exp. 575. A modern example is described in detail in Selby, *Zapotec Deviance*, pp. 26–27. Drunken violence was also connected to a feeling of defenselessness, AEO *Juzgados*, bundle for 1805.

180. This point is developed in Cavan, *Liquor License*.

181. Stross, pp. 58–89, discusses the association of the tavern with machismo in modern Jalisco, a connection that may also have made colonial taverns violent places.

182. AGN *Criminal* 41 exp. 7, 95 exp. 6, 108 exps. 5, 7, 11, 14, 110 exp. 8, 111 exp. 12, 117 exp. 11, 119 exp: 11, 125 exp. 2A, 126 exp. 2, 128 exp. 4, 129 exp. 5, 130 exps. 1, 6, 150 fols. 68–, 170 fols. 109–, 202–, 246–, 172 fols. 345–, 198 exp. 3, 201 fols. 179–.

183. See note 168.

184. In Scardaville, "Urban Poor and Public Disorder."

185. AGN *Criminal* 306 exp. 1A, fol. 12r.

186. Taylor, p. 83.

187. AGN *Historia* 437 exp. 6 (1794); AGI *Audiencia de Mexico* 877, April 16, 1726, letter from the parish priest of Jalatlaco.

188. Medina, "Tratado."

189. AGN *Criminal* 29 exp. 6.

190. AGN *Inquisición* 718 exp. 18.

191. AGN *Policía* 15 exp. 1 (1794).

192. "Informe sobre pulquerías y tabernas, el año de 1784," *Boletín del Archivo General de la Nación* XVIII: 2 (1947), 208, 211; AGN *Civil* 2126 exp. 1, fol. 45v; BNM 1359 fol. 7r.

193. The recent literature on the relationship of drinking to other aspects of social life in Latin America is admirably summarized in Dwight B. Heath, "Perspectivas socioculturales del alcohol," and "Anthropological Approaches to Alcohol."

194. Fenna et al., pp. 472–75.

195. MacAndrew and Edgerton, pp. 165–71.

196. Madsen and Madsen, pp. 701–18.

197. Ronald Spores has found alcohol used as a "levelling mechanism" to reduce social differences and social distance in Yucuita, Mixteca Alta (personal communication).

198. See Cinquemani for a recent discussion of drinking patterns and their relationship to violence in three modern Mexican villages (Mixtec Indians of Justlahuaca, Oaxaca; Nahuatl-speaking Tecospans near Mexico City; and mestizo villagers of El Cerrito, Guerrero). In agreement with MacAndrew and Edgerton, she concludes that "the forms of violent and non-violent behavior exhibited while drinking are highly structured by cultural expectations and

cultural context" (p. 4). Violence does not occur in any of these communities during ritual, ceremonial, and a few types of secular gatherings where alcohol is consumed even in prodigious quantities.

199. Horton, pp. 199–320.

Chapter Three

1. Beattie, pp. 47–95, provides a valuable discussion of the limitations and biases of arrest records.

2. Edgerton, p. 170; Bohannon, *African Homicide*, p. 84; Romanucci-Ross, p. 132; Lester, pp. 466–68; Whyte, pp. 373–92; Taggart, "'Ideal' and 'Real' Behavior," pp. 347–57; Given, p. 213.

3. AGN *Criminal* 55, fol. 111–(1721), is an example of the colonial authorities punishing alcaldes indios who were lax in complying with the requirement of reporting homicides.

4. PNE VI pp. 95–6, 101, 107, 124, 129, 134, 139, 146, 188, 223, 277, IV pp. 18, 34, 167–68, 198; Guerra, p. 39; Carbajal, pp. 86–92; Clavijero, p. 218; Bandelier, pp. 625–26; *Epistolario* vol. 14, p. 146; DII, vol. 4, p. 541.

5. See especially Bohannon, *African Homicide*, passim.

6. Bloch and Geis, p. 255; Samaha, p. 21; Cinquemani, pp. 76, 79; Jane Collier, *Law and Social Change*, p. 55; Nader, "Zapotec Law Cases," p. 120; Quiroz et al., p. 111.

7. Dollar and Jensen, p. 14.

8. The legal costs were defrayed by the *medio real de ministros*, a tax levied on male tributaries, Florescano, p. 13.

9. Calderón Quijano et al., II, 348. Especially for lesser crimes, the Juzgado de Indios was in perpetual conflict with lieutenants of the alcaldes mayores who passed judgments and executed sentences without consulting the court. See, for example, AGN *Criminal* 184, fols. 45–.

10. Doughty, "Social Uses," p. 187; Romanucci-Ross, p. 138.

11. Modern variations in different societies are described in Landau and Drapkin, pp. 24–39.

12. In AGN *Criminal* 118 exp. 5, the offender specifically said, "It was because of the anger that rose up in me when he used those words."

13. AGN *Criminal* 140 exp. 4.

14. Paz distinguishes between the Spanish "hijo de puta" and the Mexican "hijo de la chingada," in *Labyrinth*, pp. 75–88.

15. CDCh *Oaxaca*, roll 5, exp. 36; roll 14, exp. 26.

16. Wolfgang and Ferracuti, p. 154.

17. *Ibid.*, pp. 258–59.

18. Favre, "Notas," pp. 305–22.

19. Wolfgang and Ferracuti, p. 260.

20. Landau and Drapkin, p. 40. I have not found comparable figures for other eighteenth-century societies. A ratio of 2.3:1 is suggested for thirteenth-century England by figures in Given, p. 48. Some anthropologists have explained these patterns of female victims over female assailants by suggesting that peasant women vent their aggressions through gossip and verbal abuse rather than violence: Romanucci-Schwartz, p. 153, and Edgerton, p. 164. Examples of colonial peasant women making malicious insults are found in AGN *Criminal* 27 exp. 8, and 49 exp. 5.

21. Wolfgang and Ferracuti, p. 267.

22. Steinmetz and Straus, p. v; Parsons, p. 484, notes that the village *presidente* usually handles such cases informally.

23. CDCh *Oaxaca*, roll 14, exp. 211.

24. AGN *Criminal* 50 exp. 26.

25. Similar tensions within the peasant household have been noted for modern African communities by Bohannon, *African Homicide*, p. 241, and Gluckman, p. 73.

26. Patrilocal and neolocal residence patterns have been described for sixteenth-century Tepoztlán (Morelos) by Carrasco, "Family Structure," pp. 185–210.

27. CDCh *Oaxaca*, roll 13, exp. 178.

28. AGN *Criminal* 61 exp. 17.

29. Jane Collier, *Law and Social Change*, p. 44.

30. AGN *Criminal* 145 fol. 493, 148 fols. 94–105, 175 exp. 4.

31. AGN *Criminal* 129 exp. 6 fols. 408–409.

32. CDCh *Oaxaca*, roll 5, exp. 179; roll 8, exp. 311; roll 9, exp. 513.

33. CDCh *Oaxaca*, roll 12, exp. 153.

34. CDCh *Oaxaca*, roll 2, 1600, San Francisco, sujeto of Yolotepec; roll 4, exp. 136bis; roll 5, exps. 180, 188; roll 6, exps. 199, 218; roll 11, exp. 575.

35. AGN *Criminal* 25 exp. 19, 41 exp. 3, 111 exp. 10, 118 exp. 5, 119 exp. 8, 123 exps. 8, 25, 125 exp. 2, 131 exp. 33, 203 fol. 366. A state of extreme anger (*cólera, rabia*) is frequently alleged by the central Mexico husband-offenders.

36. CDCh *Oaxaca*, roll 2, 1598, Tiltepec; 1600, San Francisco, sujeto of Yolotepec; 1601, Yanhuitlán; 1602, Teposcolula; roll 3, 1605, Santa María Gatlasclauaca; roll 4, exp. 108; roll 5, exp. 186; roll 6, exp. 199; roll 8, exps. 299, 302; roll 10, exps. 533, 556; roll 14, exp. 210.

37. AGN *Criminal* 213 fols. 93bis–112.

38. AGN *Criminal* 137 exp. 17. Other examples appear in AGN *Criminal* 111 exp. 10, 123 exp. 13, 155 fols. 148–.

39. AGN *Criminal* 111 exp. 10, 123 exp. 13, 139 exp. 17, and 155 fols. 148–51.

40. CDCh *Oaxaca*, roll 10, exp. 565; roll 9, exp. 513; roll 8, exp. 311; roll 5, exp. 179; AGN *Criminal* 98 exp. 16, 110 exp. 4, 113 exp. 22, 122 exp. 5, 127 exp. 2, 139 exp. 17.

41. Central Mexico sentences: 1600–1650 (5), 1710–1789 (14), 1790–1809 (89), 1810–1819 (30); Mixteca Alta sentences: 1600–1650 (17), 1680–1739 (5), 1740–1780 (13), 1781–1809 (15).

42. AGN *Criminal* 95 exp. 1, 166 fols. 185–, 215 exp. 1; Bancroft Library, University of California, Berkeley, Mexican MS 1722 doc. 87.

43. Muro Orejón, p. 443.

44. AGN *Criminal* 72 exp. 11.

45. CDCh *Oaxaca*, roll 3.

46. AGN *Criminal* 121 exp. 7, 61 exp. 3, 56 exp. 4, Bancroft Library Mexican MS 1722 doc. 87. The Mixteca Alta records for the seventeenth century contain numerous examples of whippings.

47. For example, AGN *Criminal* 95 exp. 1.

48. UT Mexican MS JGI-970.

49. Perkins, pp. 397–409.

50. For example, AGN *Criminal* 56 exp. 4. The rare use of capital punishment was decried by the bishop of Oaxaca in 1809, AGN *Intendentes* 12 exp. 1, fol. 6v.

51. Perkins, pp. 410–12.

52. AGN *Criminal* 95 exp. 1, November 1793.

53. *Epistolario*, 5, pp. 86–89.   54. *Siete Partidas* 7-8-9.

55. *Recopilación* 7-7-14.   56. *Recopilación* 7-8-12.

57. AGN *Criminal* 179 fols. 266–, 224 fol. 371; CDCh *Oaxaca*, roll 14, exps. 216, 216A.

58. AGN *Criminal* 224 fols. 369–75.

59. Presidio sentences: AGN *Criminal* 145 fol. 78r, 170 exp. 1, 170 fols. 202–, 170 fols. 246–, 113 exp. 18, 122 exp. 3, 123 exp. 8, 125 exps. 2 and 4, 126 exps. 2 and 4, 127 exp. 2, 190 fols. 365–, 198 exp. 2, 201 fols. 179–, 25 exp. 1, 95 exp. 5, 108 exps. 2 and 5, 113 exp. 22, 203 fols. 325–, 366–, 404–, 61 exp. 3, 63 exps. 4 and 7, 280 exp. 9, 50 exp. 26, 56 exp. 4, 280 exp. 8. Public works, obraje, and recogidas sentences: AGN *Criminal* 140 exp. 6, 152 fols. 173–, 170 fols. 134–, 176 fols. 266–, 188 fols. 328–, 114 exp. 2, 127 exp. 4, 64 exps. 2 and 10, 236 fols. 138–, 270 exp. 10, 280 exp. 8; *General de Parte* 21 exp. 49. Penal servitude in the Mexican textile industry has been examined by Kagan, "Penal Servitude in New Spain." The importance of convict labor to the maintenance of this major industry is clear.

60. Provision for such pardons was made in the *Siete Partidas* 7-32-1.

61. AGN *Criminal* 2 exp. 2 (1787).

62. There are documented cases of indultos applied for and denied: AGN *Criminal* 26 exp. 1, 68 exp. 7.

63. Drapkin, p. 317: "As elsewhere in Europe during the Middle Ages, deprivation of liberty as a means of punishment was practically unknown in Spain. There existed a number of cárceles where those suspected or accused were held until they were brought before the judge."

64. AGN *Criminal* 95 exp. 4.

65. Calderón Quijano, IV, 78–79.

66. *Siete Partidas* 7-31-4.

67. *Siete Partidas* 7-8-3: A man who finds his daughter, sister, or wife being molested by another man; a man who encounters an armed robber in his house and kills him while trying to apprehend him; a nobleman protecting his lord; a person who kills an arsonist trying to burn his house or fields; if the offender is a known robber; if the offender is a demented person or a child under ten and one-half years old; 7-8-4: accidental homicide (example of a man cutting down a tree which falls on a passerby); 7-8-5: negligent accident (example of a sleepwalker, who knows he is capable of violence, leaving a knife handy at bedtime).

68. *Recopilación* 6-10-21.

69. AGN *Criminal* 215 exp. 1.

70. Cases in which the excepción de ebriedad was not accepted by the court: CDCh *Oaxaca*, roll 5, exps. 20, 25; roll 14, exps. 32, 38; AGN *Criminal* 129 exp. 6, 17 exp. 8, 170 fols. 246–, 127 exp. 2, 132 exp. 15.

71. For example, AGN *Criminal* 63 exp. 4, 203 fols. 325–, 270 exp. 10, 180 fols. 137–, 137 exp. 6, 64 exp. 10, 128 exp. 4, 171 fols. 429–, 170 fols. 246–, 152 fols. 173–, 15 exp. 22.

72. Given, p. 105.

73. Hay, pp. 17–18.
74. Erikson, *Wayward Puritans*, p. 189.
75. This point is made implicitly in many studies of Mexican villages. See especially Foster, "The Dyadic Contract," pp. 1173–92, and Kearney, *The Winds of Ixtepeji*, pp. 76–77.
76. Whyte, pp. 373–92. Redfield argues that family strife is the best index of social disorganization in rural Yucatán (pp. 186–88). Taggart has challenged this point, asserting that family problems in Mexican peasant villages are a chronic condition rather than an indication of accelerating social disorganization ("'Ideal' and 'Real,'" pp. 347–57). The findings of Romanucci-Ross for a village in Morelos agree with Taggart's hypothesis (p. 146). There is considerable debate among social scientists over the relationships between homicide and social breakdown. Henry and Short view rising homicide rates as direct evidence of social breakdown. Lester claims there is no clear association between actual homicide rates and socialization. In several cases drawn from African evidence, it appears that the breakdown of institutions in villages is associated with fewer homicides, Bohannon, *African Homicide*, pp. 84, 264–65.
77. O'Nell and Selby, p. 99. O'Nell and Selby also describe differing village norms for aggression by men and women: "Young boys are permitted even encouraged to manifest aggressive behavior, whereas girls rarely exhibit aggressive tendencies and run the risk of punishment if they do exhibit them. This is particularly evident in teasing behavior and the maltreatment of small animals. . . . A woman is expected to control herself—woman's loss of composure is associated with temporary possession of mal de ojo" (pp. 98–99).
78. Rogers, passim; Harris, p. 85.
79. Bohannon, *African Homicide*, p. 161.
80. Nieburg, p. 83. Machismo is not always an inevitable effect or cause of weakening community ties. It can stem from other situations as well, such as the frustration of adult men in a matrilocal setting, Brueske, "The Petapa Zapotecs."

Chapter Four

1. Charles Tilly, "Changing Place of Collective Violence," p. 140; Huizer, "'Resistance to Change' and Radical Peasant Mobilization," pp. 303–13, and *Revolutionary Potential*; Huizer and Stavenhagen, pp. 378–409; Hobsbawm, "Peasant Land Occupations," pp. 120–52; Reed, *The Caste War*; Rowe, pp. 17–47.
2. Favre, *Changement et continuité*, pp. 269ff.
3. AGN *Criminal* 123 exp. 21, 180 fols. 361–430, 430–475, 155 fol. 111–, 169 fols. 103–43, 210 fols. 189–, 229 fols. 263–, 232 exp. 2, 284 exp. 5, 304 fols. 1–4; *Civil* 865 exp. 9; Calderón Quijano, I, 306–308.
4. Calderón Quijano, I, 306–308; AGI *Audiencia de Mexico* 1934 (Papantla 1767); AGN *Criminal* 54 exp. 14, 57 exp. 1, 75 exps. 3–4, 90 (November 1773), 104 fol. 452r, 117 exp. 7, 123 exp. 21, 180 fols 361–430 and 430–75, 203 exp. 4, 155 fols. 111–; *Civil* 241 exp. 1, 1599 exp. 9, 865 exp. 9, 2292 exp. 10, 1505 exp. 7.
5. AGN *Criminal* 283 exp. 3.
6. See Wasserstrom, p. 134, for a critique of the view that the Tzeltal Revolt of 1712 was led by members of the Indian cabildo.

7. AGN *Inquisición* 746 exp. 18 fols. 337–56.

8. Wasserstrom, pp. 69, 75.

9. Davis makes this distinction pp. 169–70.

10. AEO *Juzgados* bundle for 1612–83: "Como los indios se crían en el campo, verse enjaulados lo tienen por mayor pena que la muerte."

11. Manzano, I, 13 (Ixmiquilpan, 1677); AGN *Criminal* 243 exp. 1, 92 exp. 5, 218 fols. 1–19, 229 exp. 231, 107 exp. 1, 307 exp. 2, 202 exp. 1, 151 exp. 1, 306 exps. 1 and 6, 308 (August 31, 1769), 507 exp. 17; *Civil* 241 exp. 1, 865 exps. 8 and 9; AGI *Audiencia de México* 2588 report of Dr. Joseph Ruiz, fol. 4v; CDCh *Oaxaca*, roll 6, exp. 209; roll 8, exp. 286; roll 9, exp. 529; roll 15, exp. 430.

12. AGN *Criminal* 304 exp. 1 fols. 1–4.

13. AGN *Criminal* 79 exp. 1 fol. 6r.

14. AGN *Criminal* 57 exp. 1, 232 exp. 2, 243 exp. 1.

15. AGN *Criminal* 55 fols. 122–, 79 exp. 1 fol. 62v, 304 exp. 1; Calderón Quijano, II, 163–75; AEO *Juzgados* bundle for 1806.

16. AGN *Criminal* 304 fol. 366r.

17. AGN *Criminal* 283 exp. 1, 218 fols. 1–19, 54 exp. 14, 230 exp. 15, 203 exp. 4, 166 fols. 185–272, 75 exp. 3, 202 exp. 1, 241 exp. 1, 162 fols. 187–306 exp. 5; *Indios* 54 exp. 85, 70 exp. 69; *Tierras* 381 exp. 5.

18. AGN *Criminal* 306 exp. 6; *Historia* 335 exp. 1.

19. Report on the parish of Tlacochahuaya submitted by Lic. Juan José de Echarri, April 29, 1803, typescript in the possession of Lic. Luis Castañeda Guzmán, Oaxaca, Oaxaca.

20. Priestley, pp. 213–20; AGN *Criminal* 306 exp. 6.

21. AGN *Criminal* 138 exp. 2; Contreras R., p. 32.

22. AGN *Criminal* 306 exp. 5.

23. AGN *Criminal* 79 exp. 8 (March 6, 1777).

24. AGN *Criminal* 79 exp. 1 fol. 6r.

25. AGN *Criminal* 308.

26. AGN *Civil* 241.

27. AGN *Criminal* 123 exp. 21.

28. AGN *Criminal* 54 exp. 14, 241 exp. 1.

29. Smelser, *Collective Behavior*.

30. Florescano, p. 161. Davis, p. 169, and Charles Tilly, "Major Forms of Collective Action," p. 372, note a similar lack of relationship between famine and revolts. On the other hand, the Tzeltal Revolt of 1712 coincided with a long drought, UT Mexican MS G-19, fol. 191r.

31. For example, Bricker, "Les Insurrections."

32. Davis, pp. 176–78.

33. Huizer and Stavenhagen, p. 403; Casarrubias, p. vii.

34. Buve, "Movimientos campesinos," pp. 423–47.

35. Huizer and Stavenhagen, p. 403, make this point, but also emphasize elite intransigence and a "culture of repression" rather than an elite losing vitality.

36. In contrast to these findings, many works stress monopolistic landlords as the structural underpinning of peasant revolts, for example, Buve, "Movimientos campesinos," Huizer, "Resistance to Change," p. 311.

37. Simmel, passim; the main points of this approach are neatly summarized in Grimshaw, pp. 36–46.

38. Mousnier, p. 306; Moore, pp. 256–57, 380; Le Roy Ladurie, pp. 265, 269; C. S. L. Davies, p. 53, explains fewer peasant uprisings in England than in France on the basis of lower taxes.

39. AGN *Criminal* 210 fols. 189–205.

40. For example, AGN *Criminal* 166 fols. 354bis–.

41. For example, Calderón Quijano, II, 163–75.

42. AGN *Criminal* 166 fols. 320–, 54 exp. 14, 55 fols. 122–, 181 fols. 201–, 163 fols. 295–; *Civil* 865 exp. 8; *Historia* 334 exp. 5; *Indios* 70 exp. 69; CDCh *Oaxaca*, roll 10, exp. 551.

43. AGN *Hospital de Jesús* 307 exp. 4 fol. 5r.

44. AGN *Tierras* 381 exp. 5 fol. 1r–v.

45. AGN *Epidemias* 15 exps. 2, 8, 9, 10 exps. 1, 3, 4, 12 exp. 6.

46. AGN *Tierras* 148 exp. 3, 2384 exp. 1.

47. AGN *Indios* 3 exp. 241; *Criminal* 92 exp. 5; CDCh *Oaxaca*, roll. 21 legajo 2.

48. AGN *Criminal* 180 fols. 361–430.

49. AGN *Criminal* 104 fols. 380–, 123 exp. 21, 180 fols. 430–75, 202 exp. 1, 157 fols. 93–, 507 exp. 17, 55 fols. 122–, 92 exp. 5, 210 fols. 189–, 226 fols. 401–, 229 fols. 263–, 283 exp. 3, 284 exp. 5; *Civil* 241 exp. 1, 2166 exp. 6.

50. For example, AGN *Criminal* 284 exp. 5.

51. AGN *Civil* 241 exp. 1; Manzano, I, 13. The 1642 Ixmiquilpan rebellion was surprisingly early and centered in an area of Indian villages. The potential for insurrection there was evident again in 1677 and was momentarily realized in a millenarian movement more than one hundred years later.

52. AGI *Audiencia de Mexico* 2588, report by Dr. Joseph Ruiz, fol. 4v; Bancroft Library Mexican MS 435 p. 21; UT Mexican MS G-205; AGN *Criminal* 54 exp. 14, 283 exp. 3, 75 exps. 3–4, 306 exp. 5.

53. For example, Guridi y Alcocer, pp. 72–73.

54. AEO *Juzgados* bundle for 1807, January 7, 1744, Santiago Amatepec, jurisdiction of Villa Alta, complaint against Br. Santiago Mariano Villanueva.

55. AGN *Hospital de Jesús* 307 exp. 4; *Criminal* 180 fols. 361–; *Tierras* 318 exp. 5.

56. AGN *Criminal* 306 exp. 5A, 151 fols. 140–, 210 fols. 189–.

57. Banfield, pp. 83, 85–100; also Perrot, p. 170.

58. Foster, "Dyadic Contract," pp. 1173–92.

59. Favre, "A propos du potentiel insurrectionnel."

60. Mousnier, pp. 323, 327; Contreras, p. 15.

61. This interpretation gained popularity in the 1960's, especially in the work of Franz Fanon, *The Revolutionary Peasant* (see Coser, *Continuities*, pp. 211–14).

62. Huizer, *Revolutionary Potential* and "Resistance to Change."

63. Moore, pp. 201–2, 208, 254, 379–82; also Gately et al., p. 78.

64. Moore, p. 208.

65. Meyer, *Problemas campesinos*, p. 75.

66. The extremely localized nature of rebellion in these two regions is particularly evident when it is compared to the character of peasant uprisings in southern France in the late-sixteenth and seventeenth centuries, many of which were true insurrections with far-reaching objectives. Le Roy Ladurie, pp. 192–202.

67. González Navarro, "Tenencia de la tierra," pp. 63–86.

68. Reed, *Caste War*; Meyer, *Problemas campesinos*, pp. 11–13, 62–66.

69. Meyer, *Problemas campesinos*, pp. 10–13.

70. Paz, *Other Mexico*, p. 60.

Conclusion

1. Wolf, "On Peasant Rebellions," p. 292.

2. Romanucci-Ross, p. 46. This emphasis on village identity for colonial peasants is different in degree from the view of modern Mexican peasants of George Foster (among others), who stresses the importance of the nuclear family and posits "relative absence of a sense of association in peasant villages," in Potter et al., pp. 155, 156, 159. It is less different than might appear from James Lockhart's work on the old *altepetl* (subprovincial) boundaries in colonial central Mexico, in Altman and Lockhart, p. 101. Lockhart does not question the importance of village identity, and the actual operation of altepetl groups with villages remains to be described in detail. Also, it must be evaluated in light of the abundant evidence of boundary and political strife between villages within the old altepetl jurisdictions in the colonial period, and the urge of subject villages to achieve cabecera status and thereby liberate themselves from traditional aggregations. On the other hand, violence seems to have been more intense between villages belonging to different subprovincial districts.

3. Scott, p. 5.

4. Cohn, p. 308.

5. Huizer, *Revolutionary Potential*, p. 12; Beals and Siegel, p. 17.

6. Demos, p. 563.

7. Given, p. 164.

8. Selby, *Zapotec Deviance*, p. 48.

9. Charles Tilly, "Town and Country," p. 283.

10. Braudel, pp. 158, 166, 177; Gibson, *Aztecs*, pp. 150, 347, 409; Góngora, p. 141; Phelan, *Hispanization of the Philippines*, p. 158. Góngora, in particular, sees the repetitive work in rural areas of colonial Spanish America punctuated only by "idleness, dissipation, and drunkenness."

11. See Chapter 2, notes 193–99.

12. Beals and Siegel, pp. 163–64; Huizer, *Revolutionary Potential*, p. 63.

13. Ozouf, p. 384.

14. Stoianovich, p. 164.

15. Some examples of political caciquismo are to be found in AGN *Criminal* 221 fols. 210–, 255 exp. 20, and 560 (unmarked expediente for Tetela, 1748). In the late colonial period, political caciques in villages began to carry pistols, a symbol of the threat of force.

16. La Faye, p. 92.

17. Roseberry, p. 45.

18. Charles Tilly, "Town and Country," p. 273.

19. Frank, p. 27; Florescano, pp. 188, 196; Gibson, *Spain in America*, p. 158.

20. Chaunu, *Histoire, science social*, pp. 188–93.

21. Borah, "Race and Class," p. 337.

22. Weismann, pp. 2, 23, 31, 61, 173, makes this point in a fascinating way.

23. Aguirre Beltrán, *Regiones de refugio*; Sánchez Albornoz, pp. 64–65.

24. Diamond, p. 51.

25. Gibson, *Aztecs*, pp. 134–35.

26. Moore, p. 213.

27. Moore, p. 219; Ardrey, p. 157. The importance of the land-tenure system to the mental world of Mexican villagers described here is affirmed by the contrasting case of southern Italy, presented by Banfield, pp. 37, 67, 153, 154. In the community he examined, lack of extended family ties, of peasant identification with the village, and of organized action in the face of pressing local problems is coupled with inadequate amounts of land divided into tiny holdings (rarely large enough to support more than a small nuclear family), going back at least two generations, and a general loathing of the land by the people who work it.

28. Unpublished manuscript on Mixtec codices by David Brown (seminar paper submitted to Professor Peter Bakewell, University of New Mexico, 1975). The Techialoyan codices, a large corpus of titles purporting to date from the early sixteenth century but apparently composed in the late seventeenth or early eighteenth century to meet pressing needs for written land titles in litigation, are described in Robertson, pp. 253–80.

29. Womack, pp. 42–43.

30. This possibility of intensified ritual behavior by communities responding to rapid change has been made in more sociological terms for the Naskapi Indians of Schefferville, Quebec, by Robbins, p. 99: "It is held that when economic change results in the introduction of new ways of access of persons to goods or activities that serve to maintain identities, there will be an increase in frequency of identity struggles, and a corresponding increase in those ritualized or formalized social interactions which serve as identity-resolving forums."

31. Coser, *Functions of Social Conflict*, p. 157.

32. Migdal, p. 186.

33. Favre, *Cambio y continuidad*, pp. 45, 46, 369, 370; Góngora, p. 151.

34. C., L., and R. Tilly, p. 284.

35. This colonial pattern has its modern parallel in the mill foreman who "believes that Mexico is moving forward, and . . . approves of general government policies . . . yet in every personal experience with politicians . . . has found them crooked or useless, [and] thus . . . believes in a government whose representatives he distrusts" Kahl, p. 116.

36. Stanley and Barbara Stein, p. 117. Waldemar R. Smith draws a similar conclusion from his study of the religious fiesta system in southern Mesoamerica, p. 11: "The fiesta system, as the basis of Indian social organization, was thus politically useful to Spanish society. It provided Indians with personal satisfactions, as well as being a source of religious belief and of harmless social competition. More important, it was an institution that produced leaders, interests, and organizations that were strictly local, turning Indian villages in on themselves rather than out toward one another."

BIBLIOGRAPHY

BIBLIOGRAPHY

Manuscript Sources

Archivo General de las Indias
  Audiencia de México
  Indiferente General
Archivo General de la Nación
  Acordada
  Aguardiente de Caña
  Alcabalas
  Alcaldes Mayores
  Archivo Histórico de Hacienda
  Bienes Nacionales
  Civil
  Clero Regular y Secular
  Criminal
  General de Parte
  Historia
  Hospital de Jesús
  Impresos Oficiales
  Indios
  Inquisición
  Intendentes e Intendencias
  Ordenanzas
  Policía
  Pulques
  Reales Cédulas
  Subdelegados

  Tierras
  Tributos
  Vínculos
Archivo del Estado de Oaxaca
  Juzgados
Archivo Municipal de Teposcolula
Archivo Municipal de Tlacolula
Bancroft Library, University of
  California, Berkeley
  Mexican Manuscripts
Biblioteca Genaro V. Vásquez,
  Oaxaca, Oaxaca
Biblioteca Nacional, Mexico City
Biblioteca Nacional, Madrid
Colección Luis Castañeda Guzmán,
  Oaxaca, Oaxaca
Condumex, Centro de Estudios de
  Historia de México, Mexico City
Museo Nacional de Antropología e
  Historia
Centro de Documentación del
  Museo Nacional, Chapultepec
  microfilm, Serie Oaxaca
University of Texas, Austin
  Latin American Collection

Printed Sources

Acosta, José de. *De procuranda indorum salute.* Madrid, 1952.

Adie, Robert F. "Cooperation, Cooptation, and Conflict in Mexican Peasant Organizations." *Inter-American Economic Affairs* 24 (1970): 3–25.

Aguilar, Apolonio L. "El cuapatli o madera del pulque," *El México Antiguo* 2 (1924): 14–19.

Aguirre Beltrán, Gonzalo. "Cultura y nutrición." *Estudios antropológicos publicados en homenaje al doctor Manuel Gamio,* pp. 227–49. Mexico, 1956.

————. *Medicina y magia: el proceso de aculturación en la estructura colonial*. Mexico, 1963.

————. *Regiones de refugio*. Mexico, 1967.

————. *El señorío de Cuauhtochco, luchas agrarias en México durante el virreinato*. Mexico, 1940.

Alegre, Francisco J. *Historia de la Compañía de Jesús en Nueva España*. 3 vols. Mexico, 1841.

Altman, Ida, and James Lockhart, eds. *Provinces of Early Mexico: Variants of Spanish American Regional Evolution*. Los Angeles, 1976.

Anderson, Arthur, Frances Berdan, and James Lockhart, eds. *Beyond the Codices: An Introduction to Colonial Nahuatl Documentation*. Berkeley and Los Angeles, 1976.

Anderson, R. K., J. Calvo, G. Serrano, and G. Payne. "A Study of the Nutritional Status and Food Habits of Otomí Indians in the Mezquital Valley of Mexico." *American Journal of Public Health* 36 (1946): 883–903.

Ankerson, Dudley. "Some Aspects of Economic Change and the Origins of the Mexican Revolution, 1876–1910." Centre of Latin American Studies, Cambridge University. *Working Papers*, no. 12, n.d.

Ardrey, Robert. *The Territorial Imperative*. New York, 1975.

Askinasy, Siegfried. *México indígena: observaciones sobre algunos problemas de México*. Mexico, 1939.

Bacon, M. K., H. Barry, and I. L. Child. "A Cross-Cultural Study of Correlates of Crime." *Journal of Abnormal and Social Psychology* 66 (1963): 291–300.

Bacon, S. D. "The Classic Temperance Movement of the U.S.A.; Impact Today on Attitudes, Action, and Research." *British Journal of Addiction* 62 (1967): 5–18.

Baker, J. L. "Indians, Alcohol, and Homicide." *Journal of Social Therapy* 5 (1959): 270–75.

Balboni, Claudia. "Alcohol in Relation to Dietary Patterns." In Salvatore P. Lucia, ed., *Alcohol and Civilization*, pp. 61–74. New York, 1963.

Bales, R. F. "Cultural Differences in Rates of Alcoholism." *Quarterly Journal of Studies on Alcohol* 6 (1946): 480–99.

Bancroft, Hubert H. *History of Mexico*. 6 vols. San Francisco, 1883–88.

Bandelier, Adolph F. "On the Social Organization and Mode of Government of the Ancient Mexicans." In *Twelfth Report of the Trustees of the Peabody Museum of American Archaeology and Ethnology*, vol. 2, pp. 557–699. Cambridge, Mass., 1880.

Banfield, Edward C. *The Moral Basis of a Backward Society*. New York, 1958.

Bard, Morton, and Joseph Lacker. "Assaultiveness and Alcohol Use in Family Disputes: Police Perceptions." *Criminology* 12 (1974): 281–92.

Barlow, Robert H. "El códice de los alfareros de Cuauhtitlán." *Revista Mexicana de Estudios Antropológicos* 12 (1951): 5–8.

————. *The Extent of the Empire of the Culhua Mexica*. Berkeley and Los Angeles, 1943.

Barrera Vásquez, Alfredo. "El pulque entre los mayas." *Cuadernos Mayas* 3 (1941).

Bazán Alarcón, Alicia. "El Real Tribunal de la Acordada y la delincuencia en la Nueva España." *Historia Mexicana* 13 (1964): 317–45.

Bazant, Jan. *A Concise History of Mexico from Hidalgo to Cárdenas, 1805–1940.* Cambridge, Eng., 1977.

Beals, Alan R., and Bernard J. Siegel. *Divisiveness and Social Conflict: An Anthropological Approach.* Stanford, Calif., 1966.

Beals, Ralph. *The Aboriginal Culture of the Cáhita Indians.* Ibero-Americana: 19. Berkeley, Calif., 1943.

———. "Acculturation." *Handbook of Middle American Indians,* vol. 6, pp. 449–68. Austin, Tex., 1967.

———. *The Comparative Ethnology of Northern Mexico Before 1750.* Ibero-Americana: 2. Berkeley, Calif., 1932.

———. "Definitions of Peasants: A Commentary on Isaac." *Human Organization* 35 (1976): 201–202.

———. *Ethnology of the Western Mixe.* Berkeley, Calif., 1945.

———. "Mesoamerica: Remnant Heritage." In Betty Bell, ed., *Indian Mexico: Past and Present,* pp. 87–99. Los Angeles, 1967.

Beattie, J. M. "The Pattern of Crime in England, 1660–1800." *Past & Present,* no. 62 (1974): 47–95.

Beaumont, Fray Pablo de la Purísima Concepción. *Crónica de Michoacán.* Mexico, 1932.

Benítez, Fernando. *Tierra incógnita.* Mexico, 1972.

Berdan, Frances M. "Trade, Tribute and Market in the Aztec Empire." Unpublished Ph.D. dissertation, University of Texas, Austin, 1975.

Berger, Suzanne. *Peasants against Politics: Rural Organization in Brittany, 1911–1967.* Cambridge, Mass., 1972.

Berk, Richard A. "The Controversy Surrounding Analyses of Collective Violence: Some Methodological Notes." In James F. Short and Marvin Wolfgang, eds., *Collective Violence,* pp. 112–18. Chicago, 1972.

Bernal, Ignacio, ed. "Relación de Guautla." *Tlalocan* 4 (1962): 3–16.

Berthe, Jean-Pierre. "Transferts culturels et techniques de l'Ancien au Nouveau Monde: La Brasserie en Nouvelle-Espagne au XVIe siècle." In *Méthodologie de l'histoire et des sciences humaines: Mélanges en l'honneur de Fernand Braudel,* pp. 61–73. Toulouse, 1973.

Bertram, I.G. "New Thinking on the Peruvian Highland Peasantry." *Pacific Viewpoint* 15 (1974): 2, 89–110.

Bloch, Herbert A., and Gilbert Geis. *Man, Crime, and Society: The Forms of Criminal Behavior.* New York, 1962.

Blum, Alan F., and Peter McHugh. "The Social Ascription of Motives." *American Sociological Review* 36 (1971): 98–109.

Bobb, Bernard. *The Viceregency of Antonio María Bucareli in New Spain, 1771–1779.* Austin, Tex., 1962.

Bohannon, Paul, ed. *African Homicide and Suicide.* Princeton, N.J., 1960.

———. *Law and Warfare: Studies in the Anthropology of Conflict.* Garden City, N.Y., 1967.

———. *Social Anthropology.* New York, 1963.

Bonger, Willem. *Criminality and Economic Conditions.* Bloomington, Ind., 1969.

Borah, Woodrow. "Latin America, 1610–1660." *The New Cambridge Modern History*, vol. 4, pp. 707–26.
———. "Latin American History in World Perspective." In Charles F. Delzell, ed., *The Future of History*, pp. 151–72. Nashville, Tenn., 1977.
———. "Race and Class in Mexico." *Pacific Historical Review* 23 (1954): 331–42.
———. "Social Welfare and Social Obligation in New Spain: A Tentative Assessment." 36th International Congress of Americanists. *Actas y Memorias* 4 (1966): 45–57.
Borah, Woodrow, and Sherburne F. Cook. "A Case History of the Transition from Precolonial to the Colonial Period in Mexico: Santiago Tejupan." Paper presented at the 40th International Congress of Americanists. Mexico City, 1974.
Bottoms, A. E., and J. D. McClean. *Defendants in the Criminal Process*. London and Boston, 1976.
Bourke, John G. "Distillation by Early American Indians." *American Anthropologist* 7 (1894): 297.
Braudel, Fernand. *Capitalism and Material Life, 1400–1800*. Translated by Miriam Kochan. New York, 1973.
Bray, Warwick. "The City State in Central Mexico at the Time of the Spanish Conquest." *Journal of Latin American Studies* 4 (1972): 161–85.
Bricker, Victoria R. "Les Insurrections indigènes chez les Mayas: La Pensée sauvage." Paper presented to the Symposium Interdisciplinaire sur les Insurrections Indiennes Paysannes. 42d International Congress of Americanists. Paris, 1976.
Brooks, Francis. "Parish and Cofradía in Eighteenth-Century Mexico." Unpublished Ph.D. dissertation, Princeton University, 1976.
Brophy, John. *The Meaning of Murder*. New York, 1967.
Brownmiller, Susan. *Against Our Will: Men, Women, and Rape*. New York, 1975.
Brueske, Judith M. "The Petapa Zapotecs of the Inland Isthmus of Tehuantepec, Oaxaca, Mexico: An Ethnographic Description and an Exploration into the Status of Women." Unpublished Ph.D. dissertation, University of California, Riverside, 1976.
Bruman, Henry J. "Aboriginal Drink Areas in New Spain." Unpublished Ph.D. dissertation, University of California, Berkeley, 1940.
———. "Man and Nature in Mesoamerica: The Ecologic Base." In Betty Bell, ed., *Indian Mexico: Past and Present*, pp. 13–23. Los Angeles, 1967.
Bruun, Bettil. "Drinking Practices and Their Social Function." In Salvatore P. Lucia, ed., *Alcohol and Civilization*, pp. 218–28. New York, 1963.
Bunzel, Ruth. "Chichicastenango and Chamula." In Raymond G. McCarthy, ed., *Drinking and Intoxication: Selected Readings in Social Attitudes and Controls*, pp. 73–86. Glencoe, Ill., 1959.
———. "Ethnography of Alcoholism." In McCarthy, ed., *Drinking and Intoxication*, pp. 278–86.
Burgoa, Francisco de. *Geográfica descripción de la parte septentorial del polo ártico de la América y nueva iglesia de las indias occidentales, y sitio astronómico de esta provincia de predicadores de Antequera, valle de Oaxaca. . . .* 2 vols. Mexico, 1934.

Butterworth, Douglas. "A Study of the Urbanization Process Among Mixtec Migrants from Tilantongo to Mexico City." *América Indígena* 22 (1962): 257–74.

———. *Tilantongo: comunidad mixteca en transición.* Mexico, 1975.

Buve, Raymond, Th. J. "Movimientos campesinos mexicanos: algunos apuntes e interrogantes sobre sus orígenes en la sociedad virreinal." *Anuario de Estudios Americanos* 28 (1971): 423–57.

———. "Peasant Movements, Caudillos and Land Reform During the Revolution (1910–1917) in Tlaxcala, Mexico." *Boletín de estudios latinoamericanos y del caribe* 18 (1975): 112–52.

Cahalan, Don, Ira H. Cisin, and Helen M. Crossley. *American Drinking Practices. A National Study of Drinking Behavior and Attitudes.* New Brunswick, N.J., 1969.

Calderón de la Barca, Frances. *Life in Mexico: The Letters of Fanny Calderon de la Barca.* Edited by Howard T. and Marion H. Fisher. Garden City, N.Y., 1966.

Calderón Quijano, José Antonio, et al. *Los virreyes de Nueva España* (1759–1808). 4 vols. Seville, 1967–72.

Callahan, William J. "The Problem of Confinement: An Aspect of Poor Relief in Eighteenth-Century Spain." *Hispanic American Historical Review* 51 (1971): 1–24.

Calnek, Edward. "The Internal Structure of Tenochtitlán." In Eric R. Wolf, ed., *The Valley of Mexico: Studies in Pre-Hispanic Ecology and Society,* pp. 287–302. Albuquerque, N.M., 1976.

———. "The Sahagun Texts as a Source of Sociological Information." In Munro Edmonson, ed., *Sixteenth-Century Mexico: The Work of Sahagún,* pp. 189–204. Albuquerque, N.M., 1974.

Cancian, Francesca M. *What are Norms? A Study of Beliefs and Action in a Maya Community.* Cambridge, Eng., 1975.

Carbajal, Francisco León. *Discurso sobre la legislación de los antiguos mexicanos.* Mexico, 1864.

Carr, Edward H. *What Is History?* New York, 1961.

Carrasco, Pedro. "Central Mexican Highlands: Introduction." *Handbook of Middle American Indians,* vol. 8, part 2, pp. 579–601. Austin, Tex., 1969.

———. "The Civil-Religious Hierarchy in Mesoamerican Communities: Pre-Spanish Background and Colonial Development." *American Anthropologist* 63 (1961): 483–97.

———. "Family Structure of Sixteenth-Century Tepoztlán." In Robert A. Manners, ed., *Process and Pattern in Culture: Essays in Honor of Julian H. Steward,* pp. 185–210. Chicago, 1964.

———. "The Joint Family in Ancient Mexico: The Case of Molotla." In Hugo G. Nutini, Pedro Carrasco, and James M. Taggart, eds., *Essays on Mexican Kinship,* pp. 45–64. Pittsburgh, Pa., 1976.

———. "The Mesoamerican Indian During the Colonial Period." In Betty Bell, ed., *Indian Mexico: Past and Present,* pp. 72–86. Los Angeles, 1967.

———. *Los Otomíes: cultura e historia prehispánicas de los pueblos mesoamericanos de habla otomiana.* Mexico, 1950.

———. "Relaciones sobre la organización social indígena en el siglo XVI." *Estudios de Cultura Nahuatl* 7 (1967): 119–54.

————. "La transformación de la cultura indígena durante la colonia." *Historia Mexicana* 25 (1975): 175–202.

Casado Fernández-Mensaque, Fernando. "El tribunal de la Acordada de Nueva España." *Anuario de Estudios Americanos* 7 (1950): 279–323.

Casarrubias, Vicente. *Rebeliones indígenas de la Nueva España*. Mexico, 1945.

Cascudo, Luis da Câmara. *Prelúdio da cachaça; ethnografia, história, e sociologia da aguardente no Brasil*. Rio de Janeiro, 1968.

Caso, Alfonso, ed. "Relación de los pueblos de Peñoles del Obispado de Antequera, Valle de Guaxaca." *Revista Mexicana de Estudios Históricos* 2 suplemento (1928): 185–91.

Castan, Nicole. "La justice expeditive." *Annales: Economies, sociétés, civilisations* 31 (1976), 331–61.

Catanzaro, Ronald J. "Psychiatric Aspects of Alcoholism." In David J. Pittman, ed., *Alcoholism*, pp. 31–45. New York, 1967.

Cavan, Sherri. *Liquor License: An Ethnography of Bar Behavior*. Chicago, 1966.

Cavo, Andrés. *Los tres siglos de México durante el gobierno español*. 4 vols. Mexico, 1836.

Chafetz, Morris E., and Harold W. Demone. *Alcoholism and Society*. New York, 1962.

Chaunu, Pierre. *L'Espagne et Charles Quint*. 2 vols. Paris, 1973.

————. *Histoire, science sociale: La Durée, l'espace et l'homme à l'époque moderne*. Paris, 1974.

Chávez Orozco, Luis. *Las instituciones democráticas de los indígenas mexicanos en la época colonial*. Mexico, 1943.

Chevalier, François. *La Formation des grandes domaines au Mexique: Terre et société aux XVIe-XVIIe siècles*. Paris, 1952.

Chevalier, Louis. *Laboring Classes and Dangerous Classes in Paris During the First Half of the Nineteenth Century*. New York, 1973.

Chimalpahín Cuauhtlehuanitzin, Francisco de San Antón Muñón. *Relaciones originales de Chalco Amaquemecan*. Mexico, 1965.

Christian, William A. "Holy People in Peasant Europe." *Comparative Studies in Society and History* 15 (1973): 106–14.

The Chronicles of Michoacan. Translated and edited by Eugene R. Craine and Reginald C. Reindorp. Norman, Okla., 1970.

Cinquemani, Dorothy K. "Drinking and Violence Among Middle American Indians." Unpublished Ph.D. dissertation, Columbia University, 1975.

Clavijero, Francisco Javier. *Historia antigua de México*. Edited by R. P. Mariano Cuevas. Mexico, 1964.

Cline, Howard. "Ethnohistorical Regions of Middle America." In Howard Cline, ed., *Guide to Ethnohistorical Sources*, vol. 12 of the *Handbook of Middle American Indians*, pp. 166–82. Austin, Tex., 1972.

Cobb, R. C. *The Police and the People: French Popular Protest, 1789–1820*. Oxford, 1970.

Codex Mendoza. Edited by James C. Clark. 3 vols. London, 1938.

Coffey, T. G. "Beer Street: Gin Lane. Some Views of Eighteenth-Century Drinking." *Quarterly Journal of Studies on Alcohol* 27 (1966): 669–92.

Cohen, Albert K. *Deviance and Control*. Englewood Cliffs, N.J., 1966.

Cohen, Eugene. "Who Stole the Rabbits? Crime, Dispute, and Social Control in an Italian Village." *Anthropological Quarterly* 45 (1972): 1–14.

Cohn, Norman. *The Pursuit of the Millennium.* London, 1957.

Colby, Benjamin N., and Pierre L. van den Berghe. *Ixil Country: A Plural Society in Highland Guatemala.* Berkeley, Calif., 1969.

Colección de documentos inéditos relativos al descubrimiento, conquista y organización de las antiguas posesiones españolas de América y Oceanía, sacados de los archivos del reino, y muy especialmente del de Indias. 42 vols. Madrid, 1864–84.

Colección de documentos inéditos relativos al descubrimiento, conquista y organización de las antiguas posesiones españolas de ultramar. 25 vols. Madrid, 1885–1932.

Coleman, Emily R. "L'Infanticide dans le Haut Moyen Age." *Annales: Economies, sociétés, civilisations* 29 (1974): 315–36.

Colín, Mario. *Antecedentes agrarios del municipio de Atlacomulco, Estado de México. Documentos.* Mexico, 1963.

Collier, George. *Fields of the Tzotzil: The Ecological Bases of Tradition in Highland Chiapas.* Austin, Tex., 1975.

Collier, Jane F. *Law and Social Change in Zinacantan.* Stanford, Calif., 1973.

———. "Women in Politics." In Michelle Z. Rosaldo and Louise Lamphere, eds., *Women, Culture, and Society,* pp. 89–96. Stanford, Calif., 1974.

Contreras, R., and J. Daniel. *Una rebelión indígena en el partido de Totonicapán en 1820: el indio y la independencia.* Guatemala, 1968.

Cook, M. A. *Population Pressure in Rural Anatolia, 1450–1600.* Oxford, 1972.

Cook, Sherburne, F. *Santa María Ixcatlán: Habitat, Population, Subsistence.* Ibero-Americana: 41. Berkeley, Calif., 1958.

Cook, Sherburne F., and Woodrow Borah. *Essays in Population History: Mexico and the Caribbean.* 2 vols. Berkeley, Calif., 1971, 1974.

———. *The Indian Population of Central Mexico, 1531–1610.* Ibero-Americana: 44. Berkeley and Los Angeles, 1960.

———. *The Population of the Mixteca Alta, 1520–1960.* Ibero-Americana: 50. Berkeley and Los Angeles, 1968.

Cooper, John M. "Stimulants and Narcotics." *The Comparative Ethnology of South American Indians, Handbook of South American Indians,* vol. 5, pp. 525–58. Washington, D.C., 1949.

Coser, Lewis A. *Continuities in the Study of Social Conflict.* New York, 1967.

———. *The Functions of Social Conflict.* Glencoe, Ill., 1956.

Coy, Peter E. B. "Justice for the Indian in Eighteenth-Century Mexico." *American Journal of Legal History* 11 (1968): 41–49.

Curley, R. T. "Drinking Patterns of the Mescalero Apache." *Quarterly Journal of Studies on Alcohol* 28 (1967): 116–31.

Dahlgren de Jordán, Barbro. *La Mixteca: su cultura e historia prehispánicas.* Mexico, 1966.

Daily, R. C. "The Role of Alcohol Among North American Indian Tribes as Reported in the Jesuit Relations." *Anthropologica* 10 (1968): 45–57.

Dalton, George. "How Exactly Are Peasants 'Exploited'?" *American Anthropologist* 76 (1974): 553–61.

Davies, C. N. B. *Los señoríos independientes del imperio azteca.* Mexico, 1968.

214   Bibliography

Davies, C. S. L. "Révoltes populaires en Angleterre (1500–1700)." *Annales: Economies, sociétés, civilisations* 24 (1969): 24–60.
Davis, Natalie Z. *Society and Culture in Early Modern France*. Stanford, Calif., 1975.
Demographic Yearbook, 1964. New York, 1965.
Demos, John. "Demography and Psychology in the Historical Study of Family-Life: A Personal Report." In Peter Laslett, ed., *Household and Family in Past Time*, pp. 561–69. Cambridge, Eng., 1972.
Dennis, Philip A. *Conflictos por tierras en el Valle de Oaxaca*. Mexico, 1976.
———. "The Role of the Drunk in a Oaxacan Village." *American Anthropologist* 77 (1975): 856–63.
Devereux, George. "The Function of Alcohol in Mohave Society." *Quarterly Journal of Studies on Alcohol* 9 (1948): 207–51.
Diamond, Stanley. "The Rule of Law Versus the Order of Custom." *Social Research* 38 (1971): 42–72.
Díaz del Castillo, Bernal. *The Conquest of Mexico*. Translated by J. M. Cohen. Harmondsworth, Middlesex, 1963.
Di Tella, Torcuato S., "The Dangerous Classes in Early Nineteenth-Century Mexico." *Journal of Latin American Studies* 5 (1973): 79–105.
Dock, William. "The Clinical Value of Alcohol." In Salvatore P. Lucia, ed., *Alcohol and Civilization*, pp. 75–86. New York, 1963.
Dollar, Charles M., and Richard J. Jensen. *Historian's Guide to Statistics: Quantitative Analysis and Historical Research*. New York, 1971.
Doughty, Paul L. "La cultura, bebida, y el trabajo en un distrito mestizo andino." *América Indígena* 27 (1967): 667–87.
———. "The Social Uses of Alcoholic Beverages in a Peruvian Community." *Human Organization* 30 (1971): 187–97.
Dozier, E. P. "Problem Drinking Among American Indians: The Role of Sociocultural Deprivation." *Quarterly Studies on Alcohol* 27 (1966): 72–87.
Drapkin, Israel. "Manuel Montesinos y Molina—An Almost Forgotten Precursor of Penal Reform in Spain." In Marvin Wolfgang, ed., *Crime and Culture: Essays in Honor of Thorsten Sellin*, pp. 315–46. New York, 1968.
Driver, Edwin D. "Interaction and Criminal Homicide in India." *Social Forces* 40 (1961–62): 153–58.
Dummett, Raymond E. "The Social Impact of the European Liquor Trade on the Akan of Ghana (Gold Coast and Asante) 1875–1910." *Journal of Inter-Disciplinary History* 5 (1974): 69–101.
Dunn, Richard S. *Sugar and Slaves: The Rise of the Planter Class in the English West Indies, 1624–1713*. Chapel Hill, N.C., 1972.
Dupeux, Georges. *French Society, 1789–1970*. Translated by Peter Wait. London, 1976.
Dusenberry, William H. "Discriminatory Aspects of Legislation in Colonial Mexico." *Journal of Negro History* 33 (1948): 284–302.
Edgerton, Robert B. "Violence in East African Tribal Societies." In James F. Short and Marvin Wolfgang, eds., *Collective Violence*, pp. 159–170. Chicago, 1972.
Elizondo, Francisco Antonio de. *Práctica universal forense de los tribunales de España y de las Indias*. 8 vols. Madrid, 1791–96.

Elliott, J. H. "Revolution and Continuity in Early Modern Europe." *Past & Present*, no. 42 (1969), pp. 35–56.

Emmart, Emily W., ed. *The Badianus Manuscript (Codex Barberini, Latin 241), Vatican Library; An Aztec Herbal of 1552*. Baltimore, 1940.

Encinas, Diego de. *Cedulario indiano*. 4 vols. Madrid, 1945.

Ensayo de una memoria estadística del distrito de Tulancingo. Mexico, 1825.

Epistolario de Nueva España, 1505–1818. Edited by Francisco del Paso y Troncoso. 16 vols. Mexico, 1939–42.

Erasmus, Charles. "Comments on Gerrit Huizer's 'Resistance to Change' and Radical Peasant Mobilization: Foster and Erasmus Reconsidered." *Human Organization* 29 (1970): 314–19.

———. "Community Development and the *Encogido* Syndrome." *Human Organization* 27 (1969): 65–73.

———. *Man Takes Control; Cultural Development and American Aid*. Minneapolis, 1961.

Erikson, Kai T. "Sociology and Historical Perspective." *American Sociologist* 5 (1970): 331–38.

———. *Wayward Puritans: A Study in the Sociology of Deviance*. New York, 1966.

El Estado de Hidalgo. Su historia, su riqueza, su porvenir. Pachuca, 1933.

Fabre, Daniel. "Le Monde du carnaval." *Annales: Economies, sociétés, civilisations*. 31 (1976): 389–406.

Fabrega, Horacio, and Daniel Silver. *Illness and Shamanistic Curing in Zinacantan: An Ethnomedical Analysis*. Stanford, Calif., 1973.

Fallding, Harold. "The Source and Burden of Civilization Illustrated in the Use of Alcohol." *Quarterly Journal of Studies on Alcohol* 25 (1964): 714–24.

Faron, Louis. "Effects of Conquest on the Araucanian Picunche during the Spanish Colonization of Chile: 1536–1635." *Ethnohistory* 7 (1960): 239–307.

Farriss, Nancy M. *Crown and Clergy in Colonial Mexico, 1759–1821: The Crisis of Ecclesiastical Privilege*. London, 1968.

Favre, Henri. "A Propos du Potentiel insurrectionnel de la paysannerie indienne: Oppression, alienation, insurrection." Paper presented to the Symposium Interdisciplinaire sur les Insurrections Indiennes Paysannes. 42d International Congress of Americanists. Paris, 1976.

———. *Cambio y continuidad entre los Mayas de México*. Mexico, 1973.

———. "Notas sobre el homicidio entre los Chamulas." *Estudios de Cultura Maya* 4 (1964): 305–22.

Fenna, D., L. Mix, O. Schaefer, and J. A. L. Gilbert. "Ethanol Metabolism in Various Racial Groups." *Canadian Medical Association Journal* 105 (1971): 472–75.

Ferdinand, Theodore. "The Criminal Patterns of Boston Since 1849." *American Journal of Sociology* 73 (1967): 84–99.

Ferrara, Floreal. *Alcoholismo en América Latina*. Buenos Aires, 1961.

Fischer, David H. *Historians' Fallacies: Toward a Logic of Historical Thought*. London, 1971.

Florentine Codex. Translated with notes and illustrations by Arthur J. O. Anderson and Charles E. Dibble. 12 books in 13 parts. Santa Fe, N.M., 1950–55.

Flores Ochoa, Jorge. "Mistis and Indians: Their Relations in a Micro-Region of Cuzco." In Pierre L. Van den Berghe, ed., *Class and Ethnicity in Peru*, pp. 62–72. Leiden, 1974.

Florescano, Enrique. *Precios del maíz y crisis agrícolas en México (1708–1810)*. Mexico, 1969.

Florescano, Enrique, and Isabel Gil, eds. *Descripciones económicas generales de Nueva España, 1784–1817*. Mexico, 1973.

Ford, Thomas R. *Man and Land in Peru*. Gainesville, Fla., 1955.

Forsander, Olof A. "Influence of Alcohol on the General Metabolism of the Body." In Salvatore P. Lucia, ed., *Alcohol and Civilization*, pp. 43–60. New York, 1963.

Fossey, Mathieu. *Le Mexique*. Paris, 1857.

Foster, George M. *Culture and Conquest: America's Spanish Heritage*. New York, 1960.

———. "The Dyadic Contract: A Model for the Social Structure of a Mexican Peasant Village." *American Anthropologist* 63 (1961): 1173–92.

———. "Interpersonal Relations in Peasant Society." *Human Organization* 19 (1960–61): 174–80.

Franco, Maria Sylvia de Carvalho. *Homens livres na ordem escravocrata*. São Paulo, 1969.

Frank, André Gunder. *Lumpenbourgeoisie: Lumpendevelopment; Dependence, Class, and Politics in Latin America*. New York, 1973.

Friedl, Ernestine. "The Position of Women: Appearance and Reality." *Anthropological Quarterly* 40 (1967): 97–108.

Friedrich, Paul. *Agrarian Revolt in a Mexican Village*. Englewood Cliffs, N.J., 1970.

———. "The External Relations of An Open, Corporate Village." *Kroeber Anthropological Society Papers* 27 (1962): 27–44.

———. "El homicidio político en Acan." *Revista de Ciencias Sociales* 8 (1964): 27–51.

———. "Political Homicide in Rural Mexico." In Ivo and Rosalind Feierabend and Ted R. Gurr, eds., *Anger, Violence and Politics: Theories and Research*, pp. 269–82. Englewood Cliffs, N.J., 1972.

Fromm, Erich, and Michael Maccoby. *Social Character in a Mexican Village: A Sociopsychoanalytic Study*. Englewood Cliffs, N.J., 1970.

Gamst, Frederick C. *Peasants in Complex Society*. New York, 1974.

García Alcaraz, Agustín. "El maguey y el pulque en Tepetlaoxtoc." *Comunidad*, no. 38 (1972), pp. 460–74.

Gately, Michael O., A. Lloyd Moote, and John E. Wills, Jr. "Seventeenth-Century Peasant 'Furies': Some Problems of Comparative History." *Past & Present*, no. 51 (1971), pp. 63–80.

George, M. Dorothy. *London Life in the Eighteenth Century*. New York, 1965.

Gerhard, Peter. "Congregaciones de indios en la Nueva España antes de 1570," *Historia Mexicana* 26 (1977): 347–95.

———. *A Guide to the Historical Geography of New Spain*. Cambridge, Eng., 1972.

Gibson, Charles. *The Aztecs Under Spanish Rule: A History of the Indians of the Valley of Mexico, 1519–1810*. Stanford, Calif., 1964.

———. "The Problem of the Impact of Spanish Culture on the Indigenous

American Population." In Frederick Pike, ed., *Latin American History: Selected Problems, Identity, Integration, and Nationhood*, pp. 65–98. New York, 1969.

———. *Spain in America*. New York, 1966.

Gillin, John P. *The Culture of Security in San Carlos*. New Orleans, 1951.

———. "Mestizo America." In Ralph Linton, ed., *Most of the World*, pp. 156–211. New York, 1949.

Given, James B. *Society and Homicide: An Essay on Social Interaction in Thirteenth-Century England*. Stanford, Calif., 1977.

Gluckman, Max. *Custom and Conflict in Africa*. Oxford, 1965.

Gold, Martin. "Suicide, Homicide and the Socialization of Aggression." *The American Journal of Sociology* 63 (1957–58): 651–61.

Goldberg, Leonard. "The Metabolism of Alcohol." In Salvatore P. Lucia, ed., *Alcohol and Civilization*, pp. 23–42. New York, 1963.

Goldkind, Victor. "Ethnic Relations in Southeastern Mexico: A Methodological Note." *American Anthropologist* 65 (1963): 394–99.

Goldman, I. *The Cubeo: Indians of the Northwest Amazon*. Urbana, Ill., 1963.

Gonçalves de Lima, Oswaldo. *El maguey y el pulque en los códices mexicanos*. Mexico, 1956.

Góngora, Mario. *Studies in the Colonial History of Spanish America*. Cambridge, Eng., 1975.

González Navarro, Moisés. "*Mestizaje* in Mexico During the National Period." In Magnus Mörner, ed., *Race and Class in Latin America*, pp. 145–69. New York, 1970.

———. "El Porfiriato: la vida social." In Daniel Cosío Villegas, ed., *Historia moderna de México*, vol. 4. Mexico, 1957.

———. "Tenencia de la tierra y población agrícola (1877–1960)." *Historia Mexicana* 19 (1969): 63–86.

González Obregón, Luis. *Rebeliones indígenas y precursores de la independencia mexicana en los siglos XVI, XVII, y XVIII*. 2d ed. Mexico, 1952.

Gossen, Gary H. *Chamulas in the World of the Sun: Time and Space in a Maya Oral Tradition*. Cambridge, Mass., 1974.

Goubert, Pierre. "The French Peasantry of the Seventeenth Century: A Regional Example." *Past & Present*, no. 10 (1956), pp. 55–77.

Granado Baeza, Bartolomé. "Los indios de Yucatán." *Boletín del Archivo General de la Nación* 12 (1941): 223–36.

Granberg, Wilbur J. *People of the Maguey: The Otomí Indians of Mexico*. New York, 1970.

Greenberg, Leon A. "The Definition of an Intoxicating Beverage." *Quarterly Journal of Studies on Alcohol* 16 (1955): 316–25.

Greenberg, Leon A., and J. A. Carpenter. "The Effect of Alcoholic Beverages on Skin Conductance and Emotional Tension. I. Wine, Whiskey, and Alcohol." *Quarterly Journal of Studies on Alcohol* 18 (1957): 190–204.

Grimshaw, Allen D. "Interpreting Collective Violence: An Argument for the Importance of Social Structure." In James F. Short and Marvin Wolfgang, eds., *Collective Violence*, pp. 36–46. Chicago, 1972.

Guerra, Francisco. *The Pre-Columbian Mind*. London and New York, 1971.

Guijo, Gregorio Martín de. *Diario, 1648–1664*. 2 vols. Mexico, 1952.

218 Bibliography

Guiteras, Eusebio, translator. *Rudo ensayo, by an Unknown Jesuit Padre, 1763.* Tucson, Ariz., 1951.

Guiteras-Holmes, Calixta. *Perils of the Soul: The World of a Tzotzil Indian.* New York, 1961.

Guridi y Alcocer, José Miguel. *Apuntes de la vida de D. José Miguel Guridi y Alcocer, formados por él mismo en fines de 1801 y principios del siguiente de 1802.* Mexico, 1906.

Gurr, Ted R. *Why Men Rebel.* Princeton, N.J., 1970.

Gurr, Ted R., and Vaughn F. Bishop. "Violent Nations, and Others." *The Journal of Conflict Resolution* 20 (1976): 79–110.

Guzmán, Ignacio P. *Compendio de geografía, física, política y estadística del Estado de México.* Toluca, Mex., 1906.

Gwaltney, John L. *The Thrice Shy: Cultural Accommodation to Blindness and Other Disasters in a Mexican Community.* New York, 1970.

Haberman, Paul W., and Michael M. Baden. "Alcoholism and Violent Death." *Quarterly Journal of Studies on Alcohol* 35 (1974): 221–31.

Hamer, J. H. "Acculturation, Stress, and the Functions of Alcohol Among the Forest Potawatomi." *Quarterly Journal of Studies on Alcohol* 26 (1965): 285–302.

Hanawalt, Barbara A. "Violent Death in Fourteenth and Early Fifteenth-Century England." *Comparative Studies in Society and History* 18 (1976): 297–320.

Handbook of Middle American Indians. Edited by Robert Wauchope. 15 vols. Austin, Tex., 1964–75.

Hardoy, Jorge E. *Pre-Columbian Cities.* New York, 1973.

The Harkness Collection in the Library of Congress: Manuscripts Concerning Mexico, A Guide with selected transcriptions and translations by J. Benedict Warren. Washington, D.C., 1974.

Harris, Marvin. *Cows, Pigs, Wars and Witches: The Riddles of Culture.* New York, 1974.

Harrison, Brian. *Drink and the Victorians: the Temperance Question in England, 1815–1872.* Pittsburgh, 1971.

Hay, Douglas. "Property, Authority and the Criminal Law." In Douglas Hay et al. *Albion's Fatal Tree: Crime and Society in Eighteenth-Century England*, pp. 17–64. New York, 1975.

Hays, Samuel P. "Historical Social Research: Concept, Method, and Technique." *Journal of Inter-Disciplinary History* 4 (1974): 475–82.

Heath, Dwight B. "Anthropological Approaches to Alcohol: A Review." *Alcoholism: Journal of Alcoholism and Related Addictions* 10 (1974): 24–42.

———. "Comments on 'Alcohol and Culture.'" *Current Anthropology* 6 (1965): 289–90.

———. "Drinking Patterns of the Bolivian Camba." In David J. Pittman and Charles R. Snyder, eds., *Society, Culture, and Drinking Patterns*, pp. 22–36. New York and London, 1962.

———. "Peasants, Revolution, and Drinking: Interethnic Drinking Patterns in Two Bolivian Communities." *Human Organization* 30 (1971): 179–86.

———. "Perspectivas socioculturales del alcohol en América latina." *Acta Psiquiátrica y Psicológica de América Latina* 20 (1974): 99–111.

————. "Prohibition and Post-Repeal Drinking Patterns Among the Navaho." *Quarterly Journal of Studies on Alcohol* 25 (1964): 119–35.

Heath, Shirley B. *Telling Tongues: Language Policy in Mexico, Colony to Province.* New York, 1972.

Henry, Andrew F., and James F. Short. *Suicide and Homicide.* Glencoe, Ill., 1954.

Hernández Palomo, José Jesús. *El aguardiente de caña en México (1724–1810).* Seville, 1974.

Hibbert, Christopher. *The Roots of Evil.* London, 1963.

Hilton, R. H. *Bond Men Made Free: Medieval Peasant Movements and the English Rising of 1381.* New York, 1973.

Hobbs, A. H. "Criminality in Philadelphia: 1790–1810 Compared with 1937." *The American Sociological Review* 8 (1943): 198–202.

Hobsbawm, Eric J. "From Social History to the History of Society." *Daedalus* 100 (1971): 20–45.

————. "Peasant and Rural Migrants in Politics." In Claudio Véliz, ed., *The Politics of Conformity in Latin America*, pp. 43–65. London, 1967.

————. "Peasant Land Occupations." *Past & Present*, no. 62 (1974), pp. 120–52.

Hodgen, Margaret T. *Anthropology, History, and Cultural Change.* Tucson, Ariz., 1974.

Honigmann, John J. "Dynamics of Drinking in an Austrian Village." *Ethnology* 2 (1963): 157–69.

Horton, Donald. "The Functions of Alcohol in Primitive Societies." *Quarterly Journal of Studies on Alcohol* 4 (1943): 199–320.

Hotchkiss, John C. "Children and Conduct in a Ladino Community of Chiapas, Mexico." *American Anthropologist* 69 (1967): 711–18.

Hufton, Olwen H. *The Poor of Eighteenth-Century France, 1750–1789.* Oxford, 1975.

Huitrón, Antonio. *Metepec. Miseria y grandeza del barro.* Mexico, 1962.

Huizer, Gerrit. "'Resistance to Change' and Radical Peasant Mobilization: Foster and Erasmus Reconsidered." *Human Organization* 29 (1970): 303–13.

————. *The Revolutionary Potential of Peasants in Latin America.* Lexington, Mass., 1972.

Huizer, Gerrit, and Rodolfo Stavenhagen. "Peasant Movements and Land Reform in Latin America: Mexico and Bolivia." In Henry A. Landsberger, ed., *Rural Protest, Peasant Movements and Social Change*, pp. 378–409. London, 1974.

Humboldt, Alexander von. *Political Essay on the Kingdom of New Spain.* Edited by Mary M. Dunn. Translated by John Black. Abridged. New York, 1972.

"Informe sobre pulquerías y tabernas, el año de 1784." *Boletín del Archivo General de la Nación* 18 (1947): 187–236.

Ingham, John M. "Culture and Personality in a Mexican Village." Unpublished Ph.D. dissertation, University of California, Berkeley, 1968.

Isaac, Barry L. "Peasants in Cities: Ingenious Paradox or Conceptual Muddle?" *Human Organization* 33 (1974): 251–57.

220   Bibliography

———. "Sorting Out the Grab-Bag of Peasantry: Reply to Ralph L. Beals." *Human Organization* 35 (1976): 202–205.

Israel, J. I. *Race, Class and Politics in Colonial Mexico, 1610–1670.* London, 1975.

Jara, Alvaro. "Plata y pulque en el siglo XVIII mexicano." Centre of Latin American Studies, Cambridge University. *Working Papers*, no. 9, n.d.

Jellinek, E. M. "Cultural Differences in the Meaning of Alcoholism." In David J. Pittman and Charles R. Snyder, eds., *Society, Culture, and Drinking Patterns*. New York and London, 1962.

Jiménez Moreno, Wigberto. *Estudios de historia colonial.* Mexico, 1958.

Jiménez Moreno, Wigberto, and A. García Ruiz. *Historia de México: una síntesis.* Mexico, 1970.

Kagan, Sam. "Penal Servitude in New Spain: The Colonial Textile Industry." Unpublished Ph.D. dissertation, City University of New York, 1976.

Kahl, Joseph A. *The Measurement of Modernism.* Austin, Tex., 1968.

Katz, Friedrich. *Situación social y económica de los aztecas durante los siglos XV y XVI.* Mexico, 1966.

Kearney, Michael. "Drunkenness and Religious Conversion in a Mexican Village." *Quarterly Journal of Studies on Alcohol* 31 (1970): 132–52.

———. *The Winds of Ixtepeji: World View and Society in a Zapotec Town.* New York, 1972.

Keen, Benjamin. *The Aztec Image in Western Thought.* New Brunswick, N.J., 1971.

Kellum, Barbara A. "Infanticide in England in the Later Middle Ages." *History of Childhood Quarterly* 1 (1974): 367–88.

Kendis, Joseph B. "The Human Body and Alcohol." In David J. Pittman, ed., *Alcoholism*, pp. 23–30. New York, 1967.

Kennedy, J. G. "Tesguino-Complex: The Role of Beer in Tarahumara Culture." *American Anthropologist* 65 (1963): 620–40.

Klein, Herbert. "Peasant Communities in Revolt: The Tzeltal Republic of 1712." *Pacific Historical Review* 35 (1966): 247–63.

Konrad, Herman. "Santa Lucía, 1576–1767: A Jesuit Hacienda in Colonial Mexico." Unpublished Ph.D. dissertation, University of Chicago, 1973.

Kubler, George. *Mexican Architecture of the Sixteenth Century.* 2 vols. New Haven, Conn., 1948.

———. *The Shape of Time: Remarks on the History of Things.* New Haven, Conn., 1962.

Ladd, Doris M. *The Mexican Nobility at Independence, 1780–1826.* Austin, Tex., 1976.

La Faye, Jacques. *Quetzalcóatl and Guadalupe: The Formation of Mexican National Consciousness, 1531–1813.* Translated by Benjamin Keen. Chicago, 1976.

Lamphere, Louise. "Strategies, Cooperation and Conflict Among Women in Domestic Groups." In Michelle Z. Rosaldo and Louise Lamphere, eds., *Woman, Culture, and Society*, pp. 97–112. Stanford, Calif., 1974.

Landau, Simha F., and Israel Drapkin. *Ethnic Patterns of Criminal Homicide in Israel.* Tel Aviv, 1968.

Landsberger, Henry A., ed., *Latin American Peasant Movements.* Ithaca, N.Y., 1969.

Landsberger, Henry A., and Cynthia N. Hewitt. "Ten Sources of Weakness and Cleavage in Latin American Peasant Movements." In Rodolfo Stavenhagen, ed., *Agrarian Problems and Peasant Movements in Latin America*, pp. 559–83. Garden City, N.Y., 1970.

Lane, Roger. "Crime and Criminal Statistics in Nineteenth-Century Massachusetts." *Journal of Social History* 2 (1968): 156–63.

———. "Crime and the Industrial Revolution." *Journal of Social History* 7 (1974): 287–303.

Lanhers, Yvonne. "Crimes et criminels au XIVᵉ siècle," *Revue Historique* 240 (1968): 325–38.

Lauternari, Vittorio. "Nativistic and Socio-Religious Movements: A Reconsideration." *Comparative Studies in Society and History* 16 (1974): 483–503.

Le Barre, Weston. "Native American Beers." *American Anthropologist* 40 (1938): 224–34.

LeGrand, Catherine C. "Perspectives for the Historical Study of Rural Politics and the Colombian Case: An Overview." *Latin American Research Review* 12 (1977): 7–36.

Lehr, Howard. "Patterns of Crime in Nineteenth-Century Germany and France: A Comparative Study." Unpublished Ph.D. dissertation, Rutgers University, 1974.

Lemert, E. M. "The Use of Alcohol in Three Salish Indian Tribes." *Quarterly Journal of Studies on Alcohol* 19 (1958): 90–107.

Lerner, Victoria. "Consideraciones sobre la población de la Nueva España (1793–1810) según Humboldt y Navarro y Noriega." *Historia Mexicana* 17 (1968): 327–48.

Le Roy Ladurie, Emmanuel. *The Peasants of Languedoc.* Translated by John Day. Urbana, Ill., 1974.

Leslie, Gerald R. *The Family in Social Context.* 2d ed. New York, 1973.

Lester, David. "Suicide, Homicide, and the Effects of Socialization." *Journal of Personality and Social Psychology* 5 (1967): 466–68.

Levine, Donald N., Ellwood B. Carter, and Eleanor M. Gorman. "Simmel's Influence on American Sociology." *American Journal of Sociology* 81 (1976): 813–45, 1112–32.

LeVine, Robert A. "Anthropology and the Study of Conflict." *The Journal of Conflict Resolution* 5 (1961): 3–15.

Levy, Jerrold E., and Stephen J. Kunitz. *Indian Drinking: Navaho Practices and Anglo-American Theories.* New York, 1974.

Lewis, Leslie. "In Mexico City's Shadow: Some Aspects of Economic Activity and Social Processes in Texcoco, 1570–1620." In Ida Altman and James Lockhart, eds., *Provinces of Early Mexico: Variants of Spanish American Regional Development*, pp. 125–36. Los Angeles, 1976.

Lewis, Oscar. *Pedro Martinez; A Mexican Peasant and His Family.* New York, 1964.

Linebaugh, Peter. "The Tyburn Riot Against the Surgeons." In Douglas Hay et al., *Albion's Fatal Tree: Crime and Society in Eighteenth-Century England*, pp. 65–118. New York, 1975.

Liss, Peggy K. *Mexico Under Spain, 1521–1556: Society and the Origins of Nationality.* Chicago, 1975.

Lockhart, James. "Capital and Province, Spaniard and Indian: The Example of

Late Sixteenth-Century Toluca." In Ida Altman and James Lockhart, eds., *Provinces of Early Mexico: Variants of Spanish American Regional Evolution*, pp. 99–124. Los Angeles, 1976.

Lolli, Giorgio, et al. *Alcohol in Italian Culture: Food and Wine in Relation to Sobriety Among Italians and Italian Americans.* Glencoe, Ill., 1958.

Lomnitz, Larissa. "Patrones de ingestión de alcohol entre migrantes mapuches en Santiago." *América Indígena* 29 (1969): 43–71.

———. "Patterns of Alcohol Consumption Among the Mapuche." *Human Organization* 28 (1969): 287–96.

López, Fr. Atanasio. "Misiones o doctrina en Jalisco (Mexico) en el siglo XVII." *Estudios Históricos* 2 (1960): 1–36.

López Austin, Alfredo. "De las plantas medicinales y de otras cosas medicinales." *Estudios de Cultura Nahuatl* 9 (1971): 125–231.

López Sarrelangue, Delfina. "Población indígena de la Nueva España en el siglo XVIII." *Historia Mexicana* 12 (1963): 516–30.

———. *Una villa mexicana en el siglo XVIII.* Mexico, 1957.

Lorcin, Marie-Thérèse. "Les Paysans et la justice dans la région lyonnaise aux XIVe et XVe siècles." *Le Moyen Age* 74 (1968): 269–300.

Loyola Montemayor, Elías. *La industria del pulque.* . . . Mexico, 1956.

Lurie, Nancy O. "The World's Oldest On-Going Protest Demonstration: North American Indian Drinking Patterns." *Pacific Historical Review* 40 (1971): 311–32.

MacAndrew, Craig, and Robert Edgerton. *Drunken Comportment: A Social Explanation.* Chicago, 1969.

McCarthy, Raymond G. "Alcoholism: Attitudes and Attacks, 1775–1935." *Annals of the American Academy of Political Science* 315 (1958): 12–21.

———, ed. *Drinking and Intoxication: Selected Readings in Social Attitudes and Controls.* Glencoe, Ill., 1959.

McCord, William, and Joan McCord. *Origins of Alcoholism.* Stanford, Calif., 1960.

McHale, Vincent E., and Eric A. Johnson. "Urbanization, Industrialization and Crime in Imperial Germany: Part I." *Social Science History* 1 (1976): 79–100.

Macklin, Barbara J., and N. Ross Crumrine. "Three North Mexican Folk Saint Movements." *Comparative Studies in Society and History* 15 (1973): 89–105.

MacLachlan, Colin M. *Criminal Justice in Eighteenth-Century Mexico: A Study of the Tribunal of the Acordada.* Berkeley, Calif., 1974.

Madsen, William. "The Alcoholic Agringado." *American Anthropologist* 6 (1964): 355–61.

———. *The American Alcoholic: The Nature-Nurture Controversy in Alcoholic Research and Therapy.* Springfield, Ill., 1974.

———. "Comments on 'Alcohol and Culture'." *Current Anthropology* 6 (1965): 291–92.

———. "The Nahua." *Handbook of Middle American Indians*, vol. 8, part 2, pp. 602–37. Austin, Tex., 1969.

———. "Religious Syncretism." *Handbook of Middle American Indians*, vol. 6, pp. 369–91. Austin, Tex., 1967.

Madsen, William, and Claudia Madsen. "The Cultural Structure of Mexican

Drinking Behavior." *Quarterly Journal of Studies on Alcohol* 30 (1969): 701–18.
Malinowski, Bronislaw. *Crime and Custom in Savage Society*. New York, 1926.
Mandelbaum, David G. "Alcohol and Culture." *Current Anthropology* 6 (1965): 281–88.
Mangin, William. "Drinking Among Andean Indians." *Quarterly Journal of Studies on Alcohol* 18 (1957): 55–66.
Manners, Robert A. "Colonialism and Native Land Tenure: A Case Study in Ordained Accommodation." In Robert A. Manners, ed., *Process and Pattern in Culture: Essays in Honor of Julian H. Steward*, pp. 266–80. Chicago, 1964.
Manzano, Teodomiro. *Anales del Estado de Hidalgo desde los tiempos más remotos hasta nuestros días*. 3 vols. Pachuca, Mex., 1922–27.
Margolies, Barbara L. *Princes of the Earth: Subcultural Diversity in a Mexican Municipality*. Washington, D.C., 1975.
Marrus, Michael R. "Social Drinking in the *Belle Epoque*." *Journal of Social History* 7 (1974): 115–41.
Martín del Campo, Rafael. "El pulque en el Mexico precortesiano." *Anales del Instituto de Biología* 9 (1938): 5–23.
Martínez-Alier, Verena. *Marriage, Class and Colour in Nineteenth-Century Cuba: A Study of Racial Attitudes and Sexual Values in a Slave Society*. Cambridge, 1974.
Martínez de Alva, Ernesto. *Vida rural: los campesinos de México*. Mexico, 1934.
Maza, Francisco de la. "Unos relieves del siglo XVI." *Boletín del Instituto Nacional de Antropología e Historia* 35 (1969): 8–12.
Medina, Baltasar de. "El tratado y representación sobre el abuso del pulque y daños que causa a las buenas costumbres," September 14, 1693 (manuscript in Condumex archive).
Mejido, Manuel. *México amargo*. Mexico, 1973.
Memorias (state governor's reports), Estado de México, 1877, 1877, 1879, 1889–93; Estado de Hidalgo, 1869, 1871–72; Estado de Oaxaca, 1869–70, 1871–72, 1874–75, 1881–82, 1897–98.
Meyer, Jean. "El ocaso de Manuel Lozada." *Historia Mexicana* 18 (1969): 535–68.
———. "Historia de la vida social." In *Investigaciones contemporáneas sobre historia de México*, pp. 373–406. Mexico and Austin, Tex., 1971.
———. *Problemas campesinos y revueltas agrarias (1821–1910)*. Mexico, 1973.
———. "El reyno de Lozada en Tepic (1856–1873)." Paper presented to the Symposium Interdisciplinaire sur les Insurrections Indiennes Paysannes. 42d International Congress of Americanists. Paris, 1976.
Michaelson, Evalyn J., and Walter Goldschmidt. "Family and Land in Peasant Ritual." *American Ethnologist* 3 (1976): 87–96.
———. "Female Roles and Male Dominance Among Peasants." *Southwestern Journal of Anthropology* 27 (1971): 330–52.
Migdal, J. S. "The Role of the Family in Relation to the Tension of Societal Change." *International Journal of Group Tensions* 4 (1974): 184–207.

224   Bibliography

Mirafuentes Galván, José Luis. *Movimientos de resistencia y rebeliones indígenas en el norte de México (1680–1821), guía documental*. Mexico, 1975.

Miranda, José. "Evolución cuantitativa y desplazamiento de la población indígena de Oaxaca, en la época colonial." *Estudios de Historia Novohispana* 2 (1968): 129–48.

Mörner, Magnus. *La corona española y los foráneos en los pueblos de indios de América*. Stockholm, 1970.

———. "La rebelión de Tupac Amaru en el Cuzco desde una perspectiva nueva." Paper presented to the Symposium Interdisciplinaire sur les Insurrections Indiennes Paysannes. 41st International Congress of Americanists. Paris, 1976.

Monterrosa Prado, Mariano. "Cruces del siglo XVI." *Boletín del Instituto Nacional de Antropología e Historia* 30 (1967): 16–19.

Moore, Barrington, Jr. *Social Origins of Dictatorship: Lord and Peasant in the Making of the Modern World*. Boston, 1966.

Moreno Cebrián, Alfredo. "El ocio del indio como razón teórica del repartimiento." *Revista de Indias*, nos. 139–142 (1975), pp. 167–86.

Mousnier, Roland. *Peasant Uprisings in Seventeenth-Century France, Russia, and China*. Translated by Brian Pearce. New York, 1970.

Muro Orejón, Antonio, ed. *Cedulario americano del siglo XVIII*. Seville, 1969.

Nader, Laura. "An Analysis of Zapotec Law Cases." In Paul Bohannon, ed., *Law and Warfare: Studies in the Anthropology of Conflict*, pp. 117–38. Garden City, N.Y., 1967.

———. "The Zapotec of Oaxaca." *Handbook of Middle American Indians*, vol. 7, part 1, pp. 329–59. Austin, Tex., 1969.

Nader, Laura, and Duane Metzger. "Conflict Resolution in Two Mexican Communities." *American Anthropologist* 65 (1963): 584–92.

Nash, June. "The Betrothal: A Study of Ideology and Behavior in a Maya Indian Community." In Henning Siverts, ed., *Drinking Patterns in Highland Chiapas: A Teamwork Approach to the Study of Semantics Through Ethnography*, pp. 89–120. Bergen-Oslo-Tromsö, 1973.

———. "Death as a Way of Life: The Increasing Resort to Homicide in a Mexican Indian Town." *American Anthropologist* 69 (1967): 455–70.

———. *In the Eyes of the Ancestors: Belief and Behavior in a Maya Community*. New Haven, Conn., 1970.

———. "The Passion Play in Maya Indian Communities." *Comparative Studies in Society and History* 10 (1968): 318–27.

Nash, Manning. "The Impact of Mid-Nineteenth Century Economic Change Upon the Indians of Middle America." In Magnus Mörner, ed., *Race and Class in Latin America*, pp. 170–83. New York, 1970.

Navarrete, Carlos. "Prohibición de la danza del tigre en Tanulte, Tabasco en 1631." *Tlalocan* 6 (1971): 374–76.

Navarro de Vargas, Joseph. "Padrón del pueblo de San Mateo Huitzilopochco, inventario de su iglesia y directorio de sus obvenciones parroquiales." *Anales del Museo Nacional de Arqueología, Historia y Etnología*, época 3, vol. 1 (1909), pp. 553–99.

Navarro García, Luis. *Sublevación del Yaqui*. Seville, 1966.

Netting, Robert. "Beer as a Locus of Value Among the West African Kofyar." *American Anthropologist* 66 (1964): 375–84.

Nicholson, H. B. "The Efflorescence of Mesoamerican Civilization: A Resume." In Betty Bell, ed., *Indian Mexico: Past and Present*, pp. 46–71. Los Angeles, 1967.

Nieburg, H. L. "Agonistics—Rituals of Conflict." In James F. Short and Marvin Wolfgang, eds., *Collective Violence*, pp. 82–99. Chicago, 1972.

Núñez, Theron A. "Cultural Discontinuity and Conflict in a Mexican Village." Unpublished Ph.D. dissertation, University of California, Berkeley, 1963.

Obeyesekere, Gananath. "Sorcery, Premeditated Murder, and the Canalization of Aggression in Sri Lanka." *Ethnology* 14 (1975): 1–23.

O'Nell, Carl W., and Henry A. Selby. "Sex Differences in the Incidence of *Susto* in Two Zapotec Pueblos: An Analysis of the Relationships Between Sex Role Expectations and Folk Illness." *Ethnology* 7 (1968): 95–105.

Orozco y Berra, Manuel. *Apéndice al diccionario universal de historia y de geografía*. Vol. 8. Mexico, 1855.

Ortiz, Sutti R. *Uncertainties in Peasant Farming: A Colombian Case*. London, 1973.

Ortiz de Montellano, Bernard. "Empirical Aztec Medicine." *Science*, no. 4185 (April 18, 1975), pp. 215–20.

Osborn, Wayne S. "A Community Study of Metztitlán, New Spain, 1520–1810." Unpublished Ph.D. dissertation, State University of Iowa, 1969.

———. "Indian Land Retention in Colonial Metztitlán." *Hispanic American Historical Review* 53 (1973): 217–38.

Ozouf, Mona. "Space and Time in the Festivals of the French Revolution." *Comparative Studies in Society and History* 17 (1975): 372–84.

Paddock, John. "Antiviolent Towns: Notes from a State of Social Health." Mimeograph. Mexico, 1973.

Paige, Jeffery. *Agrarian Revolution: Social Movements and Export Agriculture in the Underdeveloped World*. New York, 1975.

Palafox y Mendoza, Juan de. *Tratados Mejicanos*. 2 vols. Edited by Francisco Sánchez-Castañer. Madrid, 1968.

Papeles de Nueva España. Edited by Francisco del Paso y Troncoso. 9 vols. Madrid and Mexico, 1905–48.

Parsons, Elsie Clews. *Mitla, Town of Souls*. Chicago, 1936.

Paynó, Manuel. "Memoria sobre el maguey mexicano y sus diversos productos." *Boletín de la Sociedad Mexicana de Geografía e Estadística*, época 1, vol. 10 (1863), pp. 383–451, 485–530.

Paz, Octavio. *The Labyrinth of Solitude: Life and Thought in Mexico*. Translated by Lysander Kemp. New York, 1961.

———. *The Other Mexico: Critique of the Pyramid*. Translated by Lysander Kemp. New York, 1972.

Pennington, Campbell W. *The Tepehuan of Chihuahua; Their Material Culture*. Salt Lake City, Utah, 1969.

Perkins, Rollin M. "The Law and Homicide." *Journal of Criminal Law and Criminology* 36 (1946): 391–454.

Perrot, Michelle. "The Strengths and Weaknesses of French Social History." *Journal of Social History* 10 (1976): 166–77.

Pesez, Jean-Marie, and Emmanuel Le Roy Ladurie. "The Deserted Villages of France: An Overview." In Robert Forster and Orest Ranum, eds., *Rural Society in France: Selections from the Annales E.S.C.*, pp. 72–106. Baltimore, 1977.

Phelan, John L. *The Hispanization of the Philippines: Spanish Aims and Filipino Responses, 1565–1700*. Madison, Wis., 1959.
———. *The Kingdom of Quito in the Seventeenth Century: Bureaucratic Politics in the Spanish Empire*. Madison, Wis., 1967.
———. "Many Conquests: Some Trends and Some Challenges in Mexican Historiography (1945–69), the Sixteenth and Seventeenth Centuries." In *Investigaciones contemporáneas sobre historia de México*, pp. 125–48. Mexico and Austin, 1971.
———. *The Millennial Kingdom of the Franciscans in the New World. A Study of the Writings of Gerónimo de Mendieta (1525–1604)*. Berkeley and Los Angeles, 1956.
Piel, Jean. "Les Guerrillas indiennes dans les guerres d'Indépendance du Perou (1819–1824)." Paper presented to the Symposium Interdisciplinaire sur les Insurrections Indiennes Paysannes. 42d International Congress of Americanists. Paris, 1976.
———. "The Place of the Peasantry in the National Life of Peru in the Nineteenth Century." *Past & Present*, no. 46 (1970), pp. 108–33.
Piga Pascual. "La lucha antialcohólica de los españoles en la época colonial." *Revista de Indias*, no. 10 (1942), pp. 711–42.
Pineda, Vicente. *Historia de la sublevaciones indígenas habidas en el estado de Chiapas*. Chiapas, Mex., 1888.
Pittman, David J., ed. *Alcoholism*. New York, 1967.
Pittman, David J., and Charles R. Snyder, eds. *Society, Culture, and Drinking Patterns*. New York and London, 1962.
Pollak, Otto. *The Criminality of Women*. Philadelphia, 1950.
Ponce, Pedro. "Breve relación de los dioses y ritos de la gentilidad." In *Tratado de las idolatrías, supersticiones, dioses, ritos, hechicerías, y otras costumbres gentílicas de las razas aborígenes de México*, vol. 1, pp. 369–80. Mexico, 1953.
Pospisil, Leopold J. *Anthropology of Law: A Comparative Theory*. New Haven, Conn., 1974.
Potter, Jack M., May N. Díaz, and George M. Foster, eds. *Peasant Society: A Reader*. Boston, 1967.
Powell, T. G. *El liberalismo y el campesinado en el centro de México (1850 a 1876)*. Mexico, 1974.
Pozas Arciniega, Ricardo. "El alcoholismo y la organización social." *Palabra y el Hombre* 1 (1957): 19–26.
———. *Juan the Chamula: An Ethnological Re-Creation of the Life of a Mexican Indian*. Translated by Lysander Kemp. Berkeley, Calif., 1962.
Pozas Arciniega, Ricardo, and Isabel H. de Pozas. *Los indios en las clases sociales de México*. Mexico, 1971.
Press, Irwin. *Tradition and Adaptation: Life in a Modern Yucatan Maya Village*. Westport, Conn., 1975.
Price, John A. "An Applied Analysis of North American Indian Drinking Patterns." *Human Organization* 34 (1975): 17–26.
Priestley, Herbert I. *José de Gálvez, Visitor-General of New Spain (1765–1771)*. Berkeley, Calif., 1916.
Primov, George. "Aymara-Quechua Relations in Puno." In Pierre L. van den Berghe, ed., *Class and Ethnicity in Peru*, pp. 47–61. Leiden, 1974.

Procesos de indios idólatras y hechiceros. Mexico, 1912.

Quiroz, Alfonso, José Gómez Robleda, and Benjamín Argüelles. *Tendencia y ritmo de la criminalidad en México, D.F.* Mexico, 1939.

Radin, Paul, and Aurelio Espinosa, eds. *El folklore de Oaxaca*. Havana, n.d.

Ramírez, José F. *Adiciones a la biblioteca de Beristáin*. 2 vols. Mexico, 1898.

Ramírez, Rafael. "The Anti-Alcoholic Campaign." In Hubert Herring and Katherine Terrill, eds., *The Genius of Mexico*, pp. 177–99. New York, 1931.

Ramírez Tovar, Delfín. "El carnaval en Huixquilucan." *Mexican Folkways* 5 (1929): 35–49.

Ramos, Demetrio. "The Chronicles of the Early Seventeenth Century: How They Were Written." *The Americas* 22 (1965): 41–53.

Ravicz, Robert, and A. Kimball Romney. "The Mixtec." *Handbook of Middle American Indians*, vol. 7, part 1, pp. 367–99. Austin, Tex., 1969.

Recopilación de leyes de los reynos de las Indias. Edición facsimilar de la cuarta impresión hecha en Madrid el año 1791. 3 vols. Madrid, 1943.

Redclift, Michael. "Peasants and Revolutionaries: Some Critical Comments." *Journal of Latin American Studies* 7 (1975): 135–44.

Redfield, Robert. *The Folk Culture of Yucatan*. Chicago, 1941.

Reed, Nelson. *The Caste War of Yucatan*. Stanford, Calif., 1964.

Reina, Ruben E. *The Law of the Saints: A Pokoman Pueblo and Its Community Culture*. Indianapolis, 1966.

"Relación de Tequisquiac, Citlaltepec y Xilocingo." *Tlalocan* 3 (1949–57): 289–308.

Rendón, Silvia. "Modern Pottery of Riotenco, San Lorenzo, Cuauhtitlán." *Middle American Research Records* 1 (1951): 251–67.

Reyes Valerio, Constantino. "La obra indígena en Tepeapulco." *Boletín del Instituto Nacional de Antropología e Historia* 37 (1969): 13–18.

Ricard, Robert. *The Spiritual Conquest of Mexico; An Essay on the Apostolate and the Evangelizing Methods of the Mendicant Orders in New Spain, 1523–72*. Berkeley, Calif., 1966.

Riley, John W., and Charles F. Marden. "The Social Pattern of Alcoholic Drinking." *Quarterly Journal of Studies on Alcohol* 8 (1947): 265–73.

Río de la Loza, L. "Apuntes sobre algunos productos del maguey." *Boletín de la Sociedad Mexicana de Geografía y Estadística* 10 (1964): 531–39.

Robbins, Richard H. "Alcohol and the Identity Struggle: Some Effects of Economic Change on Interpersonal Relations." *American Anthropologist* 75 (1973): 99–122.

Robertson, Donald. "Techialoyan Manuscripts and Paintings, with a Catalog." *Handbook of Middle American Indians*, vol. 14, pp. 253–80. Austin, Tex., 1975.

Robinson, David. *From Drinking to Alcoholism: A Sociological Commentary*. London and New York, 1976.

Robles, Antonio de. *Diario de sucesos notables (1665–1703)*. 3 vols. Mexico, 1946.

Rogers, Susan C. "Female Forms of Power and the Myth of Male Dominance: A Model of Female/Male Interaction in Peasant Society." *American Ethnologist* 2 (1975): 727–56.

Rojas, Basilio. *La rebelión de Tehuantepec*. Mexico, 1964.

Romanucci-Ross, Lola. *Conflict, Violence, and Morality in a Mexican Village.* Palo Alto, Calif., 1973.

Romanucci-Schwartz, Lola. "Conflict without Violence and Violence without Conflict in a Mexican Mestizo Village." In James F. Short and Marvin Wolfgang, eds., *Collective Violence*, pp. 149–58. Chicago, 1972.

Romero Frizzi, María de los Angeles. "Los conflictos por la tierra en San Martín Huamelulpan, Mixteca Alta, Oaxaca." Oaxaca: Instituto Nacional de Antropología e Historia, Centro Regional de Oaxaca, 1975.

Roseberry, William. "Rent, Differentiation, and the Development of Capitalism Among Peasants." *American Anthropologist* 78 (1976): 45–58.

Rosenblat, Angel. *La población indígena de América desde 1492 hasta la actualidad.* Buenos Aires, 1945.

Roubin, Lucienne. "Male Space and Female Space Within the Provençal Community." In Robert Forster and Orest Ranum, eds., *Rural Society in France: Selections from the Annales E.S.C.*, pp. 152–80. Baltimore, 1977.

Rowe, John H. "Movimiento Nacional Inca del siglo XVIII." *Revista Universitaria del Cuzco*, no. 107, 2d semester (1954), pp. 17–47.

Roys, Ralph L. *The Indian Background of Colonial Yucatan.* 2d ed. Norman, Okla., 1972.

Rubio Mañé, J. Ignacio. *Introducción al estudio de los virreyes de Nueva España, 1535–1746.* 4 vols. Mexico, 1955–61.

Rudé, George. *The Crowd in History.* New York, 1964.

Ruiz de Alarcón, H. "Tratado de las supersticiones y costumbres gentílicas entre los indios de esta Nueva España, año de 1652." In *Tratado de las idolatrías, supersticiones, dioses, ritos, hechicerías, y otras costumbres gentílicas de las razas aborígenes de México*, vol. 2, pp. 23–179. Mexico, 1953.

Ruiz Moreno, Aníbal. *La lucha antialcohólica de los Jesuitas en la época colonial.* Buenos Aires, 1939.

Samaha, Joel. *Law and Order in Historical Perspective: The Case of Elizabethan Essex.* New York and London, 1974.

Sánchez-Albornoz, Nicolás. *The Population of Latin America: A History.* Berkeley, Calif., 1974.

Sánchez Colín, Salvador. *El Estado de México: su historia, su ambiente, sus recursos.* Mexico, 1951.

Sándoval, Fernando B. *La industria del azúcar en Nueva España.* Mexico, 1951.

Santamaría, Francisco J. *Diccionario de Mexicanismos.* Mexico, 1959.

Sayres, William C. "Ritual Drinking, Ethnic Status, and Inebriety in Rural Colombia." *Quarterly Journal of Studies on Alcohol* 17 (1956):

Scardaville, Michael. "Urban Poor and Public Disorder: Léperos and Vagrants in Mexico City, 1774–1803." Paper presented at the American Historical Association annual meeting, 1976.

Scholes, France, and Ralph Roys. *The Maya Chontal Indians of Acalan-Tixchel: A Contribution to the History and Ethnography of the Yucatan Peninsula.* 2d ed. Norman, Okla., 1968.

Scott, James C. *The Moral Economy of the Peasant: Rebellion and Subsistence in Southeast Asia.* New Haven, Conn., 1976.

Selby, Henry A. "The Study of Social Organization in Traditional Mesoamerica." In Hugo G. Nutini, Pedro Carrasco, and James M. Taggart, eds., *Essays on Mexican Kinship*, pp. 29–44. Pittsburgh, Pa., 1976.

————. *Zapotec Deviance: The Convergence of Folk and Modern Sociology*. Austin, Tex., 1974.

Serna, Jacinto de la. "Tratado de las supersticiones, idolatrías, hechicerías, y otras costumbres de las razas aborígenes de México." In *Tratado de las idolatrías, supersticiones, dioses, ritos, hechicerías, y otras costumbres gentílicas de las razas aborígenes de México*, vol. 1, pp. 39–368. Mexico, 1953.

Shaw, Mary, ed. *According to Our Ancestors: Folk Texts from Guatemala and Honduras*. Norman, Okla., 1971.

Las siete partidas del sabio rey don Alfonso el IX, glosadas por el Lic. Gregoria López. 4 vols. Madrid, 1829–31.

Simmel, Georg. *Conflict* and *The Web of Group-Affiliations*. Translated by Kurt H. Wolff. New York, 1964.

Simmons, Ozzie. "Ambivalence and the Learning of Drinking Behavior in a Peruvian Community." *American Anthropologist* 62 (1960): 1018–27.

————. "The Criollo Outlook in the Mestizo Culture of Coastal Peru." *American Anthropologist* 57 (1955): 107–17.

————. "Drinking Patterns and Interpersonal Performance in a Peruvian Mestizo Community." *Quarterly Journal of Studies on Alcohol* 20 (1959): 103–11.

————. "The Sociocultural Integration of Alcohol Use; A Peruvian Study." *Quarterly Journal of Studies on Alcohol* 29 (1968): 152–71.

Simon, Rita J. *Women and Crime*. Lexington, Mass., 1975.

Singelmann, Peter. "Campesino Movements and Class Conflicts in Latin America: The Functions of Exchange and Power." *Journal of Inter-American Studies and World Affairs* 16 (1974): 39–72.

Skinner, G. W. "Chinese Peasants and the Closed Community: An Open and Shut Case." *Comparative Studies in Society and History* 13 (1971): 270–81.

Skolnick, Jerome. "Religious Affiliation and Drinking Behavior." *Quarterly Journal of Studies on Alcohol* 19 (1958): 452–70.

Slotkin, J. S. "Fermented Drinks in Mexico." *American Anthropologist* 56 (1954): 1089.

Smelser, Neil J. *Theory of Collective Behavior*. London, 1967.

Smith, Waldemar R. *The Fiesta System and Economic Change*. New York, 1977.

Soboul, Albert. "The French Rural Community in the Eighteenth and Nineteenth Centuries." *Past & Present*, no. 10 (1956), pp. 78–95.

————. "Persistence of 'Feudalism' in the Rural Society of Nineteenth-Century France." In Robert Forster and Orest Ranum, eds., *Rural Society in France: Selections from the Annales E.S.C.*, pp. 50–71. Baltimore, 1977.

Spalding, Karen. "The Colonial Indian: Past and Future Research Perspectives." *Latin American Research Review* 7 (1972): 47–76.

————. "Indian Rural Society in Colonial Peru: The Example of Huarochirí." Unpublished Ph.D. dissertation, University of California, Berkeley, 1967.

————. "Social Climbers: Changing Patterns of Mobility among the Indians of Colonial Peru." *Hispanic American Historical Review* 50 (1970): 645–64.

Spiro, Melford E. "Violence in Burmese History: A Psychocultural Explanation." In James F. Short and Marvin Wolfgang, eds., *Collective Violence*, pp. 186–91. Chicago, 1972.

Spores, Ronald. *The Mixtec Kings and Their People*. Norman, Okla., 1967.

Starr, Frederick. *In Indian Mexico: A Narrative of Travel and Labor*. Chicago, 1908.

Stavenhagen, Rodolfo. *Social Classes in Agrarian Societies*. Garden City, N.Y., 1975.

———, ed. *Agrarian Problems and Peasant Movements in Latin America*. Garden City, N.Y., 1970.

Steck, Francis B. *Motolinia's History of the Indians of New Spain*. Washington, D.C., 1961.

Stein, Stanley, and Barbara Stein. *The Colonial Heritage of Latin America; Essays on Economic Dependence in Perspective*. New York, 1970.

Stein, William W. *Hualcan: Life in the Highlands of Peru*. Ithaca, N.Y., 1961.

Steinmetz, Suzanne K., and Murray A. Straus, eds. *Violence in the Family*. New York, 1974.

Stephens, William. *The Family in Cross-Cultural Perspective*. New York, 1963.

Stewart, Omer C. "Indians and Liquor." *Dictionary of American History* vol. 3, pp. 398–99. New York, 1976.

Stoianovich, Traian. *French Historical Method: The Annales Paradigm*. Ithaca, N.Y., 1976.

Stone, Lawrence. "History and the Social Sciences in the Twentieth Century." In Charles F. Delzell, ed., *The Future of History*, pp. 3–42. Nashville, Tenn., 1977.

Stross, Brian. "The Mexican Cantina as a Setting for Interaction." *Kroeber Anthropological Society Papers* 37 (1967): 58–89.

"Sublevación de los indios tzendales, año de 1713." *Boletín del Archivo General de la Nación* 19 (1948): 499–535.

Swartz, Marc J., ed. *Local-Level Politics: Social and Cultural Perspectives*. Chicago, 1968.

Taggart, James M. "The Fissiparous Process in Domestic Groups of a Nahuat-Speaking Community." *Ethnology* 11 (1972): 132–49.

———. "'Ideal' and 'Real' Behavior in the Mesoamerican Nonresidential Extended Family." *American Ethnologist* 2 (1975): 347–57.

Tamayo, Jorge L. *Geografía general de México*. 2d ed. 4 vols. Mexico, 1962.

Taylor, William B. *Landlord and Peasant in Colonial Oaxaca*. Stanford, Calif., 1972.

Tax, Sol, ed. *Heritage of Conquest: The Ethnology of Middle America*. Glencoe, Ill., 1952.

Thomas, Keith. "Work and Leisure in Pre-Industrial Society." *Past & Present*, no. 29 (1964), pp. 50–62.

Thompson, I. A. A. "A Map of Crime in Sixteenth-Century Spain." *Economic History Review*, 2d ser., 21 (1968): 244–67.

Thompson, J. Eric. *Mexico Before Cortez*. New York, 1940.

Thrupp, Sylvia, ed. *Millennial Dreams in Action: Essays in Comparative Study*. The Hague, 1962.

Tibón, Gutierre. *Pinotepa Nacional: Mixtecos, negros y Triques*. Mexico, 1961.

Tilly, Charles. "The Changing Place of Collective Violence." In Melvin Richter, ed., *Essays in Theory and History: An Approach to the Social Sciences*, pp. 139–64. Cambridge, Mass., 1970.

————. "Collective Violence in European Perspective." In Ivo and Rosalind Feierabend, and Ted R. Gurr, eds., *Anger, Violence, and Politics: Theories and Research*, pp. 342–51. Englewood Cliffs, N.J., 1972.

————. "Major Forms of Collective Action in Western Europe, 1500–1975." *Theory and Society* 3 (1976): 365–75.

————. "Town and Country in Revolution." In John W. Lewis, ed., *Peasant Rebellion and Communist Revolution in Asia*, pp. 271–302. Stanford, Calif., 1974.

————. *The Vendée*. Cambridge, Mass., 1964.

Tilly, Charles, and Louise Tilly; and Richard Tilly. *The Rebellious Century, 1830–1930*. Cambridge, Mass., 1975.

Tilly, Richard. "Popular Disorders in Nineteenth-Century Germany: A Preliminary Survey." *Journal of Social History* 4 (1970): 1–40.

Tinklenberg, Jared R., and Richard C. Stillman. "Drug Use and Violence." In David N. Daniels et al., eds., *Violence and the Struggle for Existence*, pp. 327–65. Boston, 1970.

Tobias, J. J. *Crime and Industrial Society in the Nineteenth Century*. New York, 1967.

Toor, Frances. *A Treasury of Mexican Folkways*. New York, 1947.

Trasselli, C. "Criminalité et moralité en Sicile au début de l'époque moderne." *Annales: Economies, sociétés, civilisations* 28 (1973): 226–46.

Tratado de las idolatrías, supersticiones, dioses, ritos, hechicerías, y otras costumbres gentílicas de las razas aborígenes de México, 2 vols., Mexico, 1953.

Trens, Manuel B. "Coquinaria, yantares y bebidas mexicanas." *Boletín del Archivo General de la Nación* 24 (1953): 1–58.

Tumin, Melvin M. *Social Stratification: The Forms and Functions of Inequality*. Englewood Cliffs, N.J., 1967.

Turk, Austin T. "Conflict and Criminality." *American Sociological Review* 31 (1966): 338–52.

————. *Criminality and Legal Order*. Chicago, 1969.

Turner, Ronny E. , and Charles K. Edgley. "The Devil Made Me Do It! Popular Culture and Religious Vocabularies of Motive." *Journal of Popular Culture* 8 (1974): 28–34.

Turner, Victor. *The Ritual Process. Structure and Anti-Structure*. Chicago, 1968.

Tutino, John M. "Creole Mexico: Spanish Elites, Haciendas, and Indian Towns, 1750–1810." Unpublished Ph.D. dissertation, University of Texas, 1976.

————. "Peasant Rebellion at the Isthmus of Tehuantepec: A Socio-Historical Perspective." Paper presented to the Symposium Interdisciplinaire sur les Insurrections Indiennes Paysannes. 42d International Congress of Americanists. Paris, 1976.

————. "Provincial Spaniards, Indian Towns, and Haciendas: Interrelated Agrarian Sectors in the Valleys of Mexico and Toluca, 1750–1810." In Ida Altman and James Lockhart, eds., *Provinces of Early Mexico: Variants of Spanish American Regional Evolution*, pp. 177–94. Los Angeles, 1976.

Urbanowicz, Charles F. "Drinking in the Polynesian Kingdom of Tonga." *Ethnohistory* 22 (1975): 33–50.

Urbina, Luis G. *Psiquis enferma*. Mexico, 1922.

Vaillant, George C. *Aztecs of Mexico: Origin, Rise, and Fall of the Aztec Nation*. 2d ed. Harmondsworth, Middlesex, 1966.

Van der Kroef, Justus M. "Javanese Messianic Expectations: Their Origin and Cultural Context." *Comparative Studies in Society and History* 1 (1959): 299–323.

Velásquez, Primo Feliciano, ed. "Relación de Querétaro: descripción de Querétaro por su alcalde mayor Hernando de Vargas, 20 de enero 1582." *Colección de documentos para la historia de San Luis Potosí*. San Luis Potosí, Mex., 1897–99.

Van Zantwijk, R. A. M. *Los indígenas de Milpa Alta, herederos de los aztecas*. N.p., n.d.

Verkko, Veli. *Homicides and Suicides in Finland and Their Dependence on National Character*. Copenhagen, 1951.

Viñas y Mey, Carmelo. *El estatuto del obrero indígena en la colonización española*. Madrid, 1929.

Viqueira, C., and A. Palerm. "Alcoholismo, brujería y homicidio en las comunidades rurales de México." *América Indígena* 14 (1954): 7–36.

Vogt, Evon Z. *Zinacantan: A Maya Community in the Highlands of Chiapas*. Cambridge, Mass., 1969.

Waddell, Jack O. "For Individual Power and Social Credit: The Use of Alcohol Among Tucson Papagos." *Human Organization* 34 (1975): 9–15.

Wagley, Charles. *The Latin American Tradition; Essays on the Unity and Diversity of Latin American Culture*. New York, 1969.

——. *The Social and Religious Life of a Guatemalan Village*. American Anthropological Association Memoir 71, 1949.

Wallace, Anthony F. C. *The Death and Rebirth of the Seneca*. New York, 1972.

Wallerstein, Immanuel. *The Modern World-System: Capitalist Agriculture and the Origins of the European World-Economy in the Sixteenth Century*. New York and London, 1974.

Washburne, Chandler. *Primitive Drinking: A Study of the Uses and Functions of Alcohol in Preliterate Societies*. New Haven, Conn., 1961.

Wasserstrom, Robert F. "White Fathers and Red Souls: Indian-Ladino Relations in Highland Chiapas, 1528–1973." Unpublished Ph.D. dissertation, Harvard University, 1976.

Weinert, Richard S. "Violence in Pre-Modern Societies: Rural Colombia." *American Political Science Review* 60 (1966): 340–47.

Weismann, Elizabeth W. *Mexico in Sculpture, 1521–1821*. Cambridge, Mass., 1950.

Westman, Barbara Hanawalt. "The Female Felon in Fourteenth-Century England." *Viator* 5 (1974): 253–68.

——. "The Peasant Family and Crime in Fourteenth-Century England." *Journal of British Studies* 13 (1974): 1–18.

Wheelock Román, Jaime. *Raíces indígenas de la lucha anticolonialista en Nicaragua de Gil González y Joaquín Zavala (1523 a 1881)*. Mexico, 1974.

Whyte, William F. "Conflict and Cooperation in Andean Communities." *American Ethnologist* 2 (1975): 373–92.

Wilkinson, Rupert. *The Prevention of Drinking Problems: Alcohol Control and Cultural Influences*. New York, 1970.

Wilson, Carter. "Expression of Personal Relations Through Drinking." In Henning Siverts, ed., *Drinking Patterns in Highland Chiapas: A Teamwork Approach to the Study of Semantics Through Ethnography*, pp. 121–46. Bergen-Oslo-Tromsö, 1973.

Wilson, Iris H. "Investigación sobre la planta 'maguey' en Nueva España." *Revista de Indias*, vols. 7–12, nos. 93–94 (1963), pp. 501–10.

Wilson, Monica H. *Reaction to Conquest: Effects of Contact with Europeans on the Pondo of South Africa*. London, 1961.

Wisdom, Charles. *The Chorti Indians of Guatemala*. Chicago, 1940.

Wolf, Eric R. *Anthropology*. Englewood Cliffs, N.J., 1964.

———. "Closed Corporate Peasant Communities in Mesoamerica and Central Java." *Southwestern Journal of Anthropology* 13 (1957): 1–18.

———. "Kinship, Friendship, and Patron-Client Relations in Complex Societies." In Michael Banton, ed., *The Social Anthropology of Complex Societies*, pp. 1–22. New York, 1966.

———. "Levels of Communal Relations." *Handbook of Middle American Indians*, vol. 6, pp. 299–316. Austin, Tex., 1967.

———. "On Peasant Rebellions." *International Social Science Journal* 21 (1969): 286–93.

———. *Peasant Wars in the Twentieth Century*. New York, 1969.

———. *Sons of the Shaking Earth*. Chicago, 1959.

———. "Types of Latin American Peasantry." *American Anthropologist* 57 (1955): 452–71.

Wolff, P. H. "Ethnic Differences in Alcohol Sensitivity." *Science*, no. 4020 (1972), pp. 449–50.

Wolfgang, Marvin E., ed. *Patterns of Violence*. In *The Annals of the American Academy of Political and Social Science*, 364 (March 1966).

———, ed. *Studies in Homicide*. New York, 1967.

Wolfgang, Marvin E., and France Ferracuti. *The Subculture of Violence: Towards an Integrated Theory in Criminology*. London, 1967.

Womack, John, Jr. *Zapata and the Mexican Revolution*. New York, 1969.

Wood, Arthur L. "Murder and Other Deviance in Ceylon." In Marvin E. Wolfgang, ed., *Studies in Homicide*, pp. 238–52. New York, 1967.

Zamora y Coronado, José M. *Biblioteca de Legislación Ultramarina (1680–1844)*. 6 vols. Madrid, 1844–46.

Zavala, Silvio, and María Castelo. *Fuentes para la historia del trabajo en Nueva España*. 8 vols. Mexico, 1939–46.

Zorita, Alonso de. *Life and Labor in Ancient Mexico: The Brief and Summary Relation of the Lords of New Spain*. Translated by Benjamin Keen. New Brunswick, N.J., 1963.

INDEX

INDEX